Creativity Research Journal

Volume 13, Number 1, 2000–2001

SPECIAL ISSUE: CREATIVITY AND THE SCHIZOPHRENIA SPECTRUM

Louis A. Sass and David Schuldberg, *Guest Editors*

First Publication by Lawrence Erlbaum Associates, Inc., Publishers

Published 2011 by Psychology Press

Published 2023 by Routledge
605 Third Avenue, New York, NY 10017
4 Park Square, Milton Park, Abingdon, Oxon OX14 4RN

Routledge is an imprint of the Taylor & Francis Group, an informa business

ISBN 13: 978-0-8058-9739-5 (pbk)

Creativity Research Journal
2000–2001, Vol. 13, No. 1, 1–4

Introduction to the Special Issue: Creativity and the Schizophrenia Spectrum

Louis A. Sass
Rutgers—The State University

David Schuldberg
The University of Montana

For much of the 20th century, scholars interested in the age-old question of the relation of mental illness to creativity and genius emphasized the connection with schizophrenia and related disorders. Although some attention was paid to depression, it was primarily the cognitive rather than affective characteristics of personality and psychopathology that were assumed to account for the relation between creativity and madness. Many prominent conceptualizations of schizophrenia were highly influenced by psychoanalytic assumptions. Accordingly, schizophrenia was viewed as a "primitive" disorder involving fixation at or regression to early instinct- and affect-dominated modes of experience that are relatively devoid of the capacity for self-consciousness or of a sense of differentiation between self and world.

In recent years, there have been some radical changes in this area of research and theorizing. Apparently coinciding with greater psychiatric interest in bipolar disorder (including its cognitive aspects), with a return to nosological assumptions grounded in Kraepelin's distinction between dementia praecox and affective psychosis (Hoenig, 1983), and with the narrowing of the American diagnostic criteria for schizophrenia, attention has shifted to the role of bipolar disorder in creativity and eminence. This change can perhaps be traced back to Andreasen and Canter's (1974) article on writers, an article that also marks a transition toward interest in writers as a representative creative group.

Coinciding with Andreasen and her colleagues' apparent shift from interest in cognitive aspects of psychosis to interest in affective disorder and creativity, the preponderance of some rather impressive research data (gathered by Jamison and Richards, as well as Andreasen and others) began to point toward an empirically greater role for affective disorder rather than schizophrenia. Notably, Jamison (1993), in her widely read book, *Touched With Fire: Manic–Depressive Illness and the Artistic Temperament,* argued that the creativity–psychopathology overlap is mostly due to the creative potential of manic depression and related affective illnesses. The previous belief in the creative potential of schizophrenic disorders has been said to result from misdiagnoses based on the overly broad conceptions of schizophrenia that prevailed in the United States prior to the advent of the *Diagnostic and Statistical Manual of Mental Disorders* (3rd ed.; American Psychiatric Association, 1980). This recently popular perspective on madness and creativity is congruent with current emphases on the negative, or deficit, aspects of schizophrenia, as well as with a neo-Kraepelinian view of schizophrenia as mere dementia, that is, as a condition that lacks creative potential as well as rationality.

The articles in this special issue seek to reexamine the relation between creativity and the schizophrenia spectrum of disorders in the wake of this recent research and theorizing. They revisit both empirical and conceptual findings and issues regarding connections

---

Louis A. Sass and David Schuldberg made equal contributions to this project. Names are listed alphabetically.

Correspondence and requests for reprints should be sent to Louis A. Sass, Rutgers—The State University, GSAPP–Busch Campus, 152 Frelinghuysen Road, Piscataway, NJ 08854–8085. E-mail: lsass@rci.rutgers.edu.

between the schizophrenia spectrum of disorders, schizotypy, psychotic-like traits, and creativity. It should be noted that the schizophrenia spectrum has both a "horizontal" and a "vertical" dimension (Schuldberg & Sass, 1999), the first including different types of disorders on approximately the same level of severity (i.e., schizoaffective and schizophreniform disorders) and the second encompassing milder conditions (e.g., schizotypal and schizoid personality disorders) as well as more severe disorders.

None of the authors in this issue wish to deny the creative potential of many persons with bipolar or other affective disorders. Taken together, however, the articles in this issue argue for a "rehabilitation" and reevaluation of the role of schizophrenia and related conditions in creativity research. We hope this collection will encourage people interested in the psychology of art and creativity not to write off people with schizophrenia and other residents of the schizophrenia spectrum.

The articles in this issue fall into two groups: one focusing on empirical issues and the other emphasizing conceptual issues concerning the relation between schizophrenia and creativity.

The first, more empirical set of articles, Reevaluation and Empirical Findings, begins with an article by Schuldberg (2000–2001b), whose previous work has examined creativity in relation to subclinical, psychotic-like characteristics. Focusing on psychometric approaches that view both creative and pathology-like characteristics as continua, he reviews the association between creativity and six symptom dimensions: (a) positive schizotypal cognitive symptoms, (b) negative schizotypal cognitive symptoms, (c) negative schizotypal affective symptoms, (d) hypomania, (e) depression, and (f) impulsivity. He presents data gathered from large samples on the relation between psychological test measures of these characteristics and scores on creativity tests, then demonstrates the difficulty in separating the variance in creativity tests attributable to affective, schizotypal, and impulsive traits.

In the second article, Kinney et al. (2000–2001), who have done research with measures of lifetime creativity, revisit creative functioning in the relatives of schizophrenic and schizotypal participants. After reviewing the literature on creativity in families of schizophrenics and on mental disorder in eminent individuals and their families, they present data on matched adoptees, 36 controls and 36 adopted-away children with a schizophrenic biological parent. Adoptees in both the index and control categories were found to have schizotypal or schizoid symptoms, and the authors present further arguments for a nonlinear, inverted-U relation in which the highest ratings of overall lifetime creativity were characteristic of those participants who had a moderate amount of schizotypal characteristics. The creativity of the participants with schizotypal characteristics was particularly apparent in avocational activities.

Russ (2000–2001), a specialist on affect, creativity, and children's play, reassesses work on play and fantasy to separate cognitive and affective characteristics of primary process. She argues that primary-process thought is central to all kinds of creativity but suggests that there may be different dimensions of primary-process thinking: a pure cognitive process that is more important in schizophrenia and a less severe and less primitive blend of cognitive–affective ideation that is more central in normal creative individuals and in the affective disorders. She calls for research to explore this and several other hypotheses about creativity in relation to affective experience and disturbance and in relation to the schizophrenia spectrum of disorders.

This set of three empirically oriented articles is followed by a commentary by Sass (2000–2001a), who highlights central points from the articles. He criticizes the tendency of researchers to rely on such concepts as positive versus negative symptoms and the primary process. He ends with a call for critical theoretical reflection on our operationalized concepts and with a plea for more research of a qualitative, ideographic, and phenomenologically oriented kind.

The second set of articles, Theoretical and Critical Reflections, begins with an article by the historical sociologist Becker (2000–2001). Becker, who is the author of an influential book-length study, *The Mad Genius Controversy* (Becker, 1978), critically examines the intellectual assumptions about creativity that have dominated speculation about mental illness and creativity since the beginning of romanticism. As Becker explains, the romantics borrowed various ideas from Greek antiquity, the Italian Renaissance, and the Enlightenment and then developed a perspective that implies that madness or mental anguish is a necessary condition for serious creative activity, at least in the arts. As a result, Becker argues, many modern writers have actually courted madness in a willful fashion or have sought to appear mad as a way of ensuring their own creative worth.

The next article is by Sass (2000–2001c), the author of *Madness and Modernism: Insanity in the Light of Modern Art, Literature, and Thought* (Sass, 1992). Sass discusses differences between romantic and postromantic as opposed to modernist and postmodernist conceptions of creativity, considering implications of adopting a more modernist or postmodernist conception. He points out that some writers, notably Jamison (1993) in *Touched With Fire,* are heavily, and rather un-self-critically, reliant on notions of creativity that derive from romanticism. Sass argues that a more flexible or diverse understanding of creative processes can help one to understand forms of creativity, in particular those characteristic of many works of modernist and postmodernist literature and art, that are likely to have a greater affinity with schizotypal or schizophrenia-like cognitive tendencies and with a schizoid form of adaptation.

This article is followed by a reply by Jamison (2000–2001) and then by a detailed rejoinder in which Sass (2000–2001b) pays particular attention to issues concerning psychiatric diagnosis.

The next article is by Ogilvie (2000–2001), a clinical psychologist with extensive training in philosophy whose doctoral dissertation (at City University of New York; Ogilvie, 1998) applied the thought of Wittgenstein to the understanding and treatment of schizophrenia. In his contribution, Ogilvie uses Wittgenstein's ambivalent attitude toward the philosophical enterprise to examine the quasiphilosophical yearnings of persons with schizophrenia, showing how these yearnings manifest creativity as well as concern with issues of self-creation. Ogilvie is particularly concerned with the consequences of schizophrenic withdrawal into a quasisolipsistic orientation, an orientation that involves an acute awareness of, and often a yearning for and striving toward, aspects of experience or mental functioning that, in normal experience, are so familiar, ubiquitous, or taken for granted as to be ignored. Ogilvie's article attempts the difficult task of evoking, yet at the same time of capturing in abstract, intellectual terms, the nearly ineffable experiences that can result from this kind of withdrawal and exaggerated self-consciousness and also from the struggle to return.

Finally, Prentky (2000–2001), author of *Creativity and Psychopathology: A Neurocognitive Perspective* (Prentky, 1980) and several influential articles in a similar vein, discusses how certain neurocognitive aspects of the major psychoses may underlie differing forms of creativity. Prentky (2000–2001) reviews a variety of research on cognitive aspects of creativity and proceeds to describe his own neurocognitive model, which hypothesizes that an optimal degree of deviation from normal patterns of information processing is necessary for creative work. This deviation can be either in the direction of expansion of awareness via extensive scanning and hyperalertness or in the direction of constriction of the field of awareness and hyperfocus on details. Whereas expanded awareness, according to Prentky (2000–2001), is likely to be associated with affective (or possibly schizoid) symptoms, he argues that constricted awareness would be more associated with schizotypal and schizophrenic conditions.

This second set of articles is followed by commentaries by two expert discussants: Schuldberg and Richards. Schuldberg (2000–2001a) discusses the limits of sociological critiques such as that of Becker, and he suggests that a focus on subclinical traits may allow researchers to see beyond the effects of playing mad and artistic roles. He also discusses different forms of creativity and thought disorder (particularly negative symptom variants) and argues for a multidimensional conceptualization and a dynamical systems approach to these phenomena.

The final commentary is by Richards (2000–2001), who has written a series of influential articles on creativity and psychological disorder beginning with her systematic 1981 typology of possible causal relations and associations between creativity and psychopathology. In her present contribution, Richards raises eight key issues concerning relations between creativity and psychopathology. She particularly emphasizes the importance of distinguishing eminent from everyday and vocational from avocational forms of creativity, as well as the differences between artistic and nonartistic work. She suggests there may be an evolutionary advantage associated with schizotypal forms of creativity that could compensate for the disadvantages also associated with such a disposition. She also offers a vivid discussion of the creative advantage that may derive from a combination of features from both the bipolar and the schizotypal spectrums.

We hope that this collection of articles and commentaries will have a significant influence on future discussion, research, and theoretical work concerning the relations between two complex and contested domains: psychopathology and creative process.

References

American Psychiatric Association. (1980). *Diagnostic and statistical manual of mental disorders* (3rd ed.). Washington, DC: Author.

Andreasen, N. C., & Canter, A. (1974). The creative writer: Psychiatric symptoms and family history. *Comparative Psychiatry, 15,* 123–131.

Becker, G. (1978). *The mad genius controversy: A study in the sociology of deviance.* Beverly Hills, CA: Sage.

Becker, G. (2000–2001). The association of creativity and psychopathology: Its cultural–historical origins. *Creativity Research Journal, 13,* 45–53.

Hoenig, J. (1983). The concept of schizophrenia: Krapelin-Bleuler-Schneider. *British Journal of Psychiatry, 142,* 547–556.

Jamison, K. R. (1993). *Touched with fire: Manic-depressive illness and the artistic temperament.* New York: Free Press.

Jamison, K. R. (2000–2001). Reply to Louis A. Sass: "Schizophrenia, modernism, and the creative imagination." *Creativity Research Journal, 13,* 75–76.

Kinney, D. K., Richards, R., Lowing, P. A., LeBlanc, D., Zimbalist, M. E., & Harlan, P. (2000–2001). Creativity in offspring of schizophrenic and control parents: An adoption study. *Creativity Research Journal, 13,* 17–25.

Ogilvie, J. (1998). *Wittgenstein and schizophrenia: On the grammar of will and the limits of metapsychology.* Unpublished doctoral dissertation, City University of New York.

Ogilvie, J. (2000–2001). On self-conceiving: Philosophical yearnings in a schizophrenic context. *Creativity Research Journal, 13,* 87–94.

Prentky, R. A. (1980). *Creativity and psychopathology.* New York: Praeger.

Prentky, R. A. (2000–2001). Mental illness and roots of genius. *Creativity Research Journal, 13,* 95–104.

Richards, R. (1981). Relationships between creativity and psychopathology. *Genetic Psychology Monographs, 103,* 261–324.

Richards, R. (2000–2001). Creativity and the schizophrenia spectrum: More and more interesting. *Creativity Research Journal, 13,* 111–132.

Russ, S. W. (2000–2001). Primary-process thinking and creativity: Affect and cognition. *Creativity Research Journal, 13,* 27–35.

Sass, L. A. (1992). *Madness and modernism: Insanity in the light of modern art, literature, and thought.* New York: Basic Books.

Sass, L. A. (2000–2001a). Eccentricity, conformism, and the primary process. *Creativity Research Journal, 13,* 37–44.

Sass, L. A. (2000–2001b). Romanticism, creativity, and the ambiguities of psychiatric diagnosis: Rejoinder to Kay Redfield Jamison. *Creativity Research Journal, 13,* 77–85.

Sass, L. A. (2000–2001c). Schizophrenia, modernism, and the creative imagination: On creativity and psychopathology. *Creativity Research Journal, 13,* 55–74.

Schuldberg, D. (2000–2001a). Creativity and psychopathology: Categories, dimensions, and dynamics. *Creativity Research Journal, 13,* 105–110.

Schuldberg, D. (2000–2001b). Six subclinical spectrum traits in normal creativity. *Creativity Research Journal, 13,* 5–16.

Schuldberg, D., & Sass, L. (1999). Schizophrenia. In M. A. Runco & S. R. Pritzker (Eds.), *Encyclopedia of creativity* (Vol. 2, pp. 501–514). San Diego, CA: Academic.

Creativity Research Journal
2000–2001, Vol. 13, No. 1, 5–16

Six Subclinical Spectrum Traits in Normal Creativity

David Schuldberg
The University of Montana

ABSTRACT: In this article, I explore conceptual and empirical connections between schizophrenia, schizotypy, psychotic-like traits, affective symptoms, and creativity. The focus is on 6 symptom-like characteristics: (a) positive schizotypal cognitive symptoms, (b) negative schizotypal cognitive symptoms, (c) negative schizotypal affective symptoms (flat affect), (d) hypomania, (e) depression, and (f) impulsivity. Attention is directed at research differentiating the cognitive symptoms associated with the schizophrenia spectrum from those of the core affective disorders, as well as distinguishing schizophrenic-like flat affect from depression. I present data on relations between paper-and-pencil measures of creativity and scales of subclinical deviant traits. I also discuss the importance of distinguishing creativity and eminence in different professional fields, artistic media, and genres, as well as the conceptual relation between continuous trait views of genius and madness and the temporal dynamics of the creative process.

Relations between creativity and madness have been noted since ancient times. Until recently, modern conceptions of this connection have emphasized the apparent similarity between the production of novel ideas in creativity and the unusual thought and behavior of persons with schizophrenia. Other symptomatic forms of affect and behavior have also been noted as relevant to creativity. In this article, I review work with relatives of schizophrenic patients, studies of mental disorder in creative people, and psychometric evaluations of creative groups. I evaluate the conceptual and empirical overlap between creative and schizophrenic cognition and distinguish different varieties of thought disorder. I dispute the claims that the overlaps between creativity and psychopathology are best accounted for as a function of the symptoms of affective disorder or of impulsivity alone. The focus is on the possible association of creativity and six symptom-like traits: (a) positive symptom thought disorder, (b) negative symptom thought disorder, (c) flat affect, (d) hypomania, (e) depression, and (f) impulsivity.

The association of insanity and creativity is embedded in more general philosophical, spiritual, and empirical questions about the relation among deviance, illness, and suffering, on the one hand, and generativity, on the other. This connection and its implications were explored by Sophocles in his drama *Philoctetes,* the story of a master archer who possesses a bow that cannot miss; his presence is essential for the Greeks to prevail in the Trojan wars, but he is also afflicted with a horribly wounded foot that will not heal and causes such intense agony that it proves insufferable to his comrades, who abandon him on a remote island. This story has become a central metaphor for the linkage between disorder and

Portions of this work were conducted with the support of National Institute of Mental Health Grant RO3 MH46628, which I gratefully acknowledge.

Portions of this article were originally presented as "Evidence for Separating Hypomanic and Schizotypal Traits in 'Normal Creativity'" in the symposium *Creativity and the Schizophrenia Spectrum: I. Re-evaluation and Empirical Findings,* and in a paper entitled "Creativity and Subclinical Mania, Depression, and Anhedonia: Implications for Dynamics" in the symposium *Creativity and Affect: Current Research and Issues,* both presented at the 105th annual meeting of the American Psychological Association, Chicago, August 1997.

I thank Ruth L. Richards, Louis A. Sass, and Shan Guisinger for their assistance. I am also grateful to the many current and former undergraduate and graduate students at The University of Montana who assisted in gathering and thinking about the data reported, notably Kaye Norris and Peg Plimpton. I am also indebted to Don Quinlan, John Strauss, Sidney J. Blatt, Frank Barron, Beth Fuller Ferris, and Glenn A. Hughes.

Correspondence and requests for reprints should be sent to David Schuldberg, Department of Psychology, The University of Montana, Missoula, MT 59812–1584. E-mail: py_das@selway.umt.edu.

creativity, a connection developed in Wilson's (1947) essay "The Wound and the Bow," in which Wilson argued that wound and bow cannot be separated. Illness is framed as a necessary (but not sufficient) condition for creativity. As is made clear in other articles in this section, the metaphor of the wound and the bow can be given either a romanticist reading, in which the profound emotional experience inherent in suffering, along with the euphoria of release from suffering, is a main inspiration of artistic creation, or else a more modernist reading, where genius is associated with social disjunction, isolation, exile, and the "cooler" mood states inherent in alienation and anxiety.

Some of the confusion in the evaluation of the schizophrenia–creativity connection derives from the fact that schizophrenia has historically been a very inclusive diagnostic category, applied to many psychotic mental disorders characterized by a break from the world of consensual reality; modern diagnostic criteria specifically emphasize disorders of perception and cognition, with more recent attention to negative behavioral symptoms. In the past 20 years, the role of schizophrenia in understanding creativity has been questioned, and recent work has underscored the role of emotional states and affective disorders in creative functioning. This leads to consideration of the role of specific affects in creativity and of affective states in schizophrenia and requires an evaluation of the place of cognition in the affective disorders.

In this article, I argue that "positive symptom" thought disorder may very well be separated into bipolar and schizophrenic types and that specifically schizophrenia-like "negative symptom" thought disorder is also important in creativity. In this article, I discuss possible roles for depressed, hypomanic, and flat affect. Finally, I evaluate the roles and confounding influences of impulsivity. I argue for further empirical evaluation of at least six relevant clinical and subclinical characteristics, all of which have at one time or another been considered related to the schizophrenia spectrum. Finally, I describe the relation of shared-trait approaches to process theories involving nonlinear dynamical systems.

The Breadth and Depth of the Schizophrenia Spectrum

Problems have arisen from the use of the term *schizophrenia spectrum* to refer to a variety of disorders presumed to be syndromally or etiologically related to schizophrenia. Much work on genetic and other causal factors in schizophrenia has used the concept of the schizophrenia spectrum to refer to a range of psychotic and psychotic-like syndromes, all presumably related, traditionally including bipolar disorder. Choices regarding what is counted within the spectrum can be very important for the results of research on such important topics as relative genetic and environmental contributions to the disorder. Diagnostic lumping has also muddied the issue of whether creativity and creative cognition are associated more with affective disorders, with antisocial behavior, or with schizophrenia. The loose spectrum concept has rendered much of the family and eminence literatures inconclusive on these points.

The term *spectrum* can have two meanings (see Schuldberg & Sass, 1999). The first suggests that different kinds of psychopathology lie in a continuous dimensional space of classification, that diagnostic groups commingle and are neither rigid nor exclusive. In this "horizontal" view of the spectrum, different disorders, such as bipolar disorder and schizophrenia, are seen as related and sometimes overlapping. The notion of a horizontal schizophrenia spectrum, like the category of schizoaffective disorder, may capture the reality and prevalence of mixed types of mental disorder evidencing several classes of symptoms. However, the concept of a horizontal spectrum has weakened research on diagnostic specificity. Some researchers in psychopathology do believe that a common factor is responsible for a broad variety of severe mental disorders; Eysenck (1993, 1995), for example, stated that schizophrenia and the affective disorders exist on a continuum and proceed from a common causal factor.

The second meaning of the term *spectrum* implies that there is a continuum of severity in psychological disturbance ranging downward from exemplary functioning to normality (however defined), through subclinical symptoms, to less severe psychopathology (e.g., schizotypal personality disorder), to the most severe mental disorders. In this "vertical spectrum" of degree of severity, the more extreme as well as the less disabling disorders are seen as being on a continuum with each other and with normality. The notion of a vertical schizophrenia spectrum allows a focus on symptoms as continuous traits, helps in understanding psychological processes underlying both creativity and psychopathology, and eventually points toward examining the ongoing and fluctuating person–environment transactions and temporal dynamics involved in both psychopathology and health. Continuum approaches lead naturally to dynamic conceptualizations of the vicissitudes, the ebb and flow (see Thorne & Miller, 1994) of creativity, as well as psychopathology and normal personality functioning, in an individual over time, in the course of daily life.

The vertical spectrum concept leads to productive continuum approaches, and the shared-trait studies described later rely on such vertical continuum views of health and psychopathology. This is in tune with recent work on the relation between, for example, normal traits or interpersonal behaviors and the diagnosis of personality disorders. However, this article also explores the horizontal differentiation of six separate trait dimensions, a notion that conflicts with positing a horizontal spectrum of indistinct overlapping syndromes and fuzzy symptoms. In shared-trait research, it is the status of the horizontal spectrum that raises the most questions: To what extent is there difference and specificity regarding the roles of distinct categories or separate dimensions of symptom-like traits? How many dimensions are there?

It is also important to treat creativity itself as a continuous, nondichotomous variable and to look at everyday, noneminent creativity. This is an approach that has been advanced greatly in the work of R. L. Richards and her collaborators (e.g., Kinney et al., 2000–2001; R. L. Richards, Kinney, Lunde, Benet, & Merzel, 1988). Thus, there is a vertical continuum between ordinary improvisation and the activities of a creative genius. An unresolved question concerns whether there are horizontally discrete types of creative syndromes or activities in different fields.

Research on Schizophrenia and Creativity

Causal and Measurement Models

This section summarizes literature on creativity and psychopathology, then focuses specifically on shared-trait approaches to studying clinical and subclinical characteristics and creative activity. It discusses the role played by six traits, all at one time or another considered part of a horizontal schizophrenia spectrum, in various forms of psychopathology and creativity.

A variety of different possible causal relations have been proposed linking genius and madness, including psychopathology causing creativity, creativity leading to psychopathology, a third variable causing both, and other plausible models involving multiple factors (see Prentky, 1980, 2000–2001; R. L. Richards, 1981). In addition, without even considering causal relations, the same cognitive variables may be viewed either as problem-solving processes or evaluated negatively in more clinical terms. *Divergent thinking,* the generating of new and possibly useful ideas, which is a core feature of creative intelligence in Guilford's (1982) theory, and *thought disorder,* cited as a defining characteristic of the schizophrenic disorders, are defined very similarly (Hasenfus & Magaro, 1976; Keefe & Magaro, 1980). This makes it difficult even to separate measured creativity and schizophrenic-like cognition as independent and dependent variables, regardless of the specific causal models proposed. Nevertheless, the equating of creative intelligence and psychotic thinking remains controversial, and Guilford himself argued that creative thinking is essentially rational.

The categorical approach to creativity and mental disorder generally employed in eminence and family studies attempts unsuccessfully to finesse these issues by treating creativity and madness as all-or-none phenomena. However, it is still difficult to separate some creators' putative mental disorder from their creations. A key distinguishing feature concerns whether new and unusual ideas are classified by others as "good," "creative," and "culturally significant," or as "bad," "psychotic," "autistic," and "useless." Social evaluations of quality enter immediately into judgments of the creative or mad product.

Eminence Studies

This first type of research looks for evidence of diagnosable psychopathology in populations of eminent individuals. The occurrence of psychopathology in creative individuals, as well as their relatives, has been documented extensively, both historically and in contemporary populations. For individuals who lived in the past, the person is generally assessed via biographical materials. Creativity is most commonly defined with reference to an individual's achieved fame or well-recognized achievement, or people are nominated as creative by mentors, teachers, or peers. Psychopathology is usually assessed, often retrospectively, by categorical diagnosis of a disorder (or spectrum disorder), the presence of specific psychiatric symptoms, or scores on psychological tests that measure symptoms.

Eminence studies and biographical research in general suffer from several methodological problems, described in more detail by Kinney et al. (2000–2001) in their article in this issue. First, psychopathology is often assessed at a distance, through contemporary reports and sometimes through the participant's own productions; this type of assessment is vulnerable to selectivity and retrospective biases. Second, the diagnostic criteria employed are often loose and vary across studies. Third, there is a problem of lack of controls. With whom is the historically eminent or contemporarily celebrated individual to be compared? Very little work has been done on base rates of psychopathology or psychological health, on symptoms, odd behavior, family problems, and environmental tribulations in noneminent people, and with some exceptions, little research has been done with biographies of "ordinary people." It is often unclear whether the sometimes lurid, dramatic behaviors and histories of the creative and eminent set them apart from the noncreative, whose histories are generally unknown. However, some controlled research does exist in this area that has found elevated rates of mental disorder in both highly creative individuals and their relatives when they are contrasted with comparison groups.

Finally, creativity may be contaminated with recognition and fame, something discussed more in the Kinney et al. (2000–2001) and Sass (2000–2001) articles. Eminence and leadership (another criterion used in biographical research) can be as difficult to define conceptually as creativity (see Sass, 2000–2001). Sass's work also exemplifies a return to aspects of the eminence approach, as he argues for an important role for schizoid, schizotypal, and schizophrenic conditions in some modern, path-breaking creative individuals.

Family Studies

Family study research explores creativity and eminence in relatives of psychiatric patients or relatives of people with schizophrenia in particular. It is well known that kin of some psychiatric patients, and sometimes patients themselves, can achieve greatly, despite (or perhaps because of) a presumably inherited predisposition for schizophrenia. Such a predisposition is, by definition, not expressed at clinical levels in "well" relatives. This research has been conducted in Iceland, Denmark, Massachusetts, and Oregon, often with case registers and an exhaustive search for patients or relatives. In some studies, adopted-away children are examined as part of family studies of the heritability of mental disorders. This research has similar methodological problems to those previously described.

Shared-Trait Research

A third methodological approach examines stylistic similarities and shared (as well as distinguishing) personality characteristics in members of creative and psychiatric populations. This research relies on the psychometric assessment of personality traits; patterns of interests; and motivational, affective, cognitive, and behavioral styles rather than diagnostic categorization or the assessment of symptomatic behaviors alone. This type of research can clarify differences among causal models and highlight the shared and unshared features of creativity and psychopathology rather than being limited to evaluation of simple models such as genius causes madness or madness causes genius.

As previously noted, partial and specific overlaps, as well as some disjunctions, have been noted in the perception, cognition, affect, and behavior of creative and eminent individuals and participants with a variety of mental disorders. Examples of traits found to be characteristic of both creative and pathological groups include psychoticism, impulsivity, hypomania, depression and other forms of affect, interpersonal abrasiveness and conflict, schizotypal traits, narcissistic features, aggression, alcohol and substance use, and other types of clinical and subclinical psychopathology. Note that these features overlap with the six traits emphasized in this article, but there are others. For example, this article does not deal in detail with interpersonal symptoms, an especially fruitful area for future work.

Some researchers have also observed that unlike members of pathological groups, creative individuals show both signs of health and signs of psychopathology, providing added support for a two-factor theory of the relation between creativity and psychopathology. Aristotle himself felt that for a melancholic individual to be a genius required a delicate balance of different humors or types of bile. This invokes a static balance or possibly dynamic equilibrium required to do creative work or to have a healthy life. (However, note that R. L. Richards [1996] and others [e.g., Zausner, 1996] have now argued that creative work may at times involve "far from equilibrium" processes. Such processes dissipate energy and are in a constant state of imbalance, as in the situation of someone who is running by constantly staying off balance, always falling forward.)

It is important to attend to positive, healthy traits, to possible mitigating and differentiating factors that can lead to creativity or exemplary functioning rather than psychopathology (see Schuldberg, 1993), and to differentiate creative and psychopathological functioning in different creative groups, such as artists, architects, scientists, mathematicians, philosophers, writers, and others. One candidate for a healthy characteristic is Barron's (1953) measure of ego strength, which has been found to distinguish members of some creative groups from schizophrenic participants, even when both groups on average show high scores on a psychometric indicator of schizotypy (e.g., Barron, 1972).

A weakness of trait studies in general is that they often use an atheoretical shotgun approach, examining participants' differences in elevations across a broad range of personality scales. Such completely empiricist methodology leaves it unclear whether trait differences are centrally related to creativity or are artefactual, possibly reflecting an irrelevant or a secondary additional factor or factors. Nevertheless, in evaluating the relative strength of the eminence, family, and shared-trait studies of schizophrenia and creativity, it now appears that the research most strongly supports a specific connection for related traits rather than for categorical diagnosis.

Six Relevant Dimensions for Pathology–Creativity Research

This article highlights six primary domains of symptoms or traits as foci for shared-trait approaches to creativity and psychopathology: (a) positive symptom schizotypal cognitive traits (positive thought disorder), (b) negative symptom schizotypal cognitive traits (negative symptom thought disorder), (c) negative symptom schizotypal affective traits (flat affect), (d) hypomania, (e) depression, and (f) impulsivity. An interesting question concerns how each of these trait dimensions can be manifested or has associated features in the domains of cognition, language, behavior, and interpersonal relations. The affective and cognitive components and correlates of each trait dimension are especially central in this discussion.

Issues in the Measurement of Symptom Dimensions

Key problems with this program concern measurement, how to define and assess each characteristic, and the determination of factorial purity and construct overlap. A current problem concerns contamination of constructs, the intercorrelation or lack of separation of measures. This issue is addressed later in this article with reference to the empirical distinctness or overlap of hypomania, impulsivity, and positive schizotypal traits.

Disordered Cognition: Form Versus Content, Positive Versus Negative

Creative and schizophrenic-like thought have been considered to overlap across several dimensions of thinking. These include cognitive styles corresponding to both positive and negative symptom subtypes of thought disorder. Sass's (2000–2001) article discusses in more detail what may be termed negative symptom forms of schizophrenic cognition and experience. Some research indicates that it is also possible to differentiate positive symptom schizophrenic from manic thought disorder (e.g., Holzman, Shenton, & Solovay, 1986; Johnston & Holzman, 1979).

Schizophrenia has been considered a disorder with central symptoms that are cognitive. These features are roughly divided into two main categories: disorders of the content of thought and disorders of the form of thought. *Disordered thought content* refers to ideas or beliefs that are generally considered false, delusional, deviant, unusual, or bizarre. The delusions of schizophrenia are often bizarre and sometimes cosmic. However, schizophrenia is not the only disorder in which delusions may appear; grandiose and self-referential delusions, more limited in scope, can appear in such conditions as the *Diagnostic and Statistical Manual of Mental Disorders* (4th ed.; American Psychiatric Association, 1994) delusional disorder and in the affective disorders as well, where apparently mistaken beliefs are sometimes congruent with the elevated or depressed mood that is the central symptom of the disorder.

Disorders of the form of thought have traditionally been viewed as the hallmark of schizophrenia. *Formal thought disorder* refers to deviances in how thoughts are linked together, occur in sequence, follow from one another, and are communicated linguistically. More recently, formal thought disorder has been well documented in affective disorder patients as well (see review in Jamison, 1990b; Marengo & Harrow, 1985). A current research question concerns the specificity of different forms of thought disorder to certain forms of psychopathology. Manic patients tend to be characterized by pressure of speech, derailment, combinatory and overinclusive thinking, and a tendency to engage the examiner interpersonally (Jamison, 1990b; Johnston & Holzman, 1979). Jamison and others have argued that it is precisely such fluent and overproductive cognitive disturbances that are most akin to the processes of creativity.

In contrast, specifically schizophrenic thought disorder is more likely to include the categories of poverty of speech, illogicality, loose associations, tangentiality, poverty of content of speech, underinclusive reasoning, absurdity, confusion, the loss of conceptual boundaries in "contamination" and "fluidity," and the use of unusual and highly idiosyncratic language (Cuesta & Peralta, 1993; Jamison, 1990b; see Berenbaum & Barch, 1995, for disconfirming findings[1]).

It is also possible to distinguish between positive symptom and negative symptom forms of thought disorder. The study of negative symptoms is potentially a very interesting area, which can also be connected to current interest in gifted or high-functioning autistic or Aspberger's syndrome individuals, whose symptoms overlap with schizophrenic negative symptoms (Frith & Frith, 1991). Differentiating forms of unusual cognition may also illuminate the understanding of varieties of creative cognition as well. An unresolved issue involves evaluating the degree to which different types of thought disorder are present or absent in different creative endeavors. Sass (1992, 1994, 2000–2001) suggests that specifically schizophrenic forms resemble modes of thought characteristic of the modernism and postmodernism of the past 100 years.

[1]These issues are also taken up in a recent book by Klieger (1999).

Flat Affect

Flat affect serves as a shorthand expression for schizotypal and negative symptom schizophrenic-like affective characteristics, also including anhedonia and perhaps inappropriate affect. Unpublished work has investigated normal personality characteristics and creativity test scores in a group of nonclinical high scorers on the Physical Anhedonia scale (Chapman, Chapman, & Raulin, 1976), indicative of a lack of experienced pleasure akin to flat affect. Analyses of a sample including participants described in Schuldberg, French, Stone, and Heberle (1988) compared controls and participants who scored 2 *SD* or more above the Wisconsin investigators' means on this scale. As a group, the anhedonic participants scored lower on all creativity measures. This effect was accounted for by the How Do You Think total score, with a trend for lower scores on the Domino (1970) Adjective Check List (ACL) scale (Gough & Heilbrun, 1980), in which male anhedonics received low scores. In contrast, both male and female anhedonics also received ACL scores indicative of high *origence,* a construct that refers to creative, nonintellective thought, and male anhedonic participants scored high on the Barron–Welsh Revised Art Scale (Welsh & Barron, 1963). (These creativity scales are discussed in more detail later.)

This partially positive picture of anhedonic participants is enriched by results from other personality instruments, which contribute to a view of these individuals as socially alienated and marching to the beats of different drummers, perhaps having positive "outsider" characteristics. There is also interesting recent work on social anhedonia and creativity (Cox & Leon, 1999).

Hypomania

This form of expansive mood and behavioral acceleration is central to the creativity–psychopathology connections drawn by Andreasen (1987; Andreasen & Glick, 1988), R. L. Richards et al. (1988), and Jamison (1990a, 1993). Hypomanic affect is also associated with some of the forms of positive symptom thought disorder just described, and an ongoing project will be to separate, if this is possible, specifically manic and specifically positive symptom schizotypal forms of positive thought disorder.

Depression

Some workers have focused on the connection between depressed affect, with its associated emotional sensitivity and awareness, and creativity (e.g., Haynal, 1985). A role for depression is included in some of the theoretical and empirical work on bipolar affective disorder and creativity (e.g., Andreasen & Canter, 1974; Jamison, Gerner, Hammen, & Padesky, 1980). Recent experimental work was conducted by Kaufman and his associates (Kaufman & Vosburg, 1997) linking depressive-like experience and creative work. Some authors (R. L. Richards, 1997; Schuldberg, 1994) have suggested that mixtures of depressed and elated affect may be key in the creative process.

Impulsivity

A number of investigators, including Barron (1963), have suggested a positive association between impulsive, antisocial behavior and creativity. Specifically, the norm-breaking behavior of antisocial individuals may parallel and co-occur with (or, perhaps, be equivalent to or indistinguishable from) the originality of creative individuals, particularly those who depart from existing artistic conventions and smash genres—"revolutionary" artists.

Impulsivity also enters this discussion via the construct of psychoticism, thought by Eysenck (e.g., Eysenck, 1993, 1995) to be a central trait in creativity. The scales developed by Eysenck and colleagues to measure psychoticism, notably the P scale of the Eysenck Personality Questionnaire (Eysenck & Eysenck, 1975), have been demonstrated to be contaminated with the constructs of impulsivity and antisocial behavior (Bishop, 1977; Block, 1977; see Eysenck, 1977a, 1977b, for replies).

The remainder of this article provides empirical illustrations of these conceptual relations.

Method

Participants

These data were gathered together from several large samples drawn from a nonclinical, noneminent college student population. For a full description of participant selection procedures, as well as details of the instrumentation in these studies, see Schuldberg et al. (1988) and Schuldberg (1988, 1990, 1995). All told, data are presented here on a total of 1,108 participants.

Measures

Symptom and trait measures.

1. Positive schizotypal symptoms were measured by the Wisconsin investigators' Perceptual Aberration–Magical Ideation scale (Per–Mag scale; Chapman & Chapman, 1985) and the Minnesota Multiphasic Personality Inventory–2 (MMPI–2; Butcher, Dahlstrom, Graham, Tellegen, & Kaemmer, 1989) Scale *8* (Schizophrenia).
2. Negative schizotypal cognitive symptoms were not addressed directly in this study. However, it appears possible that the Golden and Meehl (1979) Schizoid Taxon scale taps a negative symptom rather than a positive symptom form of schizotypy.
3. Negative schizotypal affective symptoms were tapped by means of the construct of *anhedonia,* or lack of experienced pleasure, measured by the Physical Anhedonia scale (Chapman et al., 1976), one of the Wisconsin scales of hypothetical psychosis proneness.
4. Hypomanic characteristics were measured by MMPI–2 Scale *9* (Hypomania) and the Wisconsin Hypomanic Traits scale (Eckblad & Chapman, 1986).
5. Depressive symptoms were measured by MMPI–2 Scale *2* (Depression).
6. Impulsivity was measured by the Wisconsin Impulsive Nonconformity scale (Chapman et al., 1984). This scale is correlated with the Wisconsin investigators' Per–Mag scale but was also developed to sharpen the discrimination of at-risk individuals. As noted, the P scale from the Eysenck Personality Questionnaire may also primarily tap antisocial and impulsive characteristics (Bishop, 1977; Block, 1977).

Creativity tests. Creativity tests included the Barron–Welsh Revised Art Scale (Welsh & Barron, 1963), sometimes given in computer-administered form (Schuldberg & Nichols, 1990), the How Do You Think (Davis & Subkoviak, 1975), the Gough (1979), the Domino (1970) creativity scales from the ACL (Gough & Heilbrun, 1980), a modified version of Alternate

Uses (Guilford, Christensen, Merrifield, & Wilson, 1978), the Independent Activities Questionnaire (IAQ; J. M. Richards, Holland, & Lutz, 1967), and the scales of Everyday Vocational and Avocational Creativity (R. L. Richards et al., 1988; only representative data on the maximum of the Peak Vocational and Avocational Creativity ratings are reported from these latter scales).

Results

Table 1 presents the correlations of a variety of subclinical symptom measures with a series of creativity tests. Creativity measures were positively correlated with positive schizotypal symptoms, hypomania, and impulsivity, with the largest correlations occurring for hypomania. The creativity scores were generally negatively correlated with the measures of negative schizotypal symptoms and depression. Physical Anhedonia was negatively correlated with a variety of creativity tests, including the How Do You Think, the IAQ, the Domino and Gough ACL scales, and the Richards Maximum Peak measure (see Table 1). The Schizoid Taxon scale was negatively correlated with the Gough ACL scale.

Evidence for Separate Roles for the Different Traits

As a demonstration of the different roles of schizotypal symptoms, subclinical affective symptomatology, and impulsivity in creativity, several regression models were constructed to predict scores on creativity measures with an index of hypomania (the Wisconsin Hypomanic Traits scale or MMPI–2 Scale *9*), schizotypal symptoms (the Per–Mag scale), impulsivity (the Wisconsin Impulsive Nonconformity scale), and the schizotypal negative symptom of flat affect (the Wisconsin Physical Anhedonia scale) as independent variables. In constructing these equations, scores on these four scales were entered into the final equation in this order. In the first equation, the dependent variable was the How Do You Think. Table 2 reports the results of this analysis.

The Hypomanic Traits scale accounted for approximately 39% of the variance in the How Do You Think. After the Hypomanic traits scale was entered in the equation, the Per–Mag scale, as well as impulsive nonconformity, added virtually nothing to the accounting for variance in the How Do You Think; Physical Anhedonia contributed to the prediction of about 9% of the remaining variance after these other tests were

Table 1. *Correlations of Positive Schizotypal Symptoms, Negative Schizotypal Symptoms, Impulsivity, Depression, and Hypomania With Creativity Test Scores*

	Creativity Test				
Symptom and Measure	How Do You Think	Barron–Welsh Revised Art Scale	ACL CPS	ACL Domino	Richards Maximum Peak
1. Positive Schizotypal					
Per–Mag	.38**	.14**	.08*	.17**	.17*
MMPI–2 Schizophrenia	.28**	.11	–.04	.13*	–.02
2. and 3. Negative Schizotypal					
Physical Anhedonia	–.36**	–.06	–.16**	–.18**	–.34**
Taxon	–.03	–.02	–.21**	–.05	–.05
4. Hypomania					
Hypomanic Traits	.61**	.11*	.25**	.29**	—
MMPI–2 Hypomania	.43**	.09	.17**	.34**	.08
5. Depression					
MMPI–2 Depression	–.21**	–.04	–.30**	–.22**	–.16*
6. Impulsivity					
Impulsive Nonconformity	.30**	.13**	.00	.17**	–.10
EPQ P	.20**	.02	.01	.03	—

Note: n = 198–1,108. ACL = Adjective Check List; CPS = Creative Personality Scale; Per–Mag = Perceptual Abberation–Magical Ideation scale; MMPI–2 = Minnesota Multiphasic Personality Inventory–2; EPQ = Eysenck Personality Questionnaire.
*$p \leq .05$. **$p \leq .005$.

Table 2. *Separating Variance in Creativity Test Scores Accounted for by Hypomania, the Perceptual Abberation–Magical Ideation Scale, Impulsivity, and Anhedonia*

Independent Variable	R^2	ΔR^2	*p*	β
Hypomanic Traits (Wisconsin)	.39	.39	< .0005	.56
Perceptual Abberation–Magical Ideation Scale	.39	.0001	*ns*	–.03
Impulsive Nonconformity	.39	.0025	*ns*	.03
Physical Anhedonia	.45	.06	< .0005	–.27

Note: $n = 352$. Dependent variable = How Do You Think.

Table 3. *Separating Variance in Everyday Creativity Accounted for by Hypomania, the Perceptual Abberation–Magical Ideation Scale, Impulsivity, and Anhedonia*

Independent Variable	R^2	ΔR^2	*p*	β
Hypomania (MMPI–2 Scale 9)	.005	.005	*ns*	.06
Perceptual Abberation–Magical Ideation Scale	.02	.02	.06	.12
Impulsive Nonconformity	.08	.05	.001	–.19
Physical Anhedonia	.12	.05	.002	–.24

Note: $n = 196$. Dependent variable = Maximum Peak Vocational or Avocational Creativity. MMPI–2 = Minnesota Multiphasic Personality Inventory–2.

entered into the equation. This indicates that with this creativity scale as the dependent variable, schizotypal characteristics, particularly positive symptom ones, as well as impulsivity, added very little to Hypomania in the prediction of creativity test scores.

In a second analysis, R. L. Richards and her colleagues' Maximum Peak (Vocational and Avocational) creativity measure was used as the dependent variable (see Table 3). In this analysis, hypomania now contributed nonsignificantly to the variance in the creativity measure. The Per–Mag scale accounted for approximately 2% of the variance, Impulsive Nonconformity for 5% of the remaining variance, and Physical Anhedonia for 5% of the variance that was left.

It appears at this point that the relative contributions of schizotypal and affective symptoms to scores on creativity measures depend very much on the specific measures used.

Discussion and Conclusions

Across several data sets, correlations indicated positive associations between creativity and both schizophrenic-like positive schizotypal symptoms and hypomanic characteristics. Behavioral impulsivity, which can also occur in hypomania, was also related to creativity measures. There was some but not strong justification for separating the roles of cognitive (schizophrenia-like) and affective (hypomanic) characteristics. There was substantial overlap in the variance that creativity tests shared with psychometric measures of hypomania and subclinical schizophrenic-like positive symptoms. Hypomania was generally the construct accounting for the lion's share of the variance in these creativity test scores.

Contributions of the Six Traits

This work argues for a degree of specificity in the relations between schizotypal-like traits and creativity. In these data sets, the data indicate the following:

1. *Positive symptoms and positive symptom thought disorder.* These traits appear related to creativity. They are not readily separable from hypomanic symptoms, and their empirical contribution to creativity test performance is not as great as that of hypomanic characteristics.

2. and 3. *Negative symptom thought disorder and flat affective symptoms.* Contrary to the theoretical suggestions discussed in the introduction, psychometric indicators of negative symptoms (although not specifically of negative thought disorder) are negatively correlated with the creativity tests. Higher levels of flat affect are associated with lower creativity scores, although there

have been tantalizing indications in other work that some anhedonic participants may perform better on certain creativity tests. The research of Cox and Leon (1999), who focused on social anhedonia, is also interesting. The data sets do not address specifically cognitive aspects of negative symptoms, and this is a fruitful line of future inquiry.

4. *Hypomania.* This construct has the highest correlations with creativity test scores and "soaks up" a good deal of the variance associated with other characteristics (see also Nadasi, 1997).[2]

5. *Depression.* Contrary to romanticist views of the relationship between depression and creativity and the work of Haynal (1985) and others, psychometrically assessed depressive symptoms are negatively correlated with creativity test scores.

6. *Impulsivity.* This characteristic also appears related to some creativity test scores, and it is also correlated with both positive symptom schizotypy measures and with hypomania.

Several points are important to note for future research in this area. First, attention must be paid to mitigating factors, such as ego strength, and their role in the creativity–psychopathology connection. Second, both measurement and causal modeling approaches are important. For example, a preliminary path model reported by Schuldberg and Norris (1996) suggests that positive psychotic-like symptoms and creative problem solving may actually both derive from a prior causal risk or "diathesis" factor rather than from psychopathology contemporaneously causing creativity or vice versa.

Addressing both pathology-like traits and creativity as continua also means that one can observe varying levels of these characteristics, both across individuals (as in the individual differences approach to research) and within the same individual over time. If we accept the view put forward by Kinney et al. (2000–2001), R. L. Richards et al. (1988), Akiskal and Akiskal (1988), Russ (1993), and others of a curvilinear relation between pathological-like traits and creativity, we allow nonlinearity into our picture of creativity–pathology causal relations. (Note that as soon as one speaks of an optimum level of a characteristic with regard to a particular outcome, in this case, creative functioning, one acknowledges nonlinearity.)

Finally, if dynamics, or changes with time, are also included in models of psychopathology and creativity, the result is a picture of human functioning in both its sublime and its more troubling aspects that can be described as a *nonlinear dynamical system.* This follows by definition if we view the creative process (as well, perhaps, as the onset and course of disorder) as emerging from a system of interacting components, changing with time, and with nonlinear causal connections linking at least some of the contributing variables. An interesting feature of such a system is that under certain conditions, it may be capable of chaotic behavior (see Schuldberg, 1998, 1999).

Several characteristics of chaotic systems are especially relevant to the problems of understanding creativity. First, systems in chaotic regimes are extremely sensitive to initial conditions. Small differences in starting point, as well as small chance environmental influences, can have large and increasingly divergent effects on course and outcome. This provides a way to understand the role of serendipity and a number of other phenomena. Second, the path of a chaotic system never returns to the same place while also going in the same direction. This provides a definition of novelty and originality. Finally, the behavior of chaotic systems can manifest so-called fractal properties of self-similarity, symmetry, and scaling phenomena. I argued elsewhere (Schuldberg, 1999) that these properties provide a way to understand the style of an artist's work.

The creative process then emerges not as a straight-line path of progress toward a creative product but rather involving possibly complex trajectories around attractors, regions (corresponding to genres and styles) where the creative process may orbit and then leave. Creative endeavors may be expected to exhibit sometimes apparently cyclic, sometimes more complicated, sometimes catastrophically changing trajectories and to encompass both narrative and nonnarrative structures (see Schuldberg, 1998).

A more differentiated picture of the dynamic relations between trait-like personal characteristics and temporal shifts in creative behavior should shed light on the mysteries of everyday as well as eminent creativity. A step that must precede modeling the dynamics of creativity is the selection of relevant dimensions

[2]Indeed, when the correlations in Table 1 between the How Do You Think and hypomanic traits and the Per–Mag scale were compared using Fisher's z transformation, the difference between the two correlations was highly significant ($z = 5.00, p < .00005$).

that tap the underlying processes leading to creative behavior and the understanding of the causal relations between dimensions of personal style and the criteria of creativity. This article argues for the importance of six psychological dimensions that have traditionally been associated with more conventional diagnostic notions of the schizophrenia spectrum.

References

Akiskal, H. S., & Akiskal, K. (1988). Reassessing the significance of bipolar disorders: Clinical significance and artistic creativity. *Psychiatry and Psychobiology, 3,* 29S–36S.

American Psychiatric Association. (1994). *Diagnostic and statistical manual of mental disorders* (4th ed.). Washington, DC: Author.

Andreasen, N. J. C. (1987). Creativity and mental illness: Prevalence rates in writers and their first degree relatives. *American Journal of Psychiatry, 144,* 1288–1292.

Andreasen, N. J. C., & Canter, A. (1974). The creative writer: Psychiatric symptoms and family history. *Comprehensive Psychiatry, 15,* 123–131.

Andreasen, N. C., & Glick, I. D. (1988). Bipolar affective disorder and creativity: Implications and clinical management. *Comprehensive Psychiatry, 29,* 207–217.

Barron, F. (1953). An ego-strength scale which predicts response to psychotherapy. *Consulting Psychology, 5,* 327–333.

Barron, F. (1963). *Creativity and psychological health: Origins of personal vitality and creative freedom.* New York: Van Nostrand.

Barron, F. (1972). *Artists in the making.* New York: Seminar.

Berenbaum, H., & Barch, D. (1995). The categorization of thought disorder. *Journal of Psycholinguistic Research, 24,* 349–376.

Bishop, D. V. (1977). The P scale and psychosis. *Journal of Abnormal Psychology, 86,* 127–134.

Block, J. (1977). The P scale and psychosis: Continued concerns. *Journal of Abnormal Psychology, 86,* 431–434.

Butcher, J. N., Dahlstrom, W. G., Graham, J. R., Tellegen, A., & Kaemmer, B. (1989). *MMPI–2: Minnesota Multiphasic Personality Inventory–2: Manual for administration and scoring.* Minneapolis: University of Minnesota Press.

Chapman, L. J., & Chapman, J. P. (1985). Psychosis-proneness. In M. Alpert (Ed.), *Controversies in schizophrenia: Changes and constancies* (pp. 157–174). New York: Guilford.

Chapman, L. J., Chapman, J. P., Numbers, J. S., Edell, W. S., Carpenter, B. N., & Beckfield, D. (1984). Impulsive nonconformity as a trait contributing to the prediction of psychotic-like and schizotypal symptoms. *Journal of Nervous and Mental Disease, 172,* 681–691.

Chapman, L. J., Chapman, J. P., & Raulin, M. L. (1976). Scales for physical and social anhedonia. *Journal of Abnormal Psychology, 85,* 374–382.

Cox, A. J., & Leon, J. L. (1999). Negative schizotypal traits in the relation of creativity to psychopathology. *Creativity Research Journal, 12,* 25–36.

Cuesta, M. J., & Peralta, V. (1993). Does formal thought disorder differ among patients with schizophrenic, schizophreniform, and manic schizoaffective disorders? *Schizophrenia Research, 10,* 151–158.

Davis, G. A., & Subkoviak, M. J. (1975). Multidimensional analysis of a personality-based test of creative potential. *Journal of Educational Measurement, 12,* 37–43.

Domino, G. (1970). Identification of potentially creative persons from the Adjective Check List. *Journal of Consulting and Clinical Psychology, 35,* 48–51.

Eckblad, M., & Chapman, L. J. (1986). Development and validation of a scale for hypomanic personality. *Journal of Abnormal Psychology, 95,* 214–222.

Eysenck, H. J. (1977a). Block and psychoticism. *Journal of Abnormal Psychology, 86,* 651–652.

Eysenck, H. J. (1977b). Psychosis and psychoticism: A reply to Bishop. *Journal of Abnormal Psychology, 86,* 427–430.

Eysenck, H. J. (1993). Creativity and personality: Suggestions for a theory. *Psychological Inquiry, 4,* 147–178.

Eysenck, H. J. (1995). *Genius: The natural history of creativity.* Cambridge, England: Cambridge University Press.

Eysenck, H. J., & Eysenck, S. B. G. (1975). *Manual for the Eysenck Personality Questionnaire.* London: Hodder & Stoughton.

Frith, C. D., & Frith, U. (1991). Elective affinities in schizophrenia and childhood autism. In P. E. Bebbington (Ed.), *Social psychiatry: Theory, methodology, and practice* (pp. 65–89). New Brunswick, NJ: Transaction.

Golden, R. R., & Meehl, P. E. (1979). Detection of the schizoid taxon with MMPI indicators. *Journal of Abnormal Psychology, 88,* 217–233.

Gough, H. G. (1979). A creative personality scale for the Adjective Check List. *Journal of Personality and Social Psychology, 39,* 1398–1405.

Gough, H. G., & Heilbrun, A. B. (1980). *The Adjective Check List manual.* Palo Alto, CA: Consulting Psychologists Press.

Guilford, J. P. (1982). Is some creative thinking irrational? *Journal of Creative Behavior, 16,* 151–154.

Guilford, J. P., Christensen, P. R., Merrifield, P. R., & Wilson, R. C. (1978). *Alternate uses: Manual of instructions and interpretations.* Palo Alto, CA: Mind Garden.

Hasenfus, N., & Magaro, P. (1976). Creativity and schizophrenia: An equality of empirical constructs. *British Journal of Psychiatry, 129,* 346–349.

Haynal, A. (1985). *Depression and creativity.* New York: International Universities Press.

Holzman, P. S., Shenton, M. E., & Solovay, M. R. (1986). Quality of thought disorder in differential diagnosis. *Schizophrenia Bulletin, 12,* 360–372.

Jamison, K. R. (1990a). Manic–depressive illness and accomplishment: Creativity, leadership, and social class. In F. K. Goodwin & K. R. Jamison (Eds.), *Manic–depressive illness* (pp. 332–367). New York: Oxford University Press.

Jamison, K. R. (1990b). Thought disorder, perception, and cognition. In F. K. Goodwin & K. R. Jamison (Eds.), *Manic–depressive illness* (pp. 247–280). New York: Oxford University Press.

Jamison, K. R. (1993). *Touched with fire: Manic–depressive illness and the artistic temperament.* New York: Free Press.

Jamison, K. R., Gerner, R. H., Hammen, C., & Padesky, C. (1980). Clouds and silver linings: Positive experiences associated with primary affective disorders. *American Journal of Psychiatry, 137,* 198–202.

Johnston, M. H., & Holzman, P. S. (1979). *Assessing schizophrenic thinking*. San Francisco: Jossey-Bass.

Kaufman, G., & Vosburg, S. K. (1997). "Paradoxical" mood effects on creative problem-solving. *Cognition and Emotion, 11*, 151–170.

Keefe, J. A., & Magaro, P. A. (1980). Creativity and schizophrenia: An equivalence of cognitive processing. *Journal of Abnormal Psychology, 89*, 390–398.

Kinney, D. K., Richards, R., Lowing, P. A., LeBlanc, D., Zimbalist, M. E., & Harlan, P. (2000–2001). Creativity in offspring of schizophrenic and control parents: An adoption study. *Creativity Research Journal, 13*, 17–25.

Klieger, J. H. (1999). *Disordered thinking and the Rorschach: Theory, research, and differential diagnosis*. Hillsdale, NJ: The Analytic Press.

Marengo, J., & Harrow, M. (1985). Thought disorder: A function of schizophrenia, mania, or psychosis? *Journal of Nervous and Mental Disease, 172*, 35–41.

Nadasi, C. (1997). *The relationship between creativity, self-actualization, and hypomania*. Unpublished master's thesis, University of Montana, Missoula.

Prentky, R. A. (1980). *Creativity and psychopathology: A neurocognitive perspective*. New York: Praeger.

Prentky, R. A. (2000–2001). Mental illness and roots of genius. *Creativity Research Journal, 13*, 95–104.

Richards, J. M., Holland, J. L., & Lutz, S. W. (1967). Prediction of student accomplishment in college. *Journal of Educational Psychology, 58*, 343–355.

Richards, R. L. (1981). Relationships between creativity and psychopathology: An evaluation and interpretation of the evidence. *Genetic Psychology Monographs, 103*, 261–324.

Richards, R. L. (1996). Does the lone genius ride again? Chaos, creativity and community. *Journal of Humanistic Psychology, 36*, 44–60.

Richards, R. L. (1997). Conclusions: When illness yields creativity. In M. A. Runco & R. Richards (Eds.), *Eminent creativity, everyday creativity, and health* (pp. 485–540). Greenwich, CT: Ablex.

Richards, R. L., Kinney, D. K., Lunde, I., Benet, M., & Merzel, A. P. C. (1988). Creativity in manic depressives, cyclothymes, their normal relatives, and control subjects. *Journal of Abnormal Psychology, 97*, 281–288.

Russ, S. W. (1993). *Affect and creativity: The role of affect and play in the creative process*. Hillsdale, NJ: Lawrence Erlbaum Associates, Inc.

Sass, L. A. (1994). *Madness and modernism: Insanity in the light of modern art, literature, and thought*. Cambridge, MA: Harvard University Press.

Sass, L. A. (2000–2001). Schizophrenia, modernism, and the creative imagination: On creativity and psychopathology. *Creativity Research Journal, 13*, 55–74.

Schuldberg, D. (1988). Abstract: Perceptual–cognitive and affective components of schizotaxia and creativity in a group of college males. *Journal of Creative Behavior, 22*, 73–74.

Schuldberg, D. (1990). Schizotypal and hypomanic traits, creativity, and psychological health. *Creativity Research Journal, 3*, 219–231.

Schuldberg, D. (1993). Personal resourcefulness: Positive aspects of functioning in high-risk research. *Psychiatry: Interpersonal and Biological Processes, 56*, 137–152.

Schuldberg, D. (1994). Giddiness and horror in the creative process. In M. P. Shaw & M. A. Runco (Eds.), *Creativity and affect* (pp. 87–101). Norwood, NJ: Ablex.

Schuldberg, D. (1995, August). *Personal resourcefulness: A preventive factor in risk for positive symptoms?* Poster session presented at the 103rd annual meeting of the American Psychological Association, New York.

Schuldberg, D. (1998). Creativity, bipolarity, and the dynamics of style. In S. W. Russ (Ed.), *Affect, creative experience, and psychological adjustment* (pp. 221–237). Washington, DC: Taylor & Francis.

Schuldberg, D. (1999). Chaos theory and creativity. In M. Runco & S. Pritzker (Eds.), *Encyclopedia of creativity* (Vol. 1, pp. 259–272). New York: Wiley.

Schuldberg, D., French, C., Stone, B. L., & Heberle, J. (1988). Creativity and schizotypal traits: Creativity test scores, perceptual aberration, magical ideation, and impulsive nonconformity. *Journal of Nervous and Mental Disease, 176*, 648–657.

Schuldberg, D., & Nichols, W. G. (1990). Using HyperCard to administer a figural test on the Apple Macintosh. *Behavior Research Methods, Instruments, and Computers, 22*, 417–420.

Schuldberg, D., & Norris, K. (1996, August). *Lifetime creativity, vocational adjustment, and hypothetical psychosis-proneness*. Paper presented at the 104th annual meeting of the American Psychological Association, Toronto, Canada.

Schuldberg, D., & Sass, L. A. (1999). Schizophrenia. In M. Runco & S. Pritzker (Eds.), *Encyclopedia of creativity* (Vol. 2, pp. 501–514). New York: Wiley.

Thorne, A., & Miller, L. C. (1994). *Ebbs, flows, linkages, and other things we don't know about personality change*. Manuscript in preparation.

Welsh, G. S., & Barron, F. (1963). *Barron–Welsh Art Scale*. Palo Alto, CA: Mind Garden.

Wilson, E. (1947). *The wound and the bow and other essays*. New York: Oxford University Press.

Zausner, T. (1996). The creative chaos: Speculations on the connection between nonlinear dynamics and the creative process. In W. Sulis & A. Combs (Eds.), *Nonlinear dynamics in human behavior* (pp. 343–363). Singapore: World Scientific.

Creativity Research Journal
2000–2001, Vol. 13, No. 1, 17–25

Creativity in Offspring of Schizophrenic and Control Parents: An Adoption Study

Dennis K. Kinney
Genetics Laboratory, McLean Hospital, and Harvard Medical School

Ruth Richards
*Saybrook Graduate School
University of California, San Francisco,
McLean Hospital and Harvard Medical School*

Patricia A. Lowing
Troy, Michigan

Deborah LeBlanc, Morris E. Zimbalist, and Patricia Harlan
Genetics Laboratory, McLean Hospital

ABSTRACT: Previous studies (Heston & Denney, 1968; Karlsson, 1970; Kauffman, Grunebaum, Cohler, & Gamer, 1979) have reported that psychologically healthier biological relatives of persons with schizophrenia had unusually creative jobs and hobbies. These studies, however, examined only eminent levels of creativity in a few professions, involved serendipitous post hoc findings, assessed creativity, or both, while aware of diagnosis. We studied 36 index adult adoptees of biological parents with schizophrenia and 36 demographically matched control adoptees with no biological family history of psychiatric hospitalization. Adoptees were diagnosed with the Diagnostic and Statistical Manual of Mental Disorders *(3rd ed.; American Psychiatric Association, 1980) criteria by investigators blind to creativity assessments. Adoptees' real-life creativity was rated by other investigators blind to personal and family psychopathology with scales of demonstrated reliability and validity applied to descriptions of vocational and avocational activities obtained from interviews. It was hypothesized that adoptees with genetic liability for schizophrenia (and thus potentially unconventional modes of thinking and perceiving)—although not schizophrenia itself—would be more creative. In fact, nonschizophrenics with either schizotypal or schizoid personality disorder or multiple schizotypal signs (which other research has linked with genetic liability for schizophrenia) had significantly higher creativity than other participants. Interestingly, some control adoptees also fit these criteria and were included in analyses. Results have implications for relations of creativity to personal symptoms and familial risk for schizophrenia.*

The idea that persons with schizophrenia or their biological relatives may have unusual creative potential

This work was supported in part by a Scottish Rite Schizophrenia Research Foundation grant and National Institute of Mental Health Grants R01 MH59136 and PO MH31154.

We thank Seymour Kety, Philip Holzman, Steven Matthysse, and Alan Mirsky for their encouragement. We thank Seymour Kety, David Rosenthal, Fini Schulsinger, and Paul Wender for use of the adoption study materials. We also thank these investigators, as well as Alan Mirsky and Manuel Pereira, for their roles in diagnostic evaluations; Joseph Welner for work in conducting the interviews; and Sandra Cole and Sharon Tramer for research assistance.

Correspondence and requests for reprints should be sent to Dennis K. Kinney, Genetics Laboratory, McLean Hospital, 115 Mill Street, Belmont, MA 02478.

has long been the subject of theoretical speculation. This idea, moreover, has received some empirical support from a variety of studies (see reviews by Kinney, 1992; Richards, 1981). For example, several studies of nonclinical samples found that more creative participants tended to score higher on personality test variables that are associated with emotional maladjustment or liability for psychopathology (e.g., Barron, 1969; Gotz & Gotz, 1979; MacKinnon, 1962). After reviewing several studies that reported that nonhospitalized participants with high scores on the Schizophrenia scale of the Minnesota Multiphasic Personality Inventory (Dahlstrom & Welsh, 1972) were especially likely to be described as "inventive" or "imaginative" by people who knew them well, Gottesman (1965) speculated that there may be some adaptive value to certain genes for psychopathology. Similarly, Eysenck (1983), citing studies reporting positive correlations between creativity and high scores on his Psychoticism scale, proposed that this scale indexes a continuous personality variable, which in its milder form is associated with higher levels of creative functioning. Wiggins and Pincus (1989) found that in a large sample of college students, high scores on a schizotypal personality disorder scale were associated with high scores on a personality test of openness to experience, a measure that other studies have, in turn, found to be positively correlated with creativity.

In a study that also used college students, Schuldberg (1990) found significant associations between measures of creative traits, attitudes, and behaviors on the How Do You Think Test (Davis & Subkoviak, 1975) and two Wisconsin scales of hypothetical psychosis-proneness (Perceptual Aberration and Magical Ideation; Chapman & Chapman, 1985), although there was an even higher association with a measure of hypomanic traits. In fact, cognitive style factors considered to mediate a creativity–psychopathology association have been linked more typically with bipolar disorders than schizophrenia (Andreasen & Powers, 1974; Jamison, 1989; Richards, 1993, 1997; Richards & Kinney, 1990). These intriguing studies were limited, however, by the fact that none of them appears to have examined participants who were known to be biologically related to schizophrenics.

Of great interest, therefore, is evidence, reviewed by Sass (1992, p. 367), that a number of the most influential avant-garde or modernist artists of the 20th century may have had schizophrenia or been in the schizophrenia spectrum. Also of great interest are studies by Heston and Denney (1968), Karlsson (1970), and Kauffman, Grunebaum, Cohler, and Gamer (1979) that found unusual creativity in samples of the healthier biological relatives of diagnosed schizophrenics. In an Icelandic sample, for example, Karlsson found that the biological relatives of schizophrenics were more likely than people in the general population to be recognized for their work in creative professions. Kauffman et al. conducted tests and interviews of the U.S. children of 18 mothers with schizophrenia, 12 mothers with a bipolar or unipolar affective psychosis, and 22 mothers with no major mental disorder. Among the children of mothers with a psychotic disorder was a group of 6 children who were more "competent, creative and talented" than any of the control children. Of these 6 "super" children, all but 1 had a schizophrenic or schizoaffective mother. Heston and Denney studied 47 adult adoptees who were born in the United States to a schizophrenic mother but were separated shortly after birth. As expected, these index adoptees had a significantly higher prevalence of schizophrenia than did the matched control adoptees who were born to nonpsychotic mothers. More surprising was Heston and Denney's serendipitous discovery that among the psychologically healthier index adoptees, there was a subgroup—who were not schizophrenic, sociopathic, neurotic, or retarded—that had more creative jobs and hobbies than the control adoptees.

As interesting as these results were, however, they also involved studies with important limitations. For example, in Karlsson's (1970) study, the only creative outcome examined was whether a participant was listed in *Who's Who* as being in a profession, such as the fine arts, judged to be very creative; no direct assessment of creative activities or accomplishments was obtained for any of the participants. The findings of Heston and Denney (1968) and Kauffman et al. (1979) were—as those investigators themselves were careful to point out—serendipitous discoveries, based on post hoc analyses, using clinical impressions of anecdotal reports of participants' creative activities as the basis for creativity evaluations that were made by investigators who were not always blind to participants' personal and family histories of psychopathology. Furthermore, interpretation of some results was clouded by an earlier tendency, particularly in this country, and by current standards, to overdiagnose schizophrenia and underdiagnose bipolar disorders (e.g., see Richards, 1981).

This study was designed to investigate whether these intriguing findings could be confirmed using more rigorous methods, including national samples of adopted adult offspring of biological parents with a diagnosis of schizophrenia, demographically matched control adoptees of biological parents who had not been hospitalized for mental illness, more recent research diagnostic criteria, and creativity and diagnostic assessments that were made blindly with respect to each other. In addition, research scales with demonstrated reliability and validity (Richards, Kinney, Benet, & Merzel, 1988; Richards, Kinney, Lunde, Benet, & Merzel, 1988) were used to assess participants' creativity in a broad range of real-life avocational as well as vocational activities, so that creativity assessments were neither limited only to eminent levels of creativity nor restricted only to certain fields such as the arts and sciences.

Finally, the presence of multiple schizotypal signs was used to identify a subgroup of nonschizophrenic adoptees who were more likely to carry genetic liability for schizophrenia. Several studies have found that these signs are psychiatric features that are particularly likely to occur at significantly elevated rates among schizophrenics' nonschizophrenic biological relatives, even if the schizophrenics had been adopted shortly after birth and have had little or no contact with their biological relatives (e.g., Kendler, Gruenberg, & Kinney, 1994; Kety, 1983; Kety et al., 1994; Kinney et al., 1997; Lowing, Mirsky, & Pereira, 1983; Tienari & Wynne, 1994).

Hypotheses

Based on these prior findings, we hypothesized that a subgroup of the nonschizophrenic adoptees would be more creative on average than the control adoptees. In particular, it was hypothesized that adoptees who were (a) most likely to be carrying genetic liability for schizophrenia (and may therefore have tended to show unconventional modes of thinking and perceiving conducive to the generation of creative ideas) but (b) did not have the severe and disabling features of frank schizophrenia would tend to show greater creativity than other adoptees. This was consistent with an inverted-U model linking creativity with manifestations of psychopathology or liability for psychosis (Richards, Kinney, Lunde, et al., 1988). As our operational criterion for identifying nonschizophrenic adoptees most likely to be carrying genetic liability for schizophrenia, we used the presence of either schizotypal or schizoid personality disorder or multiple schizotypal signs. A more specific hypothesis, based in part on the findings of Schuldberg (1990) noted earlier, was that peak creativity would be particularly high for participants who had schizotypal signs of unusual thinking or perception, that is, "positive" symptoms (magical thinking, recurrent illusions, or odd speech), rather than other schizotypal signs (ideas of reference, social isolation, inadequate rapport, suspiciousness, or undue social anxiety). Finally, we hypothesized that individuals with liability for schizophrenia would tend to be more creative in avocational rather than vocational spheres because increased tendencies toward social anxiety would make it easier for them to express their creativity in avocational activities that tend to be more solitary and less competitive or stressful than vocational activities.

Method

Research Design and Sample

This study used an adoption sample that had been previously ascertained for a study that was directed by Rosenthal in collaboration with Kety, Schulsinger, Wender, and their colleagues (Kety, 1983; Lowing et al., 1983; Rosenthal et al., 1968; Rosenthal, Wender, Kety, & Welner, 1971), who made use of the unusually complete adoption, psychiatric, and social registers available in Denmark. These registers made it possible for the researchers to identify a complete national sample of index adoptees who (a) had a biological mother or father with a diagnosis of schizophrenia or a related schizophrenia-spectrum disorder, (b) were separated from their biological parents at an early age (all were adopted by 5 years of age, most by 6 months), and (c) were placed with adoptive parents to whom they were not biologically related.

The index adoptees in this article were chosen by Lowing et al. (1983) from a larger sample originally selected by Rosenthal and colleagues (Rosenthal et al., 1968; Rosenthal et al., 1971) because the adoptees had a biological parent with a schizophrenic disorder. For each index adoptee, a control adoptee was chosen whose biological parents had no history of psychiatric hospitalization. Index and control adoptees were matched on a case-by-case basis for age, sex, age at adoption, and socioeconomic status of adoptive parents. Lowing et al. limited their sample to 39 pairs in which (a) each index case had a biological parent who had been unanimously diagnosed as having a schizophrenia-spectrum disorder by the diagnostic team in the study by Rosenthal and colleagues, and (b) the biological fathers of both index and control cases had been clearly identified. At the time the adoptees were born, few of the biological parents had been hospitalized for psychosis. This fact reflected Danish policies at the time: Adoption was discouraged, and abortion encouraged, by social agencies in the case of pregnancies for which a biological parent had been diagnosed as having a schizophrenic disorder. As a result, most cases of schizophrenia among the biological parents were of relatively late onset. This in turn will have tended to minimize any potential postnatal environmental influences the biological parents might have had on the adoptees. Indeed, the adoptees themselves were unaware of any schizophrenic disorder in their biological parents. These adoption policies may also have tended to select for a sample of adoptees in whom genetic liability for schizophrenia was lower than would be true for a more representative sample of offspring whose biological parents had schizophrenia-spectrum disorders.

For this study, adoptees were further screened to eliminate three index cases (along with their matched control adoptees) because the index adoptee's parent was diagnosed as having acute schizophrenia, a subtype that other adoption studies (e.g., Kety, 1983) have found not to be familial. Thus, in contrast to the adoption study by Heston and Denney (1968), in this study sample the biological father, as well as the mother, could be unambiguously identified for each of the 36 index and 36 control adoptees. There were 19 male and 17 female participants in each sample of adoptees, and the average age at assessment was 33.8 years old for the control adoptees and 33.6 years old for the index adoptees.

Interview and Diagnostic Procedures

All adoptees were given a structured interview by a Danish psychiatrist, Joseph Welner, who was blind to the diagnostic status of the adoptees' biological and adoptive parents. This extensive interview typically lasted 3 to 5 hr. The interviewer, who was fluent in both English and Danish, completed narrative descriptions in English of the interviewees' psychological, social, and medical characteristics and history, including information about the participants' vocational and avocational histories. This information was prepared in the form of a typewritten transcript (for more details, see Rosenthal et al., 1968; Rosenthal et al., 1971).

Prior to diagnosis, the interview transcripts were carefully edited to remove any clues that may have biased diagnostic evaluations, such as whether the participant was an index or control adoptee. Copies of the interviews were sent to Kety, Rosenthal, and Wender, who diagnosed the psychiatric status of each adoptee. In a subsequent study, Lowing et al. (1983) also diagnosed these adoptees, blind to their family history, using the *Diagnostic and Statistical Manual of Mental Disorders* (3rd ed. [*DSM–III*]; American Psychiatric Association, 1980) criteria. The results of Lowing et al. (1983) confirmed the earlier finding, by Rosenthal et al. (1971), of a significant excess of schizophrenia-spectrum disorders in the index adoptees.

In this study, we wanted to identify a subgroup of participants who, although not themselves schizophrenic, had an increased likelihood of carrying genetic liability for schizophrenia. As noted earlier, previous research from this and other adoption and family studies of schizophrenia has suggested that schizotypal and schizoid personality disorder, particularly the former, are psychiatric syndromes particularly likely to be associated with genetic liability for schizophrenia. Therefore, if nonschizophrenic adoptees had either been diagnosed earlier by Lowing et al. (1983) as having either frank schizotypal or schizoid personality disorder or had at least two of the *DSM–III* schizotypal signs noted earlier (e.g., magical thinking, recurrent illusions), we classified these adoptees as *wide-schizophrenia-spectrum* (*wide-spectrum,* for short).

Procedures to Maintain Blindness

Multiple procedures were used to maintain rater blindness in the rating of creativity variables in this study. Interviews were edited by Deborah LeBlanc so that they could be rated on the creativity scales by other investigators (Dennis K. Kinney and Morris E. Zimbalist) who were blind to potentially biasing information. Thus, information bearing on a participant's vocational and avocational creative activities was abstracted from these interview materials and was then carefully reviewed to make certain that there were no references to the participant's personal or family history of psychopathology.

Creativity Ratings and Data Analyses

Creativity ratings were made using the Lifetime Creativity Scales (LCS; Kinney, Richards, & Southam, in press; Richards, Kinney, Benet, et al., 1988), which were developed for use in assessing the creativity of participants' actual vocational and avocational activities in everyday life. A more detailed description of evidence for the reliability and validity of these scales was provided in published articles (Richards, Kinney, Benet, et al., 1988; Richards, Kinney, Lunde, et al., 1988). For this study, the key scales in the LCS pertain to the quality of a participant's most creative accomplishment over the adult lifetime; this peak creativity variable was assessed for both vocational and avocational activity. Of particular interest for this study was the Overall Peak Creativity rating that indicates the highest qualitative level of creative accomplishment displayed in either vocational or avocational activities over a person's adult years. This overall rating of peak creativity was the measure viewed a priori as providing the best test of any fundamental intergroup differences in creative capability wherever it may manifest itself. Satisfactory interrater reliability was obtained in this study between two of the authors (Dennis K. Kinney and Morris E. Zimbalist) for independent ratings of this creativity variable for the entire sample of participants ($r = .75, p < .001$). When the two raters disagreed on the exact rating for a particular participant, the raters conferred and reached a consensus rating (while still blind to diagnosis) that was used for data analyses. *T* tests were used to test for differences between group means for peak creativity ratings; one-tailed tests were used when the direction of the differences between group means had been hypothesized.

Results

As expected, index and control adoptees as a whole did not differ significantly with respect to creativity and had means and standard deviations that were quite similar to each other. Means for overall peak creativity for the 36 index and 36 control adoptees were, respectively, 1.84 ($SD = 0.74$) and 1.98 ($SD = 0.65$; $p = ns$; $df = 35, 35$).

However, when the index group was limited to the key subgroup hypothesized to be most creative (the 15 nonschizophrenic adoptees with schizotypal or schizoid personality disorder or with multiple schizotypal signs), there was a noteworthy trend for these wide-spectrum index adoptees to be more creative than the nonspectrum controls, although the mean difference did not reach a conventional level of statistical significance. Thus, the means for 15 wide-spectrum index adoptees versus 24 nonspectrum controls were, respectively, 2.03 ($SD = 0.69$) versus 1.83 ($SD = 0.65$; $p = ns$; $df = 14, 23$). Only one of the 72 adoptees (an index case) had frank schizophrenia; this person had a low peak creativity rating of 1.0 (the minimum score is 0).

Moreover, within the control group of 36 adoptees, there was also a trend for wide-spectrum participants to be more creative. When all wide-spectrum participants were compared to the nonspectrum participants in the total sample (i.e., the combined index and control samples), the 27 wide-spectrum cases had a significantly higher rating for peak overall creativity ($M = 2.15$, $SD = .64$) than either the 24 nonspectrum control adoptees ($M = 1.83$, $SD = .65$; $t = 1.81$; $p < .04$; $df = 26, 23$) or all 44 nonschizophrenic nonspectrum adoptees ($M = 1.79$, $SD = .70$; $t = 2.21$; $p = .015$; $df = 26, 43$).

Moreover, as Figure 1 shows, the group means for peak overall creativity ratings did in fact follow the predicted inverted-U curve, as a function of increasing severity of symptoms along a wide spectrum of schizophrenic-like psychopathology. Thus, the peak overall creativity rating was (a) relatively low ($M = 1.64$) for the 25 participants with neither schizotypal nor schizoid personality disorders nor any schizotypal signs, (b) somewhat higher ($M = 1.98$) for the 19 participants with only one schizotypal sign, (c) highest ($M = 2.19$) for the 14 participants with two or more schizotypal signs (but not a schizotypal or schizoid personality disorder), (d) still rather high ($M = 2.12$) for the 13 participants with a schizotypal or schizoid personality disorder, and (e) markedly lower ($M = 1.0$) for the 1 schizophrenic participant.

Peak overall creativity was particularly high for the nonschizophrenic participants who had positive signs of magical thinking, recurrent illusions, odd speech, or

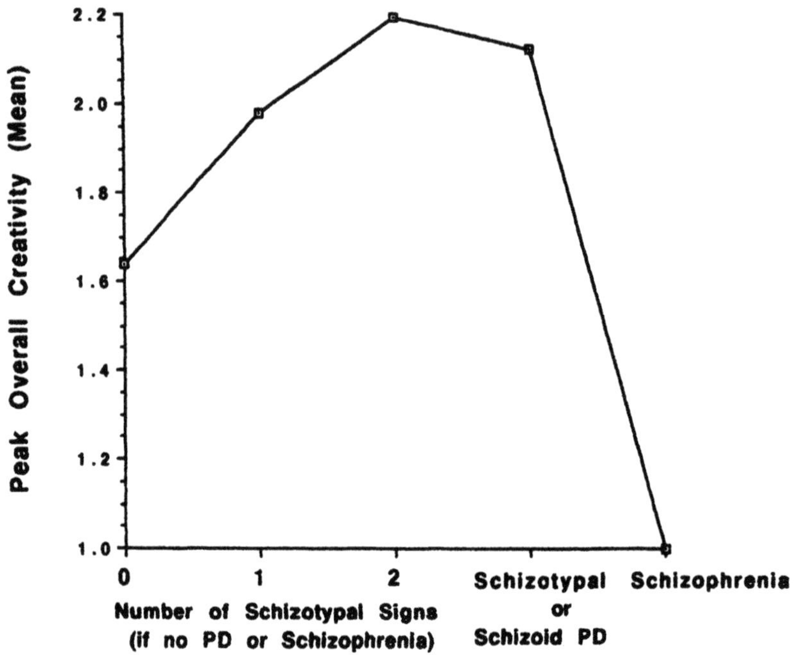

Figure 1. *Peak creativity and severity of schizophrenia-spectrum symptomatology.*

all of these; the number of these three signs present in participants was significantly correlated with overall peak creativity for all the nonschizophrenic participants ($r = .27$; $n = 71$; $p = .01$). The respective means for peak creativity were 1.78 for participants with no positive signs, 2.01 for those with one positive sign, and 2.40 for those with two or three positive signs.

The mean creativity scores on each of the peak creativity scales were somewhat higher for male participants than female participants (e.g., $M = 2.05$, $SD = .60$ vs. $M = 1.78$, $SD = .77$ on overall peak creativity for all nonschizophrenics; $df = 37, 33$), perhaps because the interview information did not permit us to assess adequately creativity displayed in homemaking, parenting, and caregiving activities. None of the gender differences in creativity ratings was statistically significant, however, nor were there statistically significant interactions between sex and diagnostic group status.

The group difference in peak creativity was more marked for avocational activities, with means of 1.60 ($SD = 0.84$) for the 27 wide-spectrum cases versus 1.20 ($SD = 0.78$) for the 44 nonspectrum cases ($t = 2.08$; $p = .02$; $df = 26, 43$), than for vocational activities, with means of 1.64 ($SD = 0.88$) for spectrum cases versus 1.58 ($SD = 0.78$) for nonspectrum cases ($t = 0.69$; $p =$ *ns*; $df = 26, 43$). Finally, in this connection, peak avocational creativity was significantly correlated with the diagnosticians' rating of social anxiety, $r = .28$ ($p = .01$). Indeed, this was the highest correlation of peak avocational creativity with any of the schizotypal signs. (By contrast, social anxiety was positively but not significantly correlated with peak vocational creativity.)

The significant group difference in overall peak creativity reflected the fact that a variety of creative jobs or hobbies were found more often among the nonschizophrenic participants with multiple schizotypal signs. Thus, these wide-spectrum participants were not only more likely to have vocations in fields such as the fine arts, which are traditionally regarded as creative (e.g., professional dancer, artisan who crafts innovative designs), but were also more likely to have jobs such as teachers or small-business entrepreneurs who had started new businesses. These wide-spectrum participants also tended to have more creative avocations, such as poetry writing, painting, and sophisticated photography. As was the case in the study by Heston and Denney (1968), in this study those participants who had been diagnosed as schizophrenic, neurotic, or retarded were not particularly creative.

Conclusion

Our findings were similar to the intriguing but serendipitous and post hoc findings by Heston and Denney (1968) and Kauffman et al. (1979) of unusual creativity in the psychologically healthier offspring of schizophrenics. Thus, in their adoption study sample, Heston and Denney noted that it was their impression that a subgroup of nonschizophrenic index adoptees (with a schizophrenic biological parent) were more likely than control adoptees to have more creative jobs and hobbies, such as musician, teacher, or collector of antique aircraft. In our sample, adoptees who were not schizophrenic but who did have schizophrenia-spectrum personality disorders or multiple schizotypal signs (psychiatric features that other research suggests are particularly likely to be associated with genetic liability for schizophrenia) were judged to have displayed a significantly higher mean level of overall peak creative accomplishment in their jobs or hobbies than were other participants. In accord with an earlier finding by Schuldberg (1990), the level of peak creativity was particularly high for participants who had schizotypal signs of magical thinking, recurrent illusions, or odd speech.

In contrast to the earlier studies, in this study researchers rated participants' creativity while blind to the participants' personal and family psychopathology and used creativity rating scales of demonstrated reliability and validity. Interpretation of study results was complicated somewhat by the fact that a number of control participants had multiple schizotypal features. However, the findings for the control adoptees augmented a trend that was also found in the relatively small group of index adoptees, which was more carefully diagnosed for schizophrenia-spectrum characteristics (with *DSM–III* criteria) than was true for samples used in previous studies. Although replication of the findings of this study is clearly needed, this study does provide important support for the hypothesis that liability for schizophrenia is related to creativity.

As we noted earlier, Danish policies regarding adoption are likely to have resulted in genetic liability for schizophrenia being weaker, on average, in this study sample of adoptees than would likely be the case for most nonadopted persons who have a biological parent with a schizophrenia-spectrum disorder. This suggests that associations between creativity and personal or family symptoms may be stronger in more representative, nonadoptee samples than in this study.

One interesting possibility suggested by these results is that genes that confer increased liability for major psychiatric disorders such as schizophrenia may also have a positive side, as appears to be the case for bipolar disorders (e.g., Richards, Kinney, Lunde, et al., 1988). That is, given a favorable environment, these genes may also be associated with personally and socially beneficial phenotypes, such as enhanced creative functioning. It is possible that—by analogy with the heterozygote advantage conferred on carriers of the sickle-cell gene—there may be some kind of compensatory advantage for a major gene or genes for schizophrenia, which helps to maintain the putative gene or genes in the population, despite the low fertility of schizophrenics themselves (e.g., Kinney & Matthysse, 1978). Enhanced creativity may represent one type of compensatory advantage.

As we noted earlier, results from a parallel set of studies point to a significantly increased prevalence of eminent creativity in the fine arts among participants with mood disorders (e.g., Akiskal & Akiskal, 1988; Andreasen, 1987; Jamison, 1989; see also reviews by Goodwin & Jamison, 1990; Kinney, 1992; Richards, 1981). This link between creativity and liability for mood disorders was also extended by research findings that even when using broader measures of "everyday" creativity (i.e., creativity not limited to eminent or socially recognized levels), creative accomplishment was significantly higher in participants with bipolar disorders and in their normal relatives than in controls (Richards, Kinney, Lunde, et al., 1988). Complementary studies (Jamison, Gerner, Hammen, & Padesky, 1980; Richards & Kinney, 1990) found that both creative artists and patients with mood disorders reported that their creativity was significantly enhanced during periods of moderately elevated mood. This research thus suggested that in the case of bipolar disorder, the association between increased creative potential and liability for mood swings extends to everyday levels of creativity and thus may be relevant to millions of people who may carry genes for bipolar disorder (including many gene carriers who have no apparent clinical symptoms). The findings on mood disorders and creativity are potentially of great clinical significance in terms of how patients and their families view liability for this illness and also for combating the social stigma that is still often attached to it.

The findings from this study suggest that similar considerations may also apply in the case of schizophrenia but perhaps with even greater implications because schizophrenia tends to be an even more disabling disease than bipolar disorder and thus may carry an even greater stigma. This study's results also, however, provide an interesting contrast to those obtained earlier for bipolar disorders, in that the creative advantage for the schizophrenia-spectrum participants was greatest for avocational activities. By contrast, the bipolar-spectrum participants displayed the greatest creative advantage for vocational activities, perhaps because some of these latter individuals tend to be temperamentally more gregarious, competitive, driven, and occupationally ambitious, whereas the schizophrenia-spectrum individuals may tend to have more social anxiety and to be better able to realize their creative potential in less competitive, avocational, spheres. Due to the fact that this study found that wide-spectrum participants tended to be more creative in a variety of everyday activities, the results seem more consistent with a view of creative potential as a broad capacity for originality that can be manifested in a wide variety of settings rather than as a capacity that is constrained to a particular field or mode of expression (Richards, in press; Richards, Kinney, Benet, et al., 1988).

Demonstrating that genes for schizophrenia are associated with creativity-enhancing traits would clearly have important implications for individual and social decisions about how to apply new genetic knowledge (e.g., see Kinney, 1992; Richards, 1997). As rapid advances in molecular biology and discovery of genetic markers make it possible to detect major genes for schizophrenic disorders (and to identify individuals who carry these genes), it becomes increasingly important to know whether such genes are indeed associated with positive, as well as negative, behavioral phenotypes or outcomes and to understand what genetic or environmental modifiers affect how the gene or genes will be expressed. For example, appropriate environmental intervention may significantly increase the likelihood that a person carrying the gene or genes in question would become an usually creative and productive adult, as well as lowering the risk of a gene carrier developing a severe and crippling psychiatric illness.

In summary, our findings provide perhaps the strongest evidence to date in support of the hypothesis that traits associated with increased liability for schizophrenia are also associated with increased creativity. The results of this study thus indicate the importance of further research on this topic that uses still larger samples and even more rigorous methods.

References

Akiskal, H. S., & Akiskal, K. (1988). Reassessing the prevalence of bipolar disorders: Clinical significance and artistic creativity. *Psychiatry and Psychobiology, 3,* 29–36.

American Psychiatric Association. (1980). *Diagnostic and statistical manual of mental disorders* (3rd ed.). Washington, DC: Author.

Andreasen, N. C. (1987). Creativity and mental illness: Prevalence rates in writers and their first-degree relatives. *American Journal of Psychiatry, 144,* 1288–1292.

Andreasen, N. C., & Powers, P. (1974). Overinclusive thinking in mania and schizophrenia. *British Journal of Psychiatry, 125,* 452–456.

Barron, F. (1969). *Creative person and creative process.* New York: Holt, Rinehart & Winston.

Chapman, L. J., & Chapman, J. P. (1985). Psychosis proneness. In M. Alpert (Ed.), *Controversies in schizophrenia: Changes and constancies* (pp. 157–172). New York: Guilford.

Dahlstrom, W. G., & Welsh, G. S. (1972). *MMPI handbook.* Minneapolis: University of Minnesota Press.

Davis, G. A., & Subkoviak, M. J. (1975). Multidimensional analysis of a personality-based test of creative potential. *Journal of Educational Measurement, 12,* 37–43.

Eysenck, H. J. (1983). The roots of creativity: Cognitive ability or personality trait. *Roeper Review, 5*(4), 10–12.

Goodwin, F., & Jamison, K. R. (Eds.). (1990). *Manic–depressive illness.* New York: Oxford University Press.

Gottesman, I. (1965). Personality and natural selection. In S. G. Vandenberg (Ed.), *Methods and goals in human behavior genetics* (pp. 63–80). New York: Academic.

Gotz, K. O., & Gotz, K. (1979). Personality characteristics of professional artists. *Perceptual and Motor Skills, 49,* 327–334.

Heston, L. L., & Denney, D. (1968). Interactions between early life experience and biological factors in schizophrenia. In D. Rosenthal & S. Kety (Eds.), *The transmission of schizophrenia* (pp. 363–376). New York: Pergamon.

Jamison, K. R. (1989). Mood disorders and patterns of creativity in British writers and artists. *Psychiatry, 52,* 125–134.

Jamison, K. R., Gerner, R. H., Hammen, C., & Padesky, C. (1980). Clouds and silver linings: Positive experiences associated with primary affective disorders. *American Journal of Psychiatry, 137,* 198–202.

Karlsson, J. L. (1970). Genetic association of giftedness and creativity with schizophrenia. *Hereditas, 66,* 177–182.

Kauffman, C., Grunebaum, H., Cohler, B., & Gamer, E. (1979). Superkids: Competent children of psychotic mothers. *American Journal of Psychiatry, 136,* 1396–1402.

Kendler, S. S., Gruenberg, A. M., & Kinney, D. K. (1994). Independent diagnoses of adoptees and relatives as defined by *DSM–III* in the provincial and national samples of the Danish

Adoption Study of Schizophrenia. *Archives of General Psychiatry, 51,* 456–468.
Kety, S. S. (1983). Mental illness in the biological and adoptive relatives of schizophrenic adoptees: Findings relevant to genetic and environmental factors in etiology. *American Journal of Psychiatry, 140,* 720–727.
Kety, S. S., Wender, P. H., Jacobsen, B., Ingraham, L. J., Jansson, L., Faber, B., & Kinney, D. K. (1994). Mental illness in the biological and adoptive relatives of schizophrenic adoptees. Replication of the Copenhagen Study in the rest of Denmark. *Archives of General Psychiatry, 51,* 442–455.
Kinney, D. K. (1992). The psychotherapist as muse: New roles for mental health professionals as catalysts of individual and institutional creativity. *American Journal of Psychotherapy, 46,* 434–453.
Kinney, D. K., Holzman, P. S., Jacobsen, B., Jansson, L., Faber, B., Hildebrand, W., Kasell, E., & Zimbalist, M. E. (1997). Thought disorder in schizophrenic and control adoptees and their relatives. *Archives of General Psychiatry, 54,* 475–479.
Kinney, D. K., & Matthysse, S. M. (1978). Genetic factors in transmission of schizophrenia. *Annual Review of Medicine, 29,* 459–473.
Kinney, D. K., Richards, R. L., & Southam, M. (in press). Everyday creativity and the Lifetime Creativity Scales. In M. A. Runco (Ed.), *Handbook of creativity research.*
Lowing, P. A., Mirsky, A. F., & Pereira, M. A. (1983). The inheritance of schizophrenia spectrum disorders: A re-analysis of the Danish adoptee study data. *American Journal of Psychiatry, 140,* 1167–1171.
MacKinnon, D. W. (1962). The personality correlates of creativity: A study of American architects. In G. S. Nielson (Ed.), *Proceedings of the 14th International Congress of Psychology* (pp. 11–39). Copenhagen, Denmark: Munksgaard.
Richards, R. (1981). Relationships between creativity and psychopathology: An evaluation and interpretation of the evidence. *Genetic Psychology Monographs, 103,* 261–324.
Richards, R. (1993). Everyday creativity, eminent creativity, and psychopathology. *Psychological Inquiry, 4,* 212–217.
Richards, R. (1997). When illness yields creativity. In M. Runco & R. Richards (Eds.), *Eminent creativity, everyday creativity, and health* (pp. 485–540). Stamford, CT: Ablex/Greenwood.
Richards, R. L., & Kinney, D. K. (1990). Mood swings and everyday creativity. *Creativity Research Journal, 3,* 202–217.
Richards, R. L., Kinney, D. K., Benet, M., & Merzel, A. P. C. (1988). Assessing everyday creativity: Characteristics of the Lifetime Creativity Scales and validation with three large samples. *Journal of Personality and Social Psychology, 54,* 476–485.
Richards, R., Kinney, D. K., Lunde, I., Benet, M., & Merzel, A. P. C. (1988). Creativity in manic–depressives, cyclothymes, their normal relatives, and control subjects. *Journal of Abnormal Psychology, 97,* 281–288.
Rosenthal, D., Wender, P., Kety, S., Schulsinger, F., Welner, J., & Ostergaard, L. (1968). Schizophrenics' offspring reared in adoptive homes. *Journal of Psychiatric Research, 6,* 377–392.
Rosenthal, D., Wender, P. H., Kety, S. S., & Welner, J. (1971). The adopted-away offspring of schizophrenics. *American Journal of Psychiatry, 128,* 307–311.
Sass, L. A. (1992). *Madness and modernism: Insanity in the light of modern art, literature, and thought.* New York: Basic Books.
Schuldberg, D. (1990). Schizotypal and hypomanic traits, creativity, and psychological health. *Creativity Research Journal, 3,* 218–230.
Tienari, P. J., & Wynne, L. C. (1994). Adoption studies in schizophrenia. *Annals of Medicine, 26,* 233–237.
Wiggins, J. S., & Pincus, A. L. (1989). Conceptions of personality disorders and dimensions of personality. *Psychological Assessment, 1,* 305–316.

Creativity Research Journal
2000–2001, Vol. 13, No. 1, 27–35

Primary-Process Thinking and Creativity: Affect and Cognition

Sandra W. Russ
Case Western Reserve University

ABSTRACT: The schizophrenia spectrum and the bipolar disorder spectrum involve different types of psychotic disorders. Both disorders have been linked to creativity.

Primary-process thinking is evident in all psychotic disorders. Primary-process thinking has also been found to relate to creativity in normal populations. One possibility is that different dimensions of primary-process thought are dominant in different disorders. The cognitive dimension may be more dominant in the schizophrenia-spectrum disorders, and the affective dimension may be more dominant in bipolar disorders. Future research should investigate how primary-process thinking differs in these disorders and the implications for creative functioning.

The schizophrenia spectrum and the bipolar disorder spectrum involve different types of psychotic disorders. Both disorders have been linked, in various ways, to creativity (Jamison, 1993; Prentky, 1989). The main thesis of this article is that these links to creativity in different clinical populations could reflect different mechanisms that underlie the creative process. The interesting theoretical question is what are the different processes that account for these relations? The role of primary-process thinking in each of these disorders could shed some light on these processes.

Primary-Process Thinking

Freud (1915/1958) first conceptualized *primary-process thought* as an early, primitive system of thought that was drive laden and not subject to rules of logic or oriented to reality. A good example of primary-process thinking is the kind of thinking that occurs in dreams. Dreams are illogical, not oriented to rules of time and space, and frequently include affect-laden content and images. Holt (1977) categorized the drive-laden content in primary-process thinking as oral, aggressive, and libidinal. As Holt developed a system to measure primary-process thinking, he defined content properties and formal properties. *Content properties* include affect-laden oral, aggressive, and libidinal content. *Formal properties* include qualities of illogical thinking, condensation (fusion of two ideas or images), and loose associations. Formal expressions and content expressions of primary process may or may not go together. These definitions of primary-process thinking imply a cognitive component and an affective component. The formal properties reflect a cognitive dimension. The affect-laden content responses reflect access to affect-laden fantasy, a blend of cognition and affect. An important aspect of both dimensions is how well they are controlled or integrated into thought.

Access to primary-process thought has been hypothesized to relate to creative thinking because associations are fluid and primitive images and ideas can be utilized. According to classic psychoanalytic theory, primary-process thinking is characterized by *mobility of cathexis* (i.e., the energy behind the ideas and images is easily displaced; Arlow & Brenner, 1964). Therefore, there is a free flow of energy not bound by specific ideas or objects. In this mode of thinking, ideas are easily interchangeable and attention is widely and flexibly distributed. Therefore, access to primary-process thinking should facilitate a fluidity

Correspondence and requests for reprints should be sent to Sandra W. Russ, Psychology Department, Case Western Reserve University, Cleveland, OH 44106–7123. E-mail: swr@po.cwru.edu.

of thought and flexibility of search among all ideas and associations. Martindale (1989) stated that "because primary process cognition is associative, it makes the discovery of new combinations of mental elements more likely" (p. 216).

Kris's (1952) concept of regression in the service of the ego stressed the importance of being in control of primary-process thinking. Kris postulated that creative individuals could regress, in a controlled fashion, and tap into primary-process thinking. The individual could go back and forth between early, primary-process thought and more mature, rational, secondary-process thinking. Regression was an important concept because the individual would, at will, go back to an earlier, primitive mode of thought and use it adaptively for creative purposes. The creative individual could be distinguished from the individual with a thought disorder in that the creative individual was in charge of this regressive process and could logically evaluate the loose, primitive associations and images. In one study (Russ, 1993), I presented creative individuals' descriptions of the creative process that described getting in touch with primary-process thinking. One good example is a description of the free flow of associations in a monologue by the comedian, Robin Williams. In commenting about the process, he said:

> And sometimes there are times when you're just on it—when you say the muse is with you and it's just flowing and that's when you know that the well is open again and you just put in the pipe and you stand back and say "yes"—you're in control but you're not—the characters are coming through you. (as cited in Culbane, 1988, pp. 1–5)

Recent conceptualizations of primary process have moved away from the energy model and from the concept of regression. Holt (1967) proposed a structural model for primary-process thought. He viewed primary process as comprising a group of structures with its own course of development. Arieti (1976) and Suler (1980) also suggested that the concept of regression to an earlier mode of thought may not be necessary. They both proposed that primary process may be a separate entity that develops simultaneously with secondary-process thought. The implication of these different conceptualizations of primary process is that the mechanism for access to primary process may not be regression but a different kind of mechanism.

One of the overlooked features of primary-process thinking is affect. Affect is an important aspect that links primary process to creativity and to contemporary theory and research in the creativity area.

Primary Process and Affect

Primary-process thinking contains both cognitive and affective elements. Some expressions are mainly cognitive, whereas other expressions have a dominant affective component. The affective elements could play as important a role in creative thinking as the cognitive elements. Theoretically, affect is a major component of much primary-process thinking. The concepts of drive-laden and instinctual energy bring us into the realm of affect. Rapaport (1951) used the term *affect-charge* in discussing primary-process thought. Primary-process content, in Holt's (1967) conceptualization, contains affect categories of oral, libidinal, and aggressive. Freud (1895/1966), in *Project for a Scientific Psychology,* stated that primary-process thought is frequently accompanied by affect.

Primary-process thinking has usually been thought of as a blend of cognitive and affective processes (Martindale, 1981; Zimiles, 1981). We need to deepen and refine our understanding of the affective processes involved so that we can theorize and measure more effectively. Earlier (Russ, 1987), I proposed that much primary process is a subtype of affective content in cognition. Primary-process content is material around which the child had experienced early intense feeling states (oral, anal, aggressive, etc.). Learning to regulate these intense emotions and affect-laden thoughts and images is a major developmental task. Children differ widely as to whether this content is thought about, how it is expressed in fantasy and play, and how it is integrated into fantasy and imagination. Pine and Holt (1960) suggested that primary process becomes a kind of cognitive style that reflects how affective material is dealt with. Earlier (Russ, 1987), I proposed that current primary-process expressions may reflect either current affect or a kind of "affective residue" in cognition left over from earlier developmental stages. How primary-process material is dealt with by the child may affect the kinds of and amounts of memories that are encoded. Recent work in the area of memory and cognition suggests that affect influences the memory process.

Empirical Findings

Most of the research investigating primary-process thinking and creativity has utilized Holt's Scoring System for Primary Process Responses on the Rorschach (Holt, 1977; Holt & Havel, 1960). Research studies have not attempted to separate the cognitive dimension from the affect dimension of primary-process thinking. Most of the research in the area was reviewed by Holt (1977), Suler (1980), and myself (Russ, 1993, 1996).

Holt made a major contribution to the field by operationalizing the construct of primary-process thinking and developing a scoring system for the Rorschach that could achieve good interrater reliability and convincing validity data. As described by me (Russ, 1993), the Holt system scores the responses that contain primary-process content (aggressive and libidinal that actually encompasses a broad range of affective content and responses that contain formal characteristics of thought processes). The system measures the percentage of primary-process content in the Rorschach protocol and the effectiveness of the control of that content. A controlled response would express primary-process content in a way that fits the form of the blot and is appropriately qualified. For example, two talking bugs can be made into a more appropriate response by making them cartoon figures. The system also measures formal characteristics of thought such as condensation and illogical associations. The scale was developed by Holt for use with adults. When used with children, the scale largely measures primary-process content and adaptiveness of that content. Scorings of formal characteristics are a very small percentage in children's protocols (Dudek, 1975; Russ, 1982). Major scores in Holt's scoring system include the percentage of primary-process responses in the entire protocol, the Defense Demand score (which measures the intensity of the content), the Defense Effectiveness score (which measures the control and cognitive integration of primary-process responses), and the Adaptive Regression (AR) score (which measures both the intensity of the primary-process content and the integration of the content). The Holt system measures both access to affect-laden material and the cognitive integration of that material. Scores on Holt's system tell us whether an individual can allow affect-laden content to surface and be expressed. Scores also tell us how well controlled and well integrated that content is in cognition.

In adults, controlled access to primary process has been significantly positively related to a number of measures of creativity (Cohen, 1961; Dudek, 1968; Pine & Holt, 1960) and to problem-solving efficiency (Blatt, Allison, & Feirstein, 1969).

In children, age, sex, and specific measures and scores emerge as important factors. Dudek (1975), one of the first to study children, found no relation between primary-process thinking on the Rorschach and divergent thinking on the Torrance tests in fourth graders. However, primary-process expression on a drawing task was related to divergent thinking. Dudek concluded that the relation between primary process and creativity is ambiguous in childhood and that children have not yet learned to use primary process adaptively. In a recent study by Dudek and Verreault (1989), creative children (fifth and sixth grade) gave significantly more total primary-process ideation than noncreative children as measured by Holt's system as applied to the Torrance Tests of Creative Thinking. Also, more creative children demonstrated more effective use of regression in the service of the ego than noncreative children when popular responses were used to determine defense effectiveness.

My research studies (Russ, 1980, 1981, 1982, 1988a) investigating primary process on the Rorschach, achievement, and creativity in children obtained positive results. (A full review of my research can be found in Russ, 1993, 1996.) However, sex differences repeatedly occurred and different scores within Holt's system predicted creativity in different studies.

In a series of studies, I specifically investigated the relation between primary-process thinking and creativity. In the first of these (Russ, 1982), I focused on the relation between primary-process thinking and transformation abilities in third-grade children, using two independent samples of third-grade children and Holt's scoring system for the Rorschach as the primary-process measure. For a measure of flexibility of thinking for young children, I adapted the Luchins's Water-Jar Test (Luchins & Luchins, 1959). The task requires the child to break out of an old set in solving a problem and to discover a new, more adaptive approach. The child must see new relations in old patterns and be able to shift sets.

The results found that for boys, the AR score was significantly related to flexibility of shifting sets in both samples of children; that is, the ability to express well-controlled primary-process content on the Rorschach was related to the ability to shift problem-solving strategies. This result was replicated with a second sample of children, suggesting the stability and robustness of this relation. When samples were combined, the size of the correlation was $r(34) = .39, p < .01$. This relation was independent of IQ.

For girls in both samples, AR was not related to the Luchins's task. In the second sample, the pure percentage of primary process predicted flexibility of shifting sets, $r(17) = .43, p < .05$.

In the next study (Russ, 1988a), I investigated the relation between divergent thinking and primary process in a fifth-grade follow-up study of 53 children who remained from the third-grade samples. The results were significant for boys but not for girls. AR and percentage of primary process were significantly related to the Alternate Uses Test (Wallach & Kogan, 1965) for boys, $r(27) = .34, p < .05$, and $r(27) = .33, p < .05$, respectively. Primary-process scores did not predict divergent thinking for girls.

My study with Grossman-McKee (Russ & Grossman-McKee, 1990) of second-grade children obtained the same pattern of sex differences. For boys, percentage of primary process on the Rorschach predicted divergent thinking on the Alternate Uses Test, $r(20) = .72, p < .001$. This relation was independent of intelligence. There was no significant relation for girls. AR did not predict divergent thinking for either sex. It may be that in children this young, the frequency of primary-process expression rather than the integration of primary process is the more important aspect of primary process in creativity. This point was also made by Dudek and Verreault (1989).

In summary, all of my studies with the Rorschach found sex differences in the magnitude of the correlations between primary process and creativity. For boys, primary process was significantly related to divergent thinking and to transformation abilities. Usually, the integration of primary-process material was the best predictor, but percentage of primary-process content was also a significant predictor in several studies. For girls, in most studies, there was no significant relation between any primary-process scores and creativity. In one study (Russ, 1982), percentage of primary process did predict flexibility on the Luchins's Water-Jar Test. The sex differences are consistent with sex differences in research findings with adults (Holt, 1977; Suler, 1980).

In my study with Grossman-McKee (Russ & Grossman-McKee, 1990), we also found a relation between the amount of primary-process thinking on the Rorschach and children's affect in play. Children who had more primary-process responses on the Rorschach had more primary process in their play, more affect in their play, and higher fantasy scores than children with less primary process on the Rorschach. This is an important finding because it shows consistency in the construct of affective expression across two different types of situations. Also, primary-process expression in pretend play was significantly related to divergent thinking in both boys and girls.

Mood-Induction Research

A second line of investigation relevant to this discussion is mood-induction research. The mood-induction paradigm provides a way of altering affect states so that the effect on cognitive processes of both adults and children can be observed.

A growing body of research has found that induced affect states facilitate creative thinking. Isen carried out a series of important, carefully controlled studies in the mood induction area. In a study by Isen and Daubman (1984), adults in a positive affect mood-induction condition categorized stimuli more inclusively than controls. Isen (1985) found that positive affect resulted in more divergent associations to neutral words than in controls. Isen, Daubman, and Nowicki (1987) found that induced positive affect (induced by a comedy film) resulted in more creative problem solving than control conditions. The problem-solving task in one study was the Duncker (1945) candle task, a measure of functional fixedness. To solve the problem, one must break a set and consider alternative solutions to the problem. This problem seems quite similar to the Luchins's Water-Jar Test used in my (Russ, 1982) study. In my study, for boys access to primary-process material was related to the ability to break the set in two separate samples. Positive results for girls occurred in one of my samples. Both the Duncker candle task and the Luchins's Water-Jar Test are measures of Guilford's (1968) transformation ability. Isen et al. (1987) reported no sex differences.

Isen et al. (1987) also found that positive affect improved performance on the Remote Associates Test (Mednick, 1962), a measure of creativity that calls for diverse associations and seeing the relatedness of ideas. They concluded that the underlying mechanism for these results is that positive affect cues positive memories and a large amount of cognitive material. This process results in defocused attention and a more complex cognitive context. This, in turn, results in a greater range of associations and interpretations. There is an increasing awareness of different aspects of stimuli and more ways of relating and combining information.

Although much of the mood-induction research has found results for positive affect states, there is evidence that negative affect states can facilitate creativity in some situations (Vosburg & Kaufmann, 1999). Also, the fact that much of the primary-process content that related to creativity was negative aggressive affect-laden expressions suggests that negative affect is also important in the creative process.

In an earlier work (Russ, 1996), I concluded that findings of the primary-process research and the mood-induction research are consistent with Bower's (1981) conceptualization of affect and memory processes (Russ, 1993). The work on mood and memory suggests that the search process for associations is broadened by the involvement of emotion. This broadened search process facilitates creative cognitive processes such as divergent thinking and transformation abilities. The role of primary-process thinking in creativity is better understood if it is conceptualized as mood-relevant cognition (Russ, 1993). When stirred, it triggers a broad associative network.

Bower's (1981) associative network theory proposed that each emotion is a memory unit: Each emotion has a special node or unit in memory. The activation of the emotion unit aids the retrieval of events associated with it. It primes emotional thematic imagery for use in free association, fantasies, and perceptual categorization. Rholes, Riskind, and Lane (1987) expanded on Bower's theory and discussed mood-related cognitions. Affect states activate a set of relevant cognitions that are mood related. A cognitive priming process occurs.

A more recent theoretical model is Getz and Lubart's (1999) emotional resonance model of creativity, in which emotions contribute to the access and association of cognitively remote concepts in memory. In this model, emotions become attached to concepts or images. These are labeled *endocepts*. Associations are emotion based and may resonate with each other when triggered. Endocepts attached to concepts resonate with each other and link concepts in memory.

In 1993, I speculated that individuals who are open to affect states and affect-laden cognition benefit in carrying out creative tasks in two ways. First, they have access to more cues that activate other nodes in the search process. More associations occur. Second, more emotionally salient material would get coded and stored when individuals were in an emotional state. For individuals open to affect, more would "get in," thus providing the individual with a richer network of affect-relevant associations. This storing of affective content would be especially important for artistic creativity, where one is often dealing with affect and the transformation of affect content into universal symbols. There is evidence that creative individuals are more sensitive and open to experience than noncreative people (McCrae & Costa, 1987; Richards, 1990).

Primary-process thinking itself may be conceptualized as mood-relevant cognition, occurring when emotion nodes are activated. Perhaps emotion and cognition are fused in many primary-process thoughts. If, as I proposed in 1987, primary process is a subtype of affect in cognition that consists of content around which the child had experienced early intense feeling states (oral, anal, aggressive), current primary-process expressions could reflect these early encodings of fused affect and cognition. The primary-process content was stored when emotion was present. Access to this primary-process material would activate emotion nodes and associations, thus broadening the search process.

It is also possible that some cognitive and affective components of primary process are separate dimensions. This conceptualization would be consistent with the view of Zajonc (1980, 1991) that affect and cognition can at times be two separate processes. Affective reactions can occur without prior involvement of cognitive processes. Cognition and affect are two interacting but independent functions. Also, some stimuli pull for affective responses without cognitive involvement.

Zajonc's (1980) hypothesis is consistent with recent work by LeDoux. In research with rats, LeDoux (1989) found that the amygdala triggers an emotional reaction before the thinking brain has fully processed the nerve signals. The amygdala can receive inputs from the senses before these inputs go through the cortex. LeDoux referred to the existence of emotional memories. The emotional system can act independently of the cognitive system. His work has discovered neural pathways that do not go through the cortex. LeDoux suggested that these precognitive emotions are functional in infants during the early formative years. Behavior is affected, but we have no conscious memory of the events.

Primary-process thinking could involve pure cognitive components. For example, Martindale (1989) theorized that creative individuals engage more than noncreative individuals in states of defocused attention, during which a large number of nodes (neurons or groups of neurons) are activated simultaneously. Defocused attention is more likely to occur during low cortical arousal. There is evidence that primary-process thinking involves defocused attention and low cortical arousal (Martindale, 1981).

Primary process could be a mode of thinking that is dominant in processing unconscious or below the level of awareness stimuli. In a review of the literature on subliminal perception, Masling (1992) concluded that the spread of associations is greater when stimuli do not quite reach awareness. A study by Spence and Holland (1962) found that subliminal presentation of a word resulted in greater recall of associated words than did no presentation or above-threshold presentation of the word. They speculated that a different pattern of cognitive activity with different associative processes operated in reduction of awareness situations. Masling (1992) hypothesized that a "subliminal message stimulates a broad band of association pathways, allowing a spread of activation over a wide area of association traces" (p. 273). This broad band of associations would be facilitative in tasks requiring divergent thinking and transformation abilities.

In summary, Bower's (1981) associative network theory and Martindale's (1989) defocused attention framework might explain different aspects of primary-process thinking. Bower's theory speaks to the importance of affect and affect-laden fantasy in facilitating creativity. Individuals who are open to affect states and to affect-laden cognition would have access to more cues that activate other nodes in the search process than individuals who are closed off to those states.

The physiological state that accompanies primary-process thinking may also facilitate creativity. Martindale's (1989) view of low cortical arousal and defocused attention hypothesizes the existence of a different cognitive process that also aids creativity. It is possible that individuals who are comfortable with affect and primary-process thinking let these low cortical arousal states occur because they are comfortable with the results. This is what Kris (1952) was saying with his concept of regression in the service of ego. Individuals who can gain controlled access to primary process are more likely to let this state occur.

Psychotic Disorders

Martindale (1989) said that the commonality among the various psychotic disorders is primary-process thinking and the cognitive disinhibition that accompanies it. One hypothesis is that different dimensions of primary process are dominant in the different disorders. Thus, the higher incidence of creativity within these populations could be partially accounted for by different mechanisms related to primary process. The cognitive dimension of primary process may be more dominant in schizophrenia-spectrum disorders and the affective dimension of affect-laden images and fantasy could be more dominant in bipolar disorders.

The most striking aspect of the schizophrenia spectrum is the presence of the formal properties of primary-process thinking. The formal deviations of thinking are often primitive, are not integrated, and are not controlled. The associations are fluid but without the integration and critical thinking necessary for creative work. Therefore, the cognitive aspects of primary-process thought cannot be used adaptively, and the fact that there may be few "normal" periods for many schizophrenics makes it less likely they can use this cognitive process at other times. It makes sense that relatives of individuals with schizophrenia may have a genetic predisposition to mild formal thinking deviations that are controlled and well integrated so that creative thought would be facilitated. Prentky (1989) speculated that it is a genetically transmitted cognitive style that is common to high creativity and to the predisposition to psychoses.

The current thinking is that for bipolar disorders, the best creative work occurs during the mild manic period (Jamison, 1993; Richards & Kinney, 1990). The positive mood state in the hypomanic phase, when thinking is not too disorganized, is the most beneficial for creative work. The mechanisms that benefit creativity appear to be those associated with positive affect. All of the research (Isen, 1999) showing that positive affect facilitates associations is relevant to the mild manic phase. Also, Jamison (1993) discussed the increased energy, expansiveness, and risk taking that is operating here that benefits productivity. The formal properties of primary-process thinking in general seem to be less severe and less primitive for the affective disorders than for schizophrenic disorders (Harrow & Marengo, 1986). This suggests that primary process is better integrated in the affective disorders and, therefore, more usable for creative work. A more important dimension of primary process could be the actual affective primary-process ideation that would facilitate emotion-laden associations.

In a study by Shenton, Solovay, and Holzman (1987), three groups (schizophrenia, mania, and schizoaffective patients) were compared on the Thought Disorder Index for the Rorschach. The manic group had a higher number of combinatory thinking responses. *Combinatory thinking* reflects the tendency to merge percepts, ideas, or images in an incongruous fashion. They at times had a playful, flippant quality not seen in the other groups. Shenton et al. concluded that extravagant combinatory efforts, flippancy, loose connections among ideas, and playfulness were characteristic of the manic group, whereas fluid thinking, confusion, elliptical and fragmented communications, and peculiar verbal productions were characteristic of the schizophrenic patients. These findings are consistent with the idea that the cognitive dimension of primary process could be dominant in schizophrenia and the affective dimension dominant in bipolar disorders.

Future research should specifically investigate how primary-process thinking differs in schizophrenia and in bipolar disorders. How are the content and formal properties different? A study that would use Holt's scoring system for primary-process comparing Rorschachs of these diagnostic groups would be very valuable. We could also look specifically at the differences in the integration of primary-process thought between groups.

Another question to investigate is whether there are really two different dimensions of primary-process thinking, one a pure cognitive process and the other a blend of cognitive–affective ideation. Are these different types of primary-process thinking related to different types of creativity?

Finally, by studying children in the schizophrenia spectrum who are in therapy, especially borderline psychotic children, we can learn about the integration of primary-process thought. Borderline psychotic children experience primary-process ideation in raw, unmodulated forms (Leichtman & Shapiro, 1980). Oral and aggressive material frequently is intense, unintegrated, and overwhelming to the child. The accompanying affect is usually anxiety or terror. These children also have many strengths. As these children progress in therapy, they are better able to control and integrate the primary process. The techniques that therapists use to help these children control primary process should be studied so that we can learn about the development of primary-process thought (Russ, 1988b). Often, the therapist uses a mix of cognitive techniques (differentiating inside from outside) and psychodynamic or attachment theory techniques of fostering better object relations and internal representations. Many theorists have pointed out the relation between the development of primary-process thought and the development of object relations and the interpersonal world. As these developmental processes work together in therapy, the primary process becomes better integrated, and in my clinical experience, these children can become quite creative. They have harnessed their primary process, as it were.

In conclusion, by studying the mechanisms underlying creativity in clinical populations, both adult and child, we can learn about the operation and the development of these mechanisms and processes.

References

Arieti, S. (1976). *Creativity: The magic synthesis.* New York: Basic Books.

Arlow, J., & Brenner, C. (1964). *Psychoanalytic concepts and structural theory.* New York: International Universities Press.

Blatt, S., Allison, O., & Feirstein, A. (1969). The capacity to cope with cognitive complexity. *Journal of Personality, 37,* 269–288.

Bower, G. H. (1981). Mood and memory. *American Psychologist, 36,* 129–148.

Cohen, I. (1961). Adaptive regression, dogmatism, and creativity. *Dissertation Abstracts, 21,* 3522–3523.

Culbane, J. (1988, January 10). Throw away the script. *The Plain Dealer,* pp. H1, H5.

Dudek, S. (1968). Regression and creativity. *Journal of Nervous and Mental Disease, 147,* 535–546.

Dudek, S. (1975). Regression in the service of the ego in young children. *Journal of Personality Assessment, 39,* 369–376.

Dudek, S., & Verreault, R. (1989). The creative thinking and ego functioning of children. *Creativity Research Journal, 2,* 64–86.

Duncker, K. (1945). On problem solving. *Psychological Monographs, 58*(5, Whole No. 270).

Freud, S. (1958). The unconscious. In J. Strachey (Ed. & Trans.), *The standard edition of the complete psychological works of Sigmund Freud* (Vol. 14, pp. 159–215). London: Hogarth. (Original work published 1915)

Freud, S. (1966). Project for a scientific psychology. In J. Strachey (Ed. & Trans.), *The standard edition of the complete psychological works of Sigmund Freud* (Vol. 1, pp. 283–413). London: Hogarth. (Original work published 1895)

Getz, I., & Lubart, T. (1999). The emotional resonance model of creativity. Theoretical and practical extensions. In S. Russ (Ed.), *Affect, creative experience and psychological adjustment* (pp. 41–56). Philadelphia: Brunner/Mazel.

Guilford, J. P. (1968). *Intelligence, creativity, and their educational implications.* San Diego, CA: Knapp.

Harrow, M., & Marengo, J. (1986). Schizophrenia thought disorder at follow-up: Its persistence and prognostic significance. *Schizophrenia Bulletin, 12,* 373–393.

Holt, R. (1967). The development of the primary process: A structural view. In R. Holt (Ed.), *Motivation and thought* (pp. 344–384). New York: International Universities Press.

Holt, R. R. (1977). A method for assessing primary process manifestations and their control in Rorschach responses. In M. Rickers-Ovsiankina (Ed.), *Rorschach psychology* (pp. 375–420). New York: Krieger.

Holt, R. R., & Havel, J. (1960). A method for assessing primary and secondary process in the Rorschach. In M. Rickers-Ovsiankina (Ed.), *Rorschach psychology* (pp. 283–315). New York: Wiley.

Isen, A. (1985). The asymmetry of happiness and sadness in effects on memory in normal college students. *Journal of Experimental Psychology: General, 114,* 388–391.

Isen, A. (1999). On the relationship between affect and creative problem solving. In S. Russ (Ed.), *Affect, creative experience and psychological adjustment* (pp. 3–17). Philadelphia: Brunner/Mazel.

Isen, A., & Daubman, K. (1984). The influence of affect in categorization. *Journal of Personality and Social Psychology, 47,* 1206–1217.

Isen, A., Daubman, K., & Nowicki, G. (1987). Positive affect facilitates creative problem solving. *Journal of Personality and Social Psychology, 52,* 1122–1131.

Jamison, K. R. (1993). *Touched with fire: Manic–depressive illness and the artistic temperament.* Toronto, Canada: Free Press.

Kris, E. (1952). *Psychoanalytic exploration in art.* New York: International Universities Press.

LeDoux, J. E. (1989). Cognitive–emotional interactions in the brain. *Cognition and Emotion, 3,* 267–289.

Leightman, M., & Shapiro, S. (1980). An introduction to the psychological assessment of borderline conditions in children: Borderline children and the test process. In J. Kwarer, H. Lerner, P. Lerner, & A. Sugarman (Eds.), *Borderline phenomena on the Rorschach test* (pp. 343–366). New York: International Universities Press.

Luchins, A., & Luchins, E. (1959). *Rigidity of behavior.* Eugene: University of Oregon Books.

Martindale, C. (1981). *Cognition and consciousness.* Homewood, IL: Dorsey.

Martindale, C. (1989). Personality, situation, and creativity. In J. Glover, R. Ronning, & C. R. Reynolds (Eds.), *Handbook of creativity* (pp. 211–232). New York: Plenum.

Masling, J. (1992). What does it all mean? In R. Bornstein & T. Pittman (Eds.), *Perception without awareness* (pp. 259–276). New York: Guilford.

McCrae, R. R., & Costa, P. T., Jr. (1987). Validation of the five-factor model across instruments and observers. *Journal of Personality and Social Psychology, 52,* 81–90.

Mednick, S. A. (1962). The associative bases of the creative process. *Psychological Review, 69,* 220–232.

Pine, R., & Holt, R. (1960). Creativity and primary process: A study of adaptive regression. *Journal of Abnormal and Social Psychology, 61,* 370–379.

Prentky, R. (1989). Creativity and psychopathology: Gamboling at the seat of madness. In J. Glover, R. Ronning, & C. R. Reynolds (Eds.), *Handbook of creativity* (pp. 243–271). New York: Plenum.

Rapaport, D. (1951). *Organization and pathology of thought.* New York: Columbia University Press.

Rholes, W., Riskind, J., & Lane, J. (1987). Emotional states and memory biases: Effects of cognitive priming and mood. *Journal of Personality and Social Psychology, 52,* 91–99.

Richards, R. (1990). Everyday creativity, eminent creativity, and health: Afterview for *CRJ* issues on creativity and health. *Creativity Research Journal, 3,* 300–326.

Richards, R., & Kinney, P. (1990). Mood swings and creativity. *Creativity Research Journal, 3,* 202–217.

Russ, S., (1980). Primary process integration on the Rorschach and achievement in children. *Journal of Personality Assessment, 44,* 338–344.

Russ, S. (1981). Primary process on the Rorschach and achievement in children: A follow-up study. *Journal of Personality Assessment, 46,* 473–477.

Russ, S. (1982). Sex differences in primary process thinking and flexibility in problem solving in children. *Journal of Personality Assessment, 45,* 569–577.

Russ, S. (1987). Assessment of cognitive affective interaction in children: Creativity, fantasy, and play research. In J. Butcher & C. Spielberger (Eds.), *Advances in personality assessment* (Vol. 6, pp. 141–155). Hillsdale, NJ: Lawrence Erlbaum Associates, Inc.

Russ, S. (1988a). Primary process thinking on the Rorschach, divergent thinking, and coping in children. *Journal of Personality Assessment, 52,* 539–548.

Russ, S. (1988b). The role of primary process thinking in child development. In H. Lerner & P. Lerner (Eds.), *Primitive mental states and the Rorschach* (pp. 601–618). Madison, CT: International Universities Press.

Russ, S. (1993). *Affect and creativity: The role of affect and play in the creative process.* Hillsdale, NJ: Lawrence Erlbaum Associates, Inc.

Russ, S. (1996). Psychoanalytic theory and creativity: Cognition and affect revisited. In J. Masling & R. Bornstein (Eds.), *Psychoanalytic perspectives on developmental psychology* (pp. 69–103). Washington, DC: American Psychological Association.

Russ, S., & Grossman-McKee, A. (1990). Affective expression in children's fantasy play, primary process thinking on the Rorschach, and divergent thinking. *Journal of Personality Assessment, 54,* 756–771.

Shenton, M., Solovay, M., & Holzman, P. (1987). Comparative studies of thought disorders. *Archives of General Psychiatry, 44,* 21–30.

Spence, D., & Holland, B. (1962). The restricting effects of awareness: A paradox and explanation. *Journal of Abnormal and Social Psychology, 64,* 163–174.

Suler, J. (1980). Primary process thinking and creativity. *Psychological Bulletin, 88,* 144–165.

Vosburg, S., & Kaufmann, G. (1999). Mood and creativity research: The view from a conceptual organizing perspective. In S. Russ (Ed.), *Affect, creative experience and psychological adjustment* (pp. 19–39). Philadelphia: Brunner/Mazel.

Wallach, M., & Kogan, N. (1965). *Modes of thinking in young children: A study of the creativity–intelligence distinction.* New York: Holt, Rinehart, & Winston.

Zajonc, R. (1980). Feeling and thinking: Preferences need no inferences. *American Psychologist, 35,* 151–175.

Zajonc, R. (1991, August). *Emotions and brain temperature.* Paper presented at the 99th annual meeting of the American Psychological Association, Boston.

Zimiles, H. (1981). Cognitive–affective interaction: A concept that exceeds the researcher's grasp. In E. Shapiro & E. Weber (Eds.), *Cognitive and affective growth* (pp. 49–63). Hillsdale, NJ: Lawrence Erlbaum Associates, Inc.

Creativity Research Journal
2000–2001, Vol. 13, No. 1, 37–44

COMMENT

Eccentricity, Conformism, and the Primary Process

Louis A. Sass
Rutgers—The State University

I am grateful for the opportunity to comment on the rich and lucid articles in the previous section. They offer compelling evidence and arguments in favor of examining the diversity that seems to exist at both poles of the creativity–psychopathology linkage and, more specifically, of considering the creative potential of persons in the schizophrenia spectrum of illnesses or personality types. I discuss the articles by Schuldberg (2000–2001), Kinney et al. (2000–2001), and Russ (2000–2001) in that order but with occasional flashforwards or flashbacks as these seem appropriate.[1]

Schuldberg (2000–2001) on Subclinical Spectrum Traits in Normal Creativity

In the first article, Schuldberg (2000–2001) offers good arguments for the need to go beyond a categorical diagnostic approach to schizophrenia. As he notes, both "horizontal" and "vertical" dimensions of the spectrum concept are necessary (Schuldberg & Sass, 1999): the first recognizing that pure schizophrenia gradually shades into schizoaffective forms, thus ultimately forming a continuum with paradigmatic forms of affective psychosis at a comparable level of severity, and the second recognizing the existence of schizoid or schizotypal conditions that manifest schizophrenia-like features of a milder sort.

The majority of the evidence that Schuldberg (2000–2001) presents or reviews indicates that hypomania, an affective feature, accounts for the lion's share of the variance on most creativity measures. This obviously supports the view, also put forward by Jamison (1993), Richards (1994), and others, for a close link between affective illness, especially manic tendencies, and creative potential and achievement. However, there is also (unpublished) evidence that physical anhedonia, a trait associated with the schizophrenia spectrum, may be associated with the presence of creative, nonintellective thought (*origence*) and with preference for more unusual or complex designs (on the Barron–Welsh Revised Art Scale). Schuldberg associates this "partially positive picture" of anhedonic participants with a view of them as "socially alienated and marching to the beats of different drummers" (p. 10), with "outsider" characteristics. Other evidence indicates that on at least one creativity measure, the Maximum Peak creativity score (an index of one's most creative accomplishment in either vocational or avocational activities), the high scores were more closely related to various schizotypal measures, Perceptual Aberration, magical thinking, and especially Physical Anhedonia, than to hypomania.

Schuldberg (2000–2001) argues for the importance of more differentiated conceptualizations that would acknowledge two features of creativity: first, the continuous nature of this variable and, second, the important role of social evaluation, which, depending on context, may classify the very same thought processes as problem solving, creative, or culturally significant or

Correspondence and requests for reprints should be sent to Louis A. Sass, Rutgers—The State University, GSAPP–Busch Campus, 152 Frelinghuysen Road, Piscataway, NJ 08854–8085. E-mail: lsass@rci.rutgers.edu.

[1]I am grateful to David Schuldberg for helpful editorial comments on a draft of this comment.

else as thought disordered, psychotic, or useless. The role of social evaluation suggests a point with which Schuldberg is likely to agree, namely, that creativity may need to be understood not only as a continuous variable but also, at times, as a heterogeneous one, given that what is required for products to be classified as creative may differ in fundamental ways from one cultural context to another. Particularly relevant examples of this are the works produced by both Friedrich Hölderlin and Antonin Artaud in the later periods of their lives. These writings, which certainly can be seen as having distinctly psychotic or schizophrenia-like qualities, have sometimes been dismissed as meaningless psychotic ramblings, mere "word salad" or the "verbigerations" of a dilapidated mind, but they have also been praised as the most interesting and creative, albeit "difficult," of their works.[2] It is worth noting that those who have appreciated this late work have generally had a modernist or perhaps postmodernist bent. (As I use the terms, *modernism* and *postmodernism* refer to various innovative or avant-garde movements in 20th-century art, literature, and thought; see my article [Sass, 2000–2001b] in this special issue for elaboration.)

I especially like Schuldberg's (2000–2001) apt description of the modernist associating of genius and creativity with what he calls "'cooler' mood states inherent in alienation and anxiety" (p. 6). This is well put, and it raises the interesting question of whether we should conceive of these mood states as tending to lack affect or emotion or as involving, instead, different kinds of affective responses. A phenomenological examination of human experience shows that affect or mood is always present in some form, even if it involves what Heidegger (1927/1962) called the "tranquil tarrying alongside" (p. 177; see also pp. 173, 238) that is characteristic of mere objective looking or theoretical knowledge. This suggests that there may be something misleading about our tendency in psychology to polarize or even dichotomize cognition and affect, which seems to be implicit in characterizations of schizophrenia as a thought disorder and manic–depression as a mood disorder. I am, therefore, uncomfortable with Russ's (2000–2001) statements to the effect that schizophrenic forms of creativity are bound up with cognitive as opposed to affective abnormalities; it seems to me that it is precisely the existence of cooler mood states that may be conducive to some of the forms of creativity that are especially characteristic of persons with schizoid or schizophrenia-like tendencies (e.g., in work like that of Marcel Duchamp or Andy Warhol; see Sass, 1992).

Schuldberg (2000–2001) states that antisocial and impulsive traits may be especially relevant to revolutionary artists because these traits make such people both able and motivated to trample boundaries and to break out of dominant intellectual or artistic frameworks. This is an eminently plausible claim. I would suggest, however, that certain forms of detachment characteristic of persons with schizoid traits may also be important for revolutionary achievements. Truly revolutionary innovation, at least of the kind described in Thomas Kuhn's (1970) classic study of scientific revolutions, may be facilitated by the ability not just to break but also to see or to objectify the framework assumptions of an earlier paradigm, which thereby comes to be subsumed within a new and more inclusive one. The capacity for distance and detachment, for a kind of metadetachment in which one detaches from and possibly takes as an object that which would normally constitute the very ground of action, thought, and experience, is especially characteristic of persons of high intelligence with schizoid traits (e.g., Descartes, Kant, Newton, or Einstein; see Storr, 1972).[3]

Finally, let me mention Schuldberg's (2000–2001) intriguing suggestions at the end of his article concerning the use of nonlinear dynamical systems to develop new ways of grasping and modeling the roles of serendipity and of novelty and originality in creative work. Although I do not have the technical competence to assess these suggestions, I nevertheless attempt to pose a couple of queries.

These notions, which derive from chaos theory, would seem to be especially relevant to the understanding of developments in the arts after the advent of modernism about a century ago because modernism has been so dominated by a demand for novelty as such, by

[2]Regarding Hölderin, see Sass (1992, p. 183). Regarding Artaud, see Artaud (1995) and Barber (1993). For an interesting exchange concerning these issues, although bearing on Artaud's early work, see the correspondence between Artaud and Jacques Riviere (Artaud, 1965, pp. 7–25), editor of *La Nouvelle Revue Francaise*, on their differing views of the esthetic value of certain poems by Artaud that Riviere had rejected for publication because of their scattered and fragmentary qualities.

[3]Einstein's remarkable capacity for schizoid detachment in personal and love relationships is clear in some recently published letters (see Overbye, 1999).

the requirement expressed in Ezra Pound's famous dictum: "Make it new!" (cited in Calinescu, 1977, p. 226). I am curious to know whether Schuldberg believes that these new conceptions from nonlinear dynamical systems are truly capable of doing justice to the specific difference between the two forms of novelty described in Kuhn's (1970) distinction between the puzzle-solving innovations of "normal science" as opposed to the more radical frame shifting of revolutionary science. I also wonder whether conceptualizations based on nonlinear dynamical systems would be able to capture the kinds of stylistic transformations that could be said to have a metadimension (i.e., which involve a reference to, and a knowing distance from, characteristics of previously dominant styles). The latter kind of metadimension emerges as especially important in the forms of irony and pastiche that are common in modernism and especially in postmodernism. According to some philosophical positions, those put forward by Frankfurt (1971) and Taylor (1985), for instance, it is just this kind of second-order capacity—the capacity not just to desire, for example, but to desire to desire in a certain way, or to have desires of a certain kind—that is the very essence of personhood or the human. Nonlinear dynamic systems and chaos theory derive from the study of the physical world. Are the concepts they deploy relevant not only to novelty and serendipity but also to these, perhaps quintessentially human, capacities that would seem to be so central to certain kinds of creative work?

Kinney et al. (2000–2001) on Creativity in Offspring of Schizophrenic and Control Parents

The main finding of the important study by Kinney et al. (2000–2001) is to confirm earlier research studies that discovered unusual creativity in nonschizophrenic individuals who were close biological relatives of persons with schizophrenia. As Kinney et al. note, the earlier studies of Karlsson (1970); Kauffman, Grunebaum, Cohler, and Gamer (1979); and Heston and Denney (1988) were vulnerable to a number of significant methodological critiques. Some of these earlier findings were post hoc and serendipitous. Also, the findings may have been marred by a tendency to overdiagnose schizophrenia and to underdiagnose affective illnesses. Hence, it could be argued that the seeming creativity–schizophrenia link that they found may have been due to the creativity of persons related to misdiagnosed patients who actually had affective disorder. (In my contribution to this symposium [Sass, 2000–2001b], I argue a converse point, namely, that a highly inclusive approach to the diagnosis of affective disorders and a tendency to neglect the possible presence of schizophrenia-spectrum disorders may have biased some of the interpretations offered in Jamison's [1993] writings on these topics.) The remarkable methodological rigor of the Kinney et al. research makes their results much less vulnerable to these and other criticisms. They are justified in their claim to have provided "perhaps the strongest evidence to date in support of the hypothesis that traits associated with increased liability for schizophrenia are also associated with increased creativity" (p. 24). Kinney et al. found evidence of an inverted-U relation between creativity and schizotypal characteristics, with the highest creativity scores being attained by participants with a moderate but significant amount of schizotypal characteristics.

The Kinney et al. (2000–2001) research produced an interesting finding regarding the difference between lifetime peak creativity in vocational as opposed to avocational spheres. Kinney et al. found only a slight and nonsignificant trend for the wide-spectrum participants (participants with at least two schizotypal signs) to demonstrate greater peak creativity in vocational activities than did their control participants who lacked such signs; however, there was a distinct, and statistically significant, tendency for this to be true in avocational activity. This finding is intriguing and can be interpreted in various ways. Kinney et al. attribute this differential finding to the higher social anxiety of schizophrenia-spectrum individuals, which causes them to be drawn toward more solitary and less competitive activities, such as (avocational) poetry writing or sophisticated photography.

A second possibility, perfectly compatible with the first, is that schizophrenia-spectrum individuals may simply be less interested in or motivated by the prospect of worldly success or acclaim. Still another possibility (also perfectly compatible) is that because of the cognitive or perhaps existential propensities of schizophrenia-spectrum individuals, their creative or expressive productions are likely to be less conventional or congruent with the usual preferences and tendencies prevailing in their social milieu and, therefore, less likely to be met with a ready or appreciative response.

Presumably, these eccentric tendencies would pose problems for vocational activities, which usually demand teamwork or the fulfillment of specific external demands, but would be far less problematic in the avocational or hobbyist domain. (It is also possible that these eccentric, perhaps radical ideas may sometimes be taken up, transformed, and eventually exploited by other people who have more social facility and worldly ambition.) Such an interpretation is consistent with a line of German psychopathological research and theory mentioned in my own symposium contribution, namely, Blankenburg's (1991) emphasis on the loss of common sense and "natural self-evidence" in schizophrenia.[4] It recalls as well the work by Tellenbach (1961) and Kraus (1982) on the greater conformism of persons in the affective than in the schizophrenia spectrum.

Both Schuldberg (2000–2001) and Kinney et al. (2000–2001) adopt the vocabulary of positive versus negative symptoms in describing the empirical findings that they report or review. Perceptual aberration, magical ideation, and odd speech signs are described as positive, whereas anhedonia and social anxiety are described as negative symptoms. The implication would seem to be that perceptual aberration can be viewed as some kind of *forme fruste* of hallucinatory phenomena, magical ideation as a *forme fruste* of delusional phenomena, and odd speech signs as a *forme fruste* of formal thought disorder.

Such categories do have a certain intuitive plausibility, and they may well be harmless enough if they are not taken too literally. It is worth noting, however, that schizophrenic formal thought disorder has actually been classified in several different ways, not only as a positive but also as a negative symptom (McGlashan & Fenton, 1992, p. 64) and, in the now-prominent tripartite system put forward by Liddle (1987), as a member of a third group of disorganization symptoms. Mostly, however, I am troubled by the implied association with the positive–negative distinction as this is used and understood with regard to full-blown schizophrenic symptoms.

Positive symptoms are typically defined as involving the presence of phenomena that would normally be absent, and negative symptoms as the absence of phenomena that would normally be present. This distinction is often said to be perfectly atheoretical, merely a behavioral description, but this is generally not the case. Negative symptoms have usually been understood on a defect or deficit model as involving the diminution or absence of underlying psychological processes and capacities, perhaps especially those involving the intensity of subjective life as well as the higher or more quintessentially human capacities for self-reflection, abstraction, or complex emotional response. A considerable amount of evidence now suggests, however, that these assumptions may be mistaken. For example, patients manifesting flat affect seem to have affective responses that are equal to or even more intense than those of normal individuals, as measured both by subjective report and by skin-conductance reactivity (Kring & Neale, 1996). In general, there seems to be little correlation between overtly manifested negative symptoms (actually, these ought to be called *negative signs*) and the patient's own subjective experience (Selten, Bosch, & Sijben, 1998). Elsewhere (Sass, 2000), I described in detail the kinds of (in a sense) positive anomalies that on the subjective plane may underlie the negative signs. As the German research on basic symptoms has clearly shown (Klosterkoetter, 1992), perceptual aberrations, which both Schuldberg and Kinney et al. classify as a positive symptom, will often be present in patients who manifest overtly negative signs.

The upshot of all of this is that the positive–negative distinction is oversimplified and can be highly misleading. It also suggests that the evidence for an association of creativity with positive more than with negative schizotypal signs may be somewhat weaker or more ambiguous than is implied by both Schuldberg (2000–2001) and Kinney et al. (2000–2001).

I certainly agree with, and vigorously applaud, Kinney et al.'s (2000–2001) comments on the relevance of research such as theirs for the issue of the potential stigmatization of schizophrenia. The Danish policy of encouraging abortion in schizophrenic mothers, which is mentioned in their article, is, of course, a particularly clear example of the kind of direct social consequences that a totally deficit-oriented view of schizophrenia can have, even in what is, by all accounts, a remarkably benign mental-health environment. As Kinney et al. note, it is also especially important for issues of self-esteem and for intrafamily attitudes. In my own contribution (Sass, 2000–2001b), I criticize what may be called the near hegemony within psychology, psychia-

[4]A translation of a key article by Blankenburg (1969) will appear in a future issue of the journal *Philosophy, Psychiatry, Psychology.*

try, and psychoanalysis of essentially romanticist views of creativity. A greater recognition of the role of hyperreflexivity and alienation in modernist and postmodernist forms of creativity may help many persons in the psychological and mental-health professions to appreciate the distinctive forms of creativity of which schizophrenics can be capable.

Russ (2000–2001) on Creativity and the Primary Process

Russ's (2000–2001) article offers a clear and useful summary of research on creativity and what has been termed *primary-process thinking.* I agree with what is perhaps her central point, namely, that there seem to be key differences in the kinds of psychological processes that are conducive to creativity in different people and, in particular, that different underlying psychological mechanisms or processes may subserve the creativity of schizophrenia-spectrum individuals as opposed to bipolar- or affective-spectrum individuals. One possible implication of this claim is that creativity itself may well be a more heterogeneous phenomenon or set of phenomena or processes than is usually recognized. I would also agree, at least to a limited extent, with Russ's claim that the creativity of affective-domain persons is more bound up with the content and that of schizophrenia-spectrum persons with the form of their thought and experience.

Recent research on thinking and thought disorder in affective and bipolar patients should make one question any overly extreme way of drawing this distinction (see Holzman, Shenton, & Solovay, 1986; Goodwin & Jamison, 1990, chap. 11). Still, it is true that, whereas the thinking patterns of schizophrenics can be highly unusual and hard to follow, those of patients with affective disorders do tend to remain more within certain familiar channels, although the pace may become accelerated and the content exaggerated and unrealistic. However, I must disagree with two assumptions that are central to Russ's (2000–2001) article and argument: her tendency to make too sharp a distinction between cognition and affect and, second, her use of the notion of the primary process itself.

As indicated earlier, I am dubious about the prospect of distinguishing, in any rigorous or theoretically grounded way, between cognition and affect, both of which seem to me to be better conceived as omnipresent aspects of virtually any instance of human experiencing. Also, as indicated earlier, I am not sure that the cognitive dimension really is more dominant in schizophrenia-like experience and expression. One of the important experiential changes that may occur in schizophrenia is a loss of the normal emotional affordances of the world, which gives rise to a quasisurrealistic fragmenting vision that can be bound up with a certain kind of creativity (a vision well exemplified by the passage from Giorgio de Chirico quoted in my article in this issue [Sass, 2000–2001b]). Although this experience does involve a loss of some kinds of emotional reactivity—of what one may call the full-bodied or full-blooded emotions that are geared into normal forms of desire and concern—it also gives rise to other types of affective and at least quasiemotional response, including startle, anxiety, wonder, ontological insecurity, and the like.

My most important disagreement, however, concerns the very notion of the primary process itself. This notion comes, of course, from Freud. According to Freud and most of those who have adopted the concept, the primary process is a primitive and illogical mode of consciousness dominated by affect and desire. However, as I have argued at length elsewhere (Sass, 1992), the most prominent and distinctive features of schizophrenic thought and experience have qualities that are almost antithetical to this. Many traditional studies of schizophrenic or psychotic thinking claimed to demonstrate the primitive and primary-process dominated nature of such persons. This, in turn, was often claimed to have provided some validation of the notion of primary process because the latter process had now, supposedly, been shown to be present in patients whom we know to be highly regressed. All of this can be quite circular, however: The notion of primary process may not be proven but simply presupposed.

If one examines a scoring system like Holt's (1977) "A Method for Assessing Primary Process Manifestations and Their Control in Rorschach Responses," which according to Russ (2000–2001) has been utilized in her own and most other research investigating primary-process thinking and creativity, one discovers that it is really a miscellany that includes a very disparate set of categories of phenomena, not only "oral–receptive" and "oral–aggressive content," peculiar verbalizations, and clang associations, but also "contamination" responses, which involve a fusion of two perspectives akin to a photographic double exposure. Independent evidence suggests, however, that whereas some of the features that do indeed have a "primitive" or regressive quality (e.g., responses suggesting domination by instinctual concerns) are not especially common in schizophrenia (Harrow & Quinlan, 1985, pp. 12–13, 45, 148), at least some of the phenomena that are distinctive of schizophrenia do not seem to be primitive at all. Thus, contamination responses, which of all Rorschach indicators are the most pathognomonic of schizophrenia, are virtually never found in young children (Exner, 1993, pp. 277–301). I argued elsewhere (Sass 1992, chap. 4) that contamination responses actually suggest an exaggerated perspectivism that is akin to modernist relativism and quite antithetical to the primitive or infantile mind. Given these considerations, one may well wonder whether the disparate phenomena included in Holt's primary-process list actually share any deep or essential quality. I would argue that the only thing they really share is negative in nature: the fact of deviating from an ill-defined yet still recognizable norm of practical and conventional thinking and speech.

It is necessary to note, however, that Russ (2000–2001) herself seems to reject the traditional conception of primary process; she allies herself with newer psychological approaches that reject the assumption of both its regressive and its drive-dominated nature. I certainly agree that this kind of cleaned-up (or perhaps we should say, denatured) notion of the primary process makes it less inappropriate for describing schizophrenic anomalies of thinking and language. The problem, however, is that it is now unclear why we should retain the notion at all. The very use of the term *primary process* implies, after all, that the forms of thought and experience so designated do have something in common, or to put the same point slightly differently, that there is really just one, somehow basic, lower, or fundamental (why else use the term *primary*?) kind of thinking that exists as an alternative to the consensual, logical, and practically oriented forms that we call the *secondary process*. However, what, really, do the hyperreflexive and alienated forms of thinking characteristic of at least some schizophrenics have in common with, say, the concretistic thinking of the patient with senile dementia, the accelerated giddiness of the manic, the delirium of alcoholic hallucinosis, or the animism and artificialism of the young child? It is far better to be a splitter than a lumper when one attempts to characterize abnormal styles of human thinking and experience. At least at this stage, we need to stay close to the actual phenomena, seeking to develop concepts, and probably some new terminology, that can capture the quiddities of different abnormal styles of thinking and speaking rather than effacing these differences in accordance with preconceived assumptions that are of dubious validity.

Conclusion

Russ (2000–2001) ends her article with a plea that is made by Schuldberg (2000–2001) and by Kinney et al. (2000–2001) as well: "More research is needed!" This, of course, is a familiar refrain, so familiar, in fact, that it may well seem treasonous (an act of guild-treason) for a psychologist to call it into question here. Actually, I will not dispute the idea that more empirical data, gathered with the kind of methodological rigor demonstrated in some of the studies previously discussed, would indeed be useful. However, there is an equally great need for work of a more critical, speculative, historical, and phenomenologically descriptive kind, for studies that would help us to criticize current concepts and to develop new ones that may be more adequate to the phenomena we seek to understand. Indeed, I would argue that in the absence of such studies, there is a sense in which we literally do not know what we are talking about (or looking at, or counting up in our research studies) when we speak of creativity, creative psychological processes, or certain types of psychopathology.

The philosopher Ludwig Wittgenstein (1953) criticized the human propensities to overgeneralize, postulate essences, and reify or hypostatize verbal concepts or abstractions. Both the general spirit and some of the specifics of what he had to say are of considerable relevance for understanding both poles of the creativity–psychopathology linkage. In my own contribution to this symposium (Sass, 2000–2001b), I try to suggest some of the heterogeneity that is inherent in the notion of creativity. In the same article and in my rejoinder to Jamison (Sass, 2000–2001a), I stress the importance of retaining a perspectivist's attitude about psychiatric diagnosis, one that recognizes the potential relevance of different kinds of diagnostic criteria and the possible incommensurability of different types of diagnostic validators. Some historical awareness of the way in which notions of creativity and the imagination and forms of diagnostic practice and conceptualization have changed and are changing over time can help to sharpen one's critical awareness and may also provide some skeptical distance from the viewpoints that happen to be currently dominant. For this reason, the history of both esthetics and psychiatry are of considerable relevance for psychologists and psychiatrists interested in the creativity–psychopathology relation.

It seems to me that we also need to take a more critical look at some of the operationalized variables that are meant to capture the psychological processes in question. Not only the notions of primary-process thinking and of negative and positive symptoms, but the more specific concepts (e.g., perceptual aberration, magical thinking, or anhedonia) also have a tendency to be reified and taken for granted. This tends to distract us from the important task of taking a close look at concrete examples of the actual experiences in question; it leads us to make assumptions about the homogeneity of the phenomena so classified, as well as about their underlying nature, that may be unjustified, invalid, or misleading. Operationalized variables are obviously a requirement for gathering statistically sound, nomothetic evidence. However, such research will need to develop in dialectical interchange with phenomenologically oriented studies of a more ideographic sort. In addition to offering a richer and more detailed perspective on the forms of experience and expression that actually occur, the careful, qualitative investigation of one or a few patients tends as well to encourage freer theoretical speculation about the kinds of psychological processes that may be involved, processes that can eventually be classified and studied in more traditional, empirically oriented ways.[5]

References

Artaud, A. (1965). *Antonin Artaud anthology.* San Francisco: City Lights.

Artaud, A. (1995). *Watchfiends and rack screams: Works from the final period* (C. Eshleman, Trans.). Boston: Exact Change.

Barber, S. (1993). *Antonin Artaud: Blows and bombs.* London: Faber & Faber.

Blankenburg, W. (1969). Ansätze zu einer Psychopathologie des "common sense" [First steps toward a psychopathology of common sense]. *Confinia Psychiatrica, 12,* 144–163.

Blankenburg, W. (1991). *La perte de l'evidence naturelle: Une contribution a la psychopathologie des schizophrenies pauci-symptomatiques* [The loss of natural self-evidence: A contribution to the study of symptom-poor schizophrenics]. Paris: Presses Universitaires de France.

[5]I have tried to carry out this kind of work in a number of articles (see Sass, 1996, 1997, 2000).

Calinescu, M. (1977). *Faces of modernity: Avant garde, decadence, kitsch.* Bloomington: Indiana University Press.

Exner, J. E., Jr. (1993). *The Rorschach: A comprehensive system: Vol. 1. Basic foundations* (3rd ed.). New York: Wiley.

Frankfurt, H. (1971). Freedom of the will and the concept of a person. *Journal of Philosophy, 67,* 5–20.

Goodwin, F. K., & Jamison, K. R. (1990). *Manic–depressive illness.* New York: Oxford University Press.

Harrow, M., & Quinlan, D. M. (1985). *Disordered thinking and schizophrenic pathology.* New York: Gardner.

Heidegger, M. (1962). *Being and time* (J. Macquarrie & E. Robinson, Trans.). New York: Harper & Row. (Original work published 1927)

Heston, L. L., & Denney, D. (1968). Interactions between early life experience and biological factors in schizophrenia. In D. Rosenthal & S. Kety (Eds.), *The transmission of schizophrenia* (pp. 363–376). New York: Pergamon.

Holt, R. (1977). A method for assessing primary process manifestations and their control in Rorschach responses. In M. Rickers-Ovsiankina (Ed.), *Rorschach psychology* (pp. 375–420). New York: Krieger.

Holzman, P. S., Shenton, M. E., & Solovay, M. R. (1986). Quality of thought disorder in differential diagnosis. *Schizophrenia Bulletin, 12,* 360–372.

Jamison, K. R. (1993). *Touched with fire: Manic–depressive illness and the artistic temperament.* New York: Free Press.

Karlsson, J. L. (1970). Genetic association of giftedness and creativity with schizophrenia. *Hereditas, 66,* 177–182.

Kauffman, C., Grunebaum, H., Cohler, B., & Gamer, E. (1979). Superkids: Competent children of psychotic mothers. *American Journal of Psychiatry, 136,* 1396–1402.

Kinney, D. K., Richards, R. L., Lowing, P. A., LeBlanc, D., Zimbalist, M. E., & Harlan, P. (2000–2001). Creativity in offspring of schizophrenic and control parents: An adoption study. *Creativity Research Journal, 13,* 17–25.

Klosterkoetter, J. (1992). The meaning of basic symptoms for the development of schizophrenic psychoses. *Neurology, Psychiatry, and Brain Research, 1,* 30–41.

Kraus, A. (1982). Identity and psychosis of the manic–depressive. In A. J. De Koning & F. A. Jenner (Eds.), *Phenomenology and psychiatry* (pp. 201–216). London: Academic.

Kring A. M., & Neale, J. (1996). Do schizophrenic patients show a disjunctive relationship among expressive, experiential, and psychophysiological components of emotion? *Journal of Abnormal Psychology, 105,* 249–257.

Kuhn, T. (1970). *The structure of scientific revolutions* (2nd ed.). Chicago: University of Chicago Press.

Liddle, P. F. (1987). The symptoms of chronic schizophrenia: A reexamination of the positive–negative dichotomy. *British Journal of Psychiatry, 151,* 145–151.

McGlashan, T. H., & Fenton, W. S. (1992). The positive–negative distinction in schizophrenia. *Archives of General Psychiatry, 49,* 63–72.

Overbye, D. (1999, August 31). Einstein, confused in love and, sometimes, physics. *New York Times,* p. F4.

Richards, R. (1994). Creativity and bipolar mood swings: Why the association? In M. Shaw & M. A. Runco (Eds.), *Creativity and affect* (pp. 44–72). Norwood, NJ: Ablex.

Russ, S. W. (2000–2001). Primary-process thinking and creativity: Affect and cognition. *Creativity Research Journal, 13,* 27–35.

Sass, L. (1992). *Madness and modernism: Insanity in the light of modern art, literature, and thought.* New York: Basic Books.

Sass, L. (1996). "The catastrophes of heaven": Modernism, primitivism, and the madness of Antonin Artaud. *Modernism/Modernity, 3,* 73–92.

Sass, L. (1997). Adolf Wolfli, spatiality, and the sublime. In E. Spoerri (Ed.), *Adolf Wolfli: Draftsman, poet, composer* (pp. 136–145). Ithaca, NY: Cornell University Press.

Sass, L. (2000). Schizophrenia, self-experience, and the so-called "negative symptoms." In D. Zahavi (Ed.), *Exploring the self: Philosophical and psychopathological perspectives on self-experience* (pp. 149–184). Philadelphia: Benjamin.

Sass, L. A. (2000–2001a). Romanticism, creativity, and the ambiguities of psychiatric diagnosis: Rejoinder to Kay Redfield Jamison. *Creativity Research Journal, 13,* 77–85.

Sass, L. A. (2000–2001b). Schizophrenia, modernism, and the "creative imagination": On creativity and psychopathology. *Creativity Research Journal, 13,* 55–74.

Schuldberg, D. (2000–2001). Six subclinical spectrum traits in normal creativity. *Creativity Research Journal, 13,* 5–16.

Schuldberg, D., & Sass, L. (1999). Schizophrenia. In M. A. Runco & S. R. Pritzker (Eds.), *Encyclopedia of creativity* (Vol. 2, pp. 501–514). San Diego, CA: Academic.

Selten, J.-P., Bosch, R. J. van den, & Sijben, A. E. S. (1998). The subjective experience of negative symptoms. In X. F. Amador & A. S. David (Eds.), *Insight and psychosis* (pp. 78–90). New York: Oxford University Press.

Storr, A. (1972). *The dynamics of creation.* New York: Atheneum.

Taylor, C. (1985). *Philosophical papers: Vol I. Human agency and language.* New York: Cambridge University Press.

Tellenbach, H. (1961). *Melancholie.* Berlin, Germany: Springer.

Wittgenstein, L. (1953). *Philosophical investigations* (G. E. M. Anscombe, Trans.). Oxford, England: Blackwell.

Creativity Research Journal
2000–2001, Vol. 13, No. 1, 45–53

The Association of Creativity and Psychopathology: Its Cultural–Historical Origins

George Becker
Vanderbilt University

ABSTRACT: The relation between creativity and mental illness has been a subject of controversy in Western society from about the 1830s to the present. Although speculations regarding the mental state of creative individuals predate this period by centuries, they typically fell short of the verdict of clinical insanity. It was the romantic movement in literature that provided the single most powerful impetus for the judgment of clinical madness. By selectively adopting and redefining certain cultural axioms from the past, the romantics produced not only a logical connection between creativity and madness but also one in which madness was simultaneously a piteous and exalted condition that stood in sharp contrast to what they regarded as dreaded normality. This article examines how the specific intellectual assumptions regarding creative individuals and the nature of the creative process that the romantics "inherited" from Greek antiquity, the Italian Renaissance, and the Enlightenment were subsequently transformed into a system of logic that precluded the possibility of total health and sanity on the part of the creative genius. This logic was so compelling, in fact, that self-admissions of mental anguish and actual manifestations of madness on the part of many romantics may be seen as little more than adherence to what had become part of a role expectation deemed appropriate for artists, writers, and other creative individuals. It is argued, moreover, that evidence abounds that the expectation of "madness" continues to be part of a professional ideology of what it means to be truly creative. Given such, it is not unreasonable to assume that even contemporary writers and artists, far from disavowing any connection to madness, may actually invite it and inadvertently volunteer evidence of madness in diagnostic and psychological examinations.

A commonplace assumption in Western society is the idea that profound creativity has an intimate connection to psychopathology (see Trilling, 1950). Despite speculations from Greek antiquity to the Renaissance and the Enlightenment regarding the mental state of individuals during the act of creation, the association of creativity with clinical madness is a modern phenomenon that does not predate the 1830s. As I argue in this article, it was the romantic movement in literature that was indispensable to the establishment of this medical verdict. Faced with obstacles to their existence, the romantics engaged in the selective redefinition of certain cultural axioms they inherited from the past. These redefinitions, although they tended to benefit the romantics by providing them with a clearer sense of their own identity (one that established their intellectual and artistic independence from the past), simultaneously invited a system of logic that left them defenseless against the label of clinical madness.

This article locates current thinking regarding the relation between creativity and psychopathology in the historical context of the changes in the intellectual assumptions regarding the nature of creative individuals. I open with a brief overview of relevant conceptions during three periods of Western history: Greek antiquity, the Italian Renaissance, and the Age of Enlightenment. In regard to the latter, particular attention is devoted to the introduction of a new model of the creative individual, the person of genius, and the prevailing view regarding the operations of the mind. I then turn to the romantics' reformulation of historically an-

Correspondence and requests for reprints should be sent to George Becker, Department of Sociology, Vanderbilt University, Nashville, TN 37235.

tecedent ideas, including the genius conception, and the subsequent reception of these changes in the field of philosophical–psychological speculation and the rising medical specialty of psychiatry. I conclude with a discussion of some of the implications of this article for current debates concerning creativity and attendant mental conditions.

Speculations on the Mental State of Creative Individuals Prior to the Romantic Age

Critical to an understanding of the ancient Greeks' ruminations regarding the nature of the creative process are the concepts of demonic possession and melancholia. The "demon," which the Greeks conceived as a semideity that presided over a person, a locality, or some other discrete entity, was believed to be endowed with powers to shape the destiny of each in either a positive or negative fashion. Somewhat different from this general view of the term, in the Socratic conception the demon was regarded as a divine gift granted to a few select individuals only. According to this view, the poet, priest, philosopher, and sage communicated with the gods through the intervention of their demon. It is in this sense that Socrates called on his demon and attributed most of his knowledge to intimations from it (Cahan, 1911, pp. 17–24). This conception of demons as the benevolent agents of the gods was generally endorsed by Plato and others and found support in Plato's doctrine of divine madness, or *enthousiasmos.* In this view, the poet, who himself is devoid of talent, is seen as divinely inspired, as an agent or servant of the gods. Inspiration and the gift of prophecy, however, were attainable only during particular states of mind, such as the loss of consciousness due to sleep or a mind affected by illness or possession (Rosen, 1969, pp. 83–84). Importantly, to Socrates, Plato, and other contemporaries, the divine disturbance that invited prophetic or poetic activity was clearly distinguished from clinical insanity. Unlike the latter, the inspired madness of seers and poets was conceived as a virtue, a state of mind greatly desired. To quote from Plato's (1974) *Phaedrus and the Seventh and Eighth Letters:* "Madness, provided it comes as a gift of heaven, is the channel by which we receive the greatest blessings. … [It] is a nobler thing than sober sense … madness comes from God, whereas sober sense is merely human" (pp. 46–47).

Also, the Aristotelian assertion that extraordinary talent is characterized by a melancholic temperament does not mean, as is frequently asserted, that Aristotle viewed insanity as the concomitant of creativity (Wittkower & Wittkower, 1963, p. 102). Insanity, according to Aristotle's reformulation of the Hippocratian humoral theory, did not occur in all melancholic individuals. To Aristotle, the term *melancholia* was descriptive of a type of individual, the *homo melancholicus,* who, depending on the particular balance of his "humors," could be either a sane person of distinction or a madman (Wittkower & Wittkower, 1963, p. 102).

Quite different from the subsequent Roman era and the Middle Ages, where there was relatively little concern or fascination with uncommonly creative individuals, the Italian Renaissance produced a renewed interest in those persons esteemed most highly in the arts and speculation. For these possessors of superior creative ability, the term *genio* was reserved. However, creativity was thought of primarily in terms of an imitation of the established masters and of nature. Unlike the modern conception of the genius, one that stresses originality as the distinguishing feature of the creative individual, the standard of the humanistic tradition involved the *imitatio-ideal.* Although some, like Leonardo and Vasari, insisted that the *genio* should not be just imitatively creative but newly creative (Lange-Eichbaum, 1930/1932, p. 6), these attacks on the *imitatio-ideal* did not become commonly accepted during the late Renaissance (Zilsel, 1926, pp. 248–255).

Similar to the Greek descriptions of the poet, philosopher, and sage, the unique attributes of the Renaissance *genio* commonly were described in terms of melancholia and *pazzia,* or madness. Again, a distinction was maintained between the sane melancholics capable of rare accomplishments and those condemned to insanity. The Florentine Ficino, who popularized the Aristotelian idea of melancholy, regarded this type of temperament, in its application to distinguished men, as a divine gift that constituted a metonymy for Plato's divine mania, only the melancholic temperament was considered capable of creative enthusiasm. Hence, assessments of scholars and artists in terms of *pazzia* were generally not intended to convey the notion of insanity. When applied to great people, the term referred to qualities associated with the melancholic temperament, such as eccentricity, sensitivity, moodiness, and solitariness. These were far from negative qualities; emulating these manifestations of melancholic behavior was turned into a fad in 16th-century Europe (Wittkower & Wittkower, 1963, pp. 98–105).

It was during the 18th century that the term *genius* was introduced in reference to individuals who displayed a high degree of creative ability (Lange-Eichbaum, 1927/1935; Tonelli, 1973; Zilsel, 1926). Different from the Renaissance *genio* and the associated *imitatio-ideal,* the Enlightenment genius was defined as one who was in possession of an innate power that manifested itself in works of great imaginative creation in which the decisive characteristic was profound novelty and the originally creative. Although most commentators on genius acknowledged certain subrational components, the leitmotiv most frequently encountered stressed the rational processes of genius (Fabian, 1966; Tonelli, 1973).

Perhaps the model exposition of the Enlightenment conception of genius is Gerard's (1774/1966) *An Essay on Genius* (see Fabian, 1966, p. xi; Wittkower, 1973, p. 306). Defined as the faculty of invention "by means of which a man is qualified for making new discoveries in science, or for producing original works of art" (p. 8), the creative power in genius was conceived as originating in an active imagination (p. 31). Asserting that an unbridled imagination constitutes a capricious and irresponsible faculty, he stipulated that it must be "subject to established laws" (p. 70). True genius, to Gerard, was only possible as a result of a synthesis or subtle interplay of four powers: (a) imagination, (b) judgment, (c) sense, and (d) memory. He argued:

> Mere imagination will not constitute genius. ... As fancy [imagination] has an indirect dependence both on sense and memory, from which it received the first elements of all its conceptions, so when it exerts itself in the way of genius, it has an immediate connexion with judgment, which must constantly attend it, and correct and regulate its suggestions. This connexion is so intimate, that a man can scarce be said to have invented till he has exercised his judgment. (pp. 36–37)

Gerard (1774/1966) was not alone in viewing genius as an interplay of different mental powers. To Duff, it was a balance of imagination, judgment, and taste; Voltaire saw imagination in conjunction with memory and judgment; Kant, in a first version of his theory of genius (developed between 1770 and 1780), viewed it as a favorable proportion of sensibility, judgment, creative spirit, and taste (see Tonelli, 1973). To Moses Mendelssohn, genius corresponded to a state of perfection of all mental powers working in harmony; to Shaftesbury, although he stressed the irrational traits of genius in terms of revelation and enthusiasm, a true genius did not infringe on the rules of art; he needed knowledge and good sense (see Tonelli, 1973).

The prevailing Enlightenment conception of genius did, therefore, recognize certain natural or subrational components rooted primarily in the creative imagination. However, it pointedly established judgment, or reason, as a counterweight to these components and buttressed judgment with memory, taste, sense, sensibility, and so forth. Judgment was not only capable of averting caprice and extravagance but also made madness a virtual impossibility for genius. As Gerard (1774/1966) observed, "a perfect judgment is seldom bestowed by Nature, even on her most favored sons; but a very considerable degree of it always belongs to real genius" (p. 73).

The conception of the man of genius as rational not only constituted an Enlightenment ideal but also, apparently, reflected the actual behavior of such men. Wittkower (1973) observed, for example, that even artists, known since antiquity for their propensity for eccentric behavior, complied with an image of the conforming artist. Since the Renaissance concept of the *melancholicus* had been supplanted by this newer image, "none of the great seventeenth-century masters—Rubens and Bernini, Rembrant and Velasquez—was ever described as melancholic. ... It was not until the romantic era ... that melancholy appears once again as a condition of mental and emotional catharsis" (p. 309).

The Romantics' Redefinition of Genius and the Functions It Tended to Serve

The late 18th and early 19th centuries, under the impact of the romantic movement, saw a profound change in the prevailing conception of genius. This change was intimately tied to the precarious state of existence of the romantic poets and men of letters.

The application of the term *genius* to select individuals during the 18th century marked, as has been noted, the arrival of a new model for man. Generally deprived of wealth or privileged status, men of genius, or those who aspired to be such, tended to challenge the existing hierarchical order by substituting innate creative ability as a superior criterion for the evaluation of men. D'Alembert (1967), an Enlightenment spokesperson for the man of letters, recognized three factors separating people: (a) birth, (b) wealth, and (c) intelligence, but only intelligence was deemed worthy of true esteem. Unlike the others, he argued, intelligence is a dependable national "resource," by its nature inexhaustible and incapable of being "taken" from its possessors (p. 354). De Saint-Simon (1803/1964), writing a few years after the demise of the Ancien Régime, was less guarded in his vision of the future society; it was to be dominated by men of genius: scientists, artists, men of ideas. In fact, he cautioned the power holders and the propertied classes not to impede the geniuses' quest for power, "great prestige," and money. Failure to comply with this warning, he feared, would lead to the almost certain extinction of the ruling elites: "To be convinced of the truth of what I have said, you have only to reflect on the course of events in France since 1789" (p. 3).

The period of reaction to all "revolutionary" ideas initiated by Napoleon's defeat and the creation of the Quadruple Alliance meant, of course, that prospects of establishing intelligence as a foremost legitimate criterion for the ranking of men had received a serious setback. The Metternich era refused to comply with the demands of this new, self-appointed intellectual aristocracy. Indeed, the events of the late 18th and early 19th centuries made the position of this aspiring group rather precarious. The disappearance of the traditional "sponsor" class, the nobility and the aristocratized bourgeoisie, and the subsequent hazards of commercialization and the modern marketplace left the status of the man of genius in question (see Graña, 1964). Generally impoverished and deprived of political power throughout most of the 19th century, the aspiring artist and person of ideas felt engulfed by the anonymous masses. Although the idea of genius may have commanded a degree of respect, even reverence, the men of genius themselves, faced with a practical world, lacked the special sense of identity necessary to separate themselves effectively from the masses.

It was the idea of a special kind of madness that could serve as a distinguishing factor, one that could mark a person as separate, unique, and even divinely chosen. The romantic artists and men of letters, in particular, revived the classical notion of divine mania or inspiration and established it as a defining mark of the extraordinary individual. It was the aura of mania that endowed the genius with a mystical and inexplicable quality that differentiated him from the typical man, the bourgeois, the philistine, and the merely talented. It established the genius as the modern heir of the ancient Greek poet and seer and, like the classical counterpart, enabled the genius to claim some of the powers and privileges granted the "possessed" prophet. In this role, the man of genius could counsel kings and blaspheme with impunity. Importantly also, the idea of mania conveyed to the romantics the notions of possession, suffering, and weltschmerz, and the display of these qualities confirmed an individual's identity as a true genius. The theme of the blessedness of some special kind of madness is clearly reflected in Poe's "Eleanora":

> I am come from a race noted for vigor of fancy and ardor of passion. Men have called me mad; but the question is not yet settled, whether madness is or is not the loftiest intelligence; whether much that is glorious, whether all that is profound, does not spring from disease of thought. (as cited in Marks, 1926, p. 22)

Similarly, the poet Wieland spoke of the "amiable insanity of the muses" (as cited in Hirsch, 1897, p. 71), and the clergyman Beecher commented on the desirability of at least some degree of madness on the part of poets (as cited in Sanborn, 1886, p. 188).

The desire of the romantics for an affirmed identity, however, constituted only one of their aspirations; a second, closely connected goal was to establish their intellectual independence from the past. Although the conception of the innately creative genius did much to advance the cause of originality in intellectual life, those engaged in literature and the arts remained tied to the authority of the academies and the ancient masters. Therefore, the romantics' attempt to appropriate certain supposed qualities of the ancients had to be effected without assuming a subservient role to traditional authority. This necessitated a redefinition of genius.

Prior to the 18th century, it was commonly accepted that the human imagination constituted a capricious and dangerous element in the lives of men. Recognized as the fountainhead of original creativity, it was simultaneously admired and feared. Pascal (1670/1968), writing in the mid-17th century, reflected this ambivalence clearly:

> Imagination—it is this dominant part in man, this mistress of error and falsity, and more often trickster than not. ... But being most often false, it gives no mark of its quality, marking the true and the false with the same nature. (pp. 362–363)

To benefit from imagination and yet contain its great potential for disaster and evil meant, as Pascal (1670/1968) cautioned the "wisest of men," that one had to consciously "resist" its intoxicating powers with all one's strength (p. 363). It is not surprising, therefore, that during the 18th century, when the genius first became recognized by many as a model of a superior person, the nature of genius was defined in a way that virtually precluded victimization by one's own imagination. As we have seen, in the typical Enlightenment explication of genius, the imagination was seen as constrained by a number of powers or faculties that were particularly developed in the great person (Fabian, 1966; Tonelli, 1973). Indispensable to the harmonious interplay of mental powers was the faculty of judgment, or reason, which, in conjunction with memory, taste, and sense, averted not only caprice and extravagance but also, as Gerard (1774/1966) observed, made "madness and frenzy" a near impossibility for genius (pp. 73–74).

The dominant Enlightenment view of the genius as an educated individual whose abundant imagination was properly tempered by good taste, training in the classics, and an appreciation for the masters proved unacceptable to the romantic spirit. To create a new independence, genius could no longer be seen in the Enlightenment terms of balance, proportion, and a synthesis of mental powers. The romantics, therefore, granted the imagination a clear predominance over those faculties traditionally seen as the rational counterweights to the imagination. Like the Schlegels, Lessing, and others (see Nordau, 1892/1900, p. 73; also Cahan, 1911, pp. 32–38), Schiller proposed that the deliberate application, far from being beneficial, would serve to obstruct the imagination and bind the potential for profound creativity:

> It is not well in works of creation that reason should too closely challenge the ideas that come thronging to the doors. Taken by itself, an idea may be highly unsuitable, even venturesome, and yet in conjunction with others, themselves equally absurd alone, it may furnish a suitable link in the chain of thought. Reason can not see this. ... In a creative brain reason has withdrawn her watch at the doors, and ideas crowd in pell-mell. (as cited in Hirsch, 1897, p. 31)

To suspend the "laws of rationally thinking reason" meant, as the Schlegels observed, to be transported "into the lovely vagaries of fancy and the primitive chaos of human nature" (as cited in Nordau, 1892/1900, p. 73).

Psychology, Physician–Psychiatrists, and the Clinical Association of Genius and Madness

The romantic redefinition of genius in terms of the imagination reigning supreme satisfied two goals simultaneously. Through its stress on the spontaneous and irrational imagination, it made possible the appropriation of mania from the past, but it did so while ensuring intellectual independence in the present. There was, however, a critical by-product: Although the new definition liberated the romantics from the past, it also disassociated them from the very qualities that previously had been seen as establishing and safeguarding sanity. Given the commonality of the belief concerning the relation of sanity to the balance of mental faculties, the romantic reformulation of genius, which removed this balance, established a logical foundation for the association of genius and madness. Most ironically, perhaps, the romantics, trapped by their premises and system of logic, began to suspect that clinical madness was indeed a likely if not inevitable end of the condition of genius.

The need of the romantics, then, for a sense of identity and for their own intellectual and artistic independence led them to adopt a system of premises that left them defenseless against the label of madness. Trapped by their own logic, they came to see their madness as inevitable. Accordingly, the romantic people of genius were among the first to suggest (e.g., Lamartine, Schopenhauer, Wieland, Poe, and others), in reference to themselves and other eminent individuals, that the ancients were indeed correct in their assessment: the "demon of madness" was more than just a stranger among their ranks. Although many of these confessions or pronouncements on the nature of genius were expressed in more general than specific terms and referred to the "inspired" madness of the ancients, some testified, quite clearly, to the fear of clinical insanity. Coleridge, for example, commented specifically on the dire consequences of a suspended judgment or reason:

> The reason may resist for a long time ... but too often, at length, it yields for a moment, and the man is mad forever. ...

> I think it was Bishop Butler who said that he was all his life struggling against the devilish suggestions on his senses, which would have maddened him if he had relaxed the stern wakefulness of his reason for a single moment. (as cited in Sanborn, 1886, p. 139)

Similarly, Byron, although often appearing to revel in a professed madness, nevertheless spoke with considerable apprehension about his future: "I picture myself slowly expiring on a bed of torture, or terminating my days like [Jonathan] Swift—a grinning idiot" (as cited in Sanborn, 1886, p. 126).

It would be erroneous to assume, however, that such trepidations and self-admissions on the part of geniuses were sufficient to establish as a medical fact the connection between genius and madness. For such to occur, there had to exist a close correspondence between the intellectual grounds on which these trepidations were based and the specialized knowledge claims associated with the rising fields of psychology and the medical–psychiatric profession. It should be noted in passing that at least one dominant philosophical–psychological tradition was unfavorably disposed and frequently hostile to the romantic conception of the extraordinary individual. The psychological empiricism of Hobbes, Locke, and Hume (which, in the hands of Hartley, Bentham, and James and John Stuart Mill, was transformed into psychological associationism) was unalterably opposed to the view that knowledge is in some way innate to humans or the result of inherent dispositions. Instead, these empiricists stressed the extrinsic nature of all human knowledge. The support the romantics needed to help articulate and legitimate their view of the extraordinary individual and the workings of the individual's mind was located in a highly speculative psychological tradition that predated the critical empiricism of Locke and Hume (see Boring, 1950).

Before 1700, Western scholars attempted to understand the nature of the mind, learning, and creativity from a modified Aristotelian position. This position recognized the existence of some half dozen more or less distinct mental components or "faculties," which to some degree, were subject to improvement through their exercise (Coladarci, 1968, p. 533). The belief in mental faculties was gradually expanded and formalized during the 18th and 19th centuries and, through the writings of Wolff, Reid, Sully, and others, became established as a school of thought known as faculty psychology (see Boring, 1950; Robinson, 1976). In Reid's reformulation of this perspective, for example, the number of components of the mind was expanded to 24 but retained such traditionally recognized intellectual powers as perception, judgment, memory, and moral taste (Boring, 1950, p. 205). Although Reid and other faculty psychologists concurred that the mental powers could be improved through training, they believed that a pronounced display of strength in any faculty was rooted, overwhelmingly, in a powerfully endowed instinct or native disposition (Robinson, 1976, p. 234). Accordingly, an individual distinguished by an extraordinary ability to memorize facts was seen to possess an unusually vigorous instinct or faculty of memory (Boring, 1950, p. 207). The belief in inherent mental dispositions supported not only the inception of the genius ideal but also its subsequent romantic reformulation.

Unlike the school of psychological empiricism, therefore, the faculty psychology of Reid, Wolff, and others, with its stress on innate powers and inherent mental dispositions, was sufficiently vague and mystical to accommodate most of the romantics' assertions regarding the transcendental nature of profound creativity. Importantly, also, faculty psychology even concurred with the romantics' position that the genius's dependence on an "overcharged" and highly impulsive imagination constituted a form of madness, divine or otherwise. It had long been an established principle, particularly for faculty psychologists, that an excessive stimulation of any faculty of mind was incompatible with perfect health and mental adjustment (see Sully, 1885, p. 326).

Whether or not, however, the supposed infirmities of genius constituted clinical pathology rather than a divine gift or mania remained, until the middle of the 19th century, a matter more of philosophical speculation than of supposedly scientific fact. The individuals, overwhelmingly, who were to establish the verdict of clinical madness as a medical fact were those who, as I argued elsewhere (Becker, 1978), had earned a medical degree and are classifiable under the general category of physician–psychiatrist. These specialists, although they embraced many of the assumptions of faculty psychology and brought to bear what then were regarded as the latest clinical concepts and diagnostic categories, relied quite heavily in their determination of genius as clinically mad on the self-admissions of illness on the part of the "gifted" (Becker, 1978, pp. 67–74). Although many of these self-admissions were expressed in terms of the inspired madness of the ancients, these physician–psychiatrists took the people of genius at their words; they decidedly were not like ordinary, healthy humans.

The first examination of genius as a purely medical problem may be dated to Lélut (1836), a French psychiatrist, who in 1836 scandalized the world of letters with the first clinical history of genius in which he claimed that Socrates's inclination "to take the inspirations of his conscience for the voice of a supernatural agent [his demon]" was evidence of a "most undeniable form of madness" (pp. 97–98). Other psychiatrists and scholars soon followed suit with their own views and analyses of other gifted persons (e.g., Galton, 1869/1962; Lombroso, 1863/1891; Maudsley, 1886, 1908; Moreau, 1859; Stekel, 1909, 1917), with the result that within a century, such works numbered in the hundreds (see Lange-Eichbaum, 1927/1935). As my survey of this literature for the period from 1836 to 1950 revealed (Becker, 1978, pp. 46–51), the judgment of genius as pathological was the dominant position on the issue, one that derived its overwhelming support from members of the medical and the developing psychiatric professions. Those who projected the image of sickness distinguished themselves from each other by identification of different types of mental illness, largely in step with the rise and fall of diagnostic categories in psychiatry then currently in favor. Whereas diagnostic labels such as *psycho–physical disequilibrium, monomania, degeneracy, neurasthenia,* and *neurosis* prevailed in the years up to 1950, the disease categories that have gained ascendancy since that time are those, such as *schizophrenia* and *manic–depressive illness,* that figure prominently in the contemporary lexicon of psychiatry.

Implications for the Contemporary Debate

As we have seen, the romantic poets and men of letters were among the first to suggest, in referring to themselves and other eminent individuals, that the ancients were indeed correct in their assessment: The demon of madness was hardly a stranger in their ranks. These pronouncements, as previously noted, played an integral part in the past in the determination of the genius as clinically afflicted. This tendency to take the gifted at their word regarding their own condition also applies to contemporary examinations of the issue. Jamison's (1993) book, *Touched With Fire: Manic–Depressive Illness and the Artistic Temperament,* provides demonstration of this fact. Jamison built a clinical connection between creativity and manic–depressive illness by allowing scores of artists, composers, and writers from across time in Western society to reflect on their own changes of mood ranging from melancholic states to feelings of euphoria, their obsessions and fears of going mad, their thoughts about suicide, their addictions to alcohol and drugs: those and other behaviors and mental states, in other words, identified as symptomatic of mood disorders.

One of the problems of treating such self-admissions as essentially reliable descriptions of mental illness is that it tends to overlook one critical fact: These pronouncements on the part of the creative individuals may involve self-serving descriptions and projections of images that were made in the context of cultural assumptions often quite different from those of contemporary society. In light of these facts, it remains unclear what meaning should be attached to the tendency on the part of many poets and other creative persons to admit to a "touch" of madness.

Two examples will have to suffice as illustrative of the difficulties involved in the interpretations of such admissions. The first concerns an excerpt of a poem from Drayton, a poem written in praise of another poet, Drayton's friend Reynolds:

> His raptures were
> All air, and fire, which made his verses clear,
> For that *fine madness* [italics added] still he did retain,
> Which *rightly should possess* [italics added] a poet's brain.
> (as cited in Jamison, 1993, p. 1)

This excerpt is open to a number of interpretations that include the reference to the divine mania of the ancients, a condition, as previously noted, that was not synonymous with clinical madness. Rather, it was a state of mind greatly desired. Given this fact, are we justified in treating this excerpt (as Jamison did) as an essentially reliable description of illness, or is it not equally possible that Drayton's reference to the presence of a "fine madness" on the part of Reynolds had little if nothing to do with clinical illness and was intended as an ultimate compliment a poet could be paid, one that confirmed his membership in the tribe of truly eminent poets?

Similarly, what are we to make of Coleridge's pronouncement who, in a defense of Swedenborg, proposed that, unlike ordinary madness, his was the madness of genius: "a madness, indeed celestial, and glowing from a divine mind" (as cited in Sanborn, 1886, p. 154). Is it not likely, as Kretschmer (1931) argued, that pronouncements such as these are confirmation of the fact that "many men of genius themselves prize madness and insanity as the highest distinction of the exceptional man" (p. 4). After all, Kretschmer observed, "the mentally normal man is, according to the conception itself, identical with the typical man, the average man, the philistine" (p. 6).

Consistent with this line of argument, the association of creativity and madness may essentially be seen as a kind of role expectation appropriate for artists and writers that originated in antiquity and received powerful reinforcement as a result of the romantics' redefinitions of the nature of genius. In the way that contemporary scientists, accountants, and engineers are expected to display attributes of objectivity, reason, and emotional stability, for poets, writers, and artists the expectations involve manifestations of intuitiveness, a fanciful imagination, sensitivity, temperament, and emotional expressiveness, in short, a manifestation of a kind of madness. It is not at all unreasonable to assume that to the extent that these expectations continue to be part of a professional ideology of what it means to be truly creative, even contemporary writers and artists, far from disavowing the label of madness, may actually invite it. Indeed, they may even inadvertently volunteer evidence of madness in diagnostic and psychological examinations. Moreover, is it not possible that these expectations may involve the elements of a self-fulfilling prophecy? In a rephrasing of a line from Orwell (1953), "they are wearing a mask, and their faces grow to fit it" (p. 152).

Such possibilities have implications for the issue of creativity and psychopathology. Indeed, they may invite conclusions at odds with the conventional association regarding these two variables. One of such conclusions is associated with the existentialist philosopher, Jaspers (1926), who maintained that the greater manifestation of mental illness in geniuses was the result of society's selective granting of fame. To Jaspers, in other words, the term *genius* was a socially applied label primarily reserved for those talented individuals who displayed certain attributes of sickness closely tied to the role expectations noted previously. He did not believe that the notion of the mad genius was applicable to all historical periods. Rather, what distinguishes the 19th and 20th centuries from the 17th and 18th, Jaspers reasoned, is a general mood or inclination in Western society that craves the mysterious, the unusual, the undefinable, and the blatantly diseased. Accordingly, although the Enlightenment tended to reward creative individuals who were healthy and rational with the distinction of genius, the 19th and 20th centuries (since the time of romanticism, that is) have shown a distinct preference for those creative individuals who are diseased and, specifically, schizophrenic (pp. 148–149). It should be noted that Lange-Eichbaum (1927/1935) provided an interesting variation of this type of argument.

All of this is not to suggest that the display of symptoms of mental illness on the part of the creative are the result of nothing more than role playing and adherence to role expectations deemed appropriate for artists and writers. Rather, it is intended as a reminder that examinations regarding the relation of creativity to mental health must take full measure of relevant historical and sociocultural developments and their impact on contemporary conceptions regarding the nature of creative individuals and the creative process as they pertain to different areas of artistic and intellectual endeavors. Whatever the connection regarding heredity, creative endeavor, and mental stability, social definitions in the form of role models must become an integral part of the debate.

References

Becker, G. (1978). *The mad genius controversy: A study in the sociology of deviance.* Beverly Hills, CA: Sage.

Boring, E. G. (1950). *A history of experimental psychology.* New York: Appleton-Century-Crofts.

Cahan, J. (1911). *Zur kritik des geniebegriffs* [Toward a criticism of the concept of genius]. Bern, Switzerland: Scheitlin.

Coladarci, A. P. (1968). Educational psychology. In D. L. Sills (Ed.), *International encyclopedia of the social sciences* (Vol. 4, pp. 533–539). New York: Macmillan.

d'Alembert, J. L. (1967). *Oeuvres complètes de d'Alembert* [Complete works of d'Alembert]. Geneva, Switzerland: Slatkine.

de Saint-Simon, H. (1964). Letters from an inhabitant of Geneva to his contemporaries. In *Social organization, the science of man and other writings* (pp. 1–11). New York: Harper & Row. (Original work published 1803)

Fabian, B. (1966). Introduction. In *An essay on genius* (pp. 1–48). Munich, Germany: Fink Verlag.

Galton, F. (1962). *Hereditary genius: An inquiry into its laws and consequences.* Cleveland, OH: Meridian. (Original work published 1869)

Gerard, A. (1966). *An essay on genius.* Munich, Germany: Fink Verlag. (Original work published 1774)

Graña, C. (1964). *Bohemian versus bourgeois: French society and the French man of letters in the nineteenth century.* New York: Basic Books.

Hirsch, W. (1897). *Genius and degeneration: A psychological study.* London: Heinemann.

Jamison, K. R. (1993). *Touched with fire: Manic–depressive illness and the artistic temperament.* New York: Free Press.

Jaspers, K. (1926). Strindberg und Van Gogh [Strindberg and Van Gogh]. *Philosophische Forschungen, 3,* 8–151.

Kretschmer, E. (1931). *The psychology of men of genius.* New York: Harcourt Brace Jovanovich.

Lange-Eichbaum, W. (1932). *The problem of genius.* New York: Macmillan. (Original work published 1930)

Lange-Eichbaum, W. (1935). *Genie: Irrsin und ruhm* [Genius: Madness and fame]. Munich, Germany: Reinhardt. (Original work published 1927)

Lélut, L. F. (1836). *Du démon de Socrate* [The demon of Socrates]. Paris: Trinquart.

Lombroso, C. (1891). *The man of genius.* New York: Scribner's. (Original work published 1863)

Marks, J. (1926). *Genius and disaster: Studies in drugs and genius.* New York: Adelphi.

Maudsley, H. (1886). Heredity in health and disease. *Fortnightly Review, 39,* 648–659.

Maudsley, H. (1908). *Heredity, variation and genius.* London: John Bale, Sons & Danielsson.

Moreau, J. J. (1859). *La psychologie morbide dans ses rapports avec la philosophie de l'histoire* [Abnormal psychology in its relation to the philosophy of history]. Paris: Masson.

Nordau, M. (1900). *Degeneration.* New York: Appleton-Century-Crofts. (Original work published 1892)

Orwell, G. (1953). Shooting an elephant. In *A collection of essays* (pp. 148–156). New York: Harcourt Brace.

Pascal, B. (1968). *Pensées et opuscules* [Reflections and small works]. Paris: Classiques Hachette. (Original work published 1670)

Plato. (1974). *Phaedrus and the seventh and eight letters* (W. Hamilton, Trans.). Middlesex, England: Penguin.

Robinson, D. N. (1976). *An intellectual history of psychology.* New York: Macmillan.

Rosen, G. (1969). *Madness in society: Chapters in the historical sociology of mental illness.* New York: Harper & Row.

Sanborn, K. (1886). *The vanity and insanity of genius.* New York: Coombes.

Stekel, W. (1909). Dichtung und neurose [Poetry and neurosis]. *Grenzfragen des Nerven-und Seelenlebens, 65,* 1–73.

Stekel, W. (1917). Nietzsche und Wagner: Eine sexualpsychologische studie zur psychogenese des freundschaftsgefühles und des freundschaftsverrates. [Nietzsche and Wagner: A sexual-psychological study to the psychological genesis of friendship and the betrayal of friends]. *Zeitschrift für Sexualwissenschaft und Sexualpolitik, 4,* 22–28, 58–65.

Sully, J. (1885). *Outlines of psychology.* New York: Appleton-Century-Crofts.

Tonelli, G. (1973). Genius from the Renaissance to 1770. In P. P. Wiener (Ed.), *Dictionary of the history of ideas* (pp. 293–298). New York: Scribner's.

Trilling, L. (1950). *The liberal imagination: Essays on literature and society.* New York: Viking.

Wittkower, R. (1973). Genius: Individualism in art and artists. In P. P. Wiener (Ed.), *Dictionary of the history of ideas* (pp. 297–312). New York: Scribner's.

Wittkower, R., & Wittkower, M. (1963). *Born under Saturn.* London: Shenval.

Zilsel, E. (1926). *Die entstehung des geniebegriffes* [The origin of the genius concept]. Tübingen, Germany: Mohr.

Creativity Research Journal
2000–2001, Vol. 13, No. 1, 55–74

Schizophrenia, Modernism, and the "Creative Imagination": On Creativity and Psychopathology

Louis A. Sass
Rutgers—The State University

ABSTRACT: In this article, I consider the relation between creativity and the schizophrenia spectrum of personality and mental disorders in the light of differing notions of creativity and the creative process. Prevailing conceptions of creativity in psychology and psychiatry derive from romanticist ideas about the creative imagination; they differ considerably from notions central in modernism and postmodernism. Whereas romanticism views creative inspiration as a highly emotional, Dionysian, or primitive state, modernism and postmodernism emphasize processes involving hyper-self-consciousness and alienation (hyperreflexivity). Although manic–depressive or cyclothymic tendencies seem especially suited to creativity of the romantic sort, schizoid, schizotypal, schizophreniform, and schizophrenic tendencies have more in common with the (in many respects, antiromantic) sensibilities of modernism and postmodernism. I criticize a book by psychologist Jamison (1993), Touched With Fire: Manic–Depressive Illness and the Artistic Temperament, *for treating romantic notions of creativity as if they defined creativity in general. I also argue that Jamison's denial or neglect of the creative potential of persons in the schizophrenia spectrum relies on certain diagnostic oversimplifications: an overly broad conception of affective illness and an excessively narrow conception of schizophrenia that ignores the creative potential of the schizophrenia spectrum.*

No one who wishes to understand the relation between creativity and the schizophrenia spectrum of personality and mental disorders can ignore the empirical findings of the last 15 or 20 years. Impressive studies by Andreasen (1987; Andreasen & Glick, 1988), Jamison (1989), Richards and Kinney (Richards, 1998; Richards & Kinney, 1990; Richards, Kinney, Lunde, Benet, & Merzel, 1988), Schuldberg (1990), and others have demonstrated a strikingly high correlation between affective disorders or propensities and various indexes of creative potential or achievement, along with an often surprisingly low association of creativity with schizophrenic conditions (Andreasen & Powers, 1974, 1975; Richards, 1981, 1993). The import of this work is not, however, immediately obvious. Perhaps even more than is usual in psychological or psychiatric research, considerable critical reflection and theoretical analysis is required to clarify the implications of these empirical findings and place them in proper context.

Creativity is not, after all, the most unproblematic or transparent of theoretical constructs. Despite the surprising confidence of some psychologists and psychiatrists who write on the topic, it seems unlikely that the term *creative* refers to a single, underlying essence or that its application can be separated from culturally determined and socially generated forms of interpretation and evaluation. It is not that a definition is so difficult to formulate. The cognitive and experimental psychologist Martindale (1989) averred that the creative process in poetry, science, and virtually all other domains is "really the same thing," and he defined the creative product in terms of three essential attributes: "It must be original, it must be useful or appropriate for the situation in which it occurs, and it must actually be put to some use" (p. 211). This seems fair enough, as far as it goes. However, on reflection one suspects that Martindale's definition may only push the problem

Correspondence and requests for reprints should be sent to Louis A. Sass, Rutgers—The State University, GSAPP–Busch Campus, 152 Frelinghuysen Road, Piscataway, NJ 08854–8085. E-mail: lsass@rci.rutgers.edu.

back a step or two. For what, after all, is the criterion of being "put to some use" (of usefulness or appropriateness), of innovativeness or originality? Can these features be readily defined? Are they not themselves highly context bound, taking on real definition only in light of the varying viewpoints and values of individuals and communities on which they depend?[1]

I am particularly concerned with how the recent research can be used, indeed to some extent already has been used, to support a purely deficit view of schizophrenia, a condescending, sometimes denigrating attitude that sees schizophrenia, the prototypical form of madness, entirely in terms of the loss of higher or more quintessentially human capacities of mind and spirit. Madness has long been seen as irrational. In the past, however, this was often compensated by acknowledgment of a special wisdom available to such persons or of the ready access they supposedly have to the deep, unconscious wellsprings of human imagination (Foucault, 1972). Such a (romantic) vision continues to be associated with the affective psychoses (Jamison, 1993). However, in the rather neo-Kraepelinian climate of contemporary psychiatric thinking, schizophrenics are said to lack not only reason but creativity and imagination as well.[2]

In the following sections, I consider four issues. In "Notions of Creativity: Romanticism and Its Legacy," the longest section of this article, I examine the concepts of creativity that have prevailed in Western culture at large, at least until fairly recently, and that have been dominant as well in psychology and psychiatry. Far from being universal or inevitable, these concepts actually have a fairly specific lineage in the history of European thought. The prevailing view is one that came to dominance with the romantic movement of the late 18th and early 19th centuries. It is a view that understands creativity in organicist, holistic, and emotivist terms, as a spontaneous rather than deliberative or mechanical process, a process that operates under the impulse of feeling and that seeks to heighten the vital sentiment of being by overcoming the felt separation between person and world, mind and body, thought and emotion (Abrams, 1971, 1984).

One may well expect such a vision of creative process to overlap less with the characteristics of schizoid, schizotypal, or schizophrenic individuals—with their sense of inner fragmentation and their lack of attunement with emotion and the social world—than with the temperament and cognitive style of persons who suffer from affective disorders or who have a predominantly cyclothymic or cycloid temperament. The latter sort of temperament is described in the classic work of Kretschmer (1925) as characterized by spontaneity, ready emotional reactivity, and a harmonious sense of unity (*syntony* is Bleuler's, 1922, term) both with the world and within the self.

In "Modernism and Postmodernism," I consider, more briefly, some alternative visions of creativity or aesthetic worth that are prominent in 20th-century modernist and postmodernist movements. (I employ *modernism* and *postmodernism* in accord with standard usage in art history and literary studies: The former term refers to the formally innovative, often avant-gardist, art and literature of approximately the first half of the 20th century, and the latter refers to cultural and artistic developments largely occurring after World War II; Sass, 1992, pp. 417–418.) In "Madness and Modernism: Affinities Between 20th-Century Culture and the Schizophrenia Spectrum," I look at the nature of schizophrenic and schizotypal conditions in relation to these latter concepts or visions, pointing out a series of close affinities or parallels between these types of psychopathology and modernist forms of creativity. By this point, some widespread assumptions about both creativity and schizophrenia are questioned, thereby opening up new possibilities for thinking about their relation.

In "Explanations of Schizophrenia," I examine some prominent explanations of schizophrenic consciousness from contemporary cognitive psychology and brain science, showing that these accounts are compatible with my emphasis on forms of hyperreflexivity and alienation akin to modernism and postmodernism. In the final two sections, I consider some limitations of previous empirical research on schizophrenia and creativity in the light of these various issues and suggest some new ways of understanding the potentially creative aspects of schizophrenia spectrum conditions. I focus on interpretations put for-

[1]Consider, in this regard, some of the bizarre concoctions produced by schizophrenics, who may build peculiar assemblages or invent imaginary machines. Certainly, these concoctions can be innovative or original; clearly, the patients find them useful and will sometimes put them to some kind of use. If one wishes to deny that these are truly creative, other criteria, probably involving external consensus judgment, will have to be introduced.

[2]Actually, this is a view that has been common since the Enlightenment (Foucault, 1972).

ward in an influential book by the psychologist Jamison (1993): *Touched With Fire: Manic–Depressive Illness and the Artistic Temperament.* After discussing diagnostic considerations in "Evaluating Recent Research: Diagnostic Issues," I turn to broader issues concerning concepts of creativity in "Evaluating Recent Research: Conceptions of Creativity." As we shall see, the modernist and postmodernist orientations appear to have much in common with the schizoid, schizotypal, or schizophrenia-like sensibility. An understanding of these orientations, which are strongly antiromantic in spirit, can help one to recognize and to appreciate the particular forms of creativity that are characteristic of persons in the so-called schizophrenia spectrum of personality types and mental disorders.

Notions of Creativity: Romanticism and Its Legacy

What is the relation between creativity and the schizophrenia spectrum of personality types and mental disorders? The question needs to be examined in light of the diversity of what is liable to be considered creative in different fields of endeavor, media, genres, stylistic traditions, cultural settings, and historical epochs. Like the concept *game,* that of creativity seems likely to be an instance of what Wittgenstein (1953) called a "family-resemblance concept," a grouping based on an open set of overlapping similarities or shared features, no one of which need be present in all instances of the category. What merits the honorific term *creative* will vary according to the context of production and the perspective, largely culturally determined, in which the product is seen, interpreted, and judged.

To deal with all the relevant forms of diversity would require more space than is available in this issue. Particularly important, however, is the profound dependence of contemporary notions of creativity on conceptions of the "creative imagination" that crystallized in European (especially English and German) romanticism in the first decades of the 19th century, a tradition that viewed the poet or artist as both the paradigm of creative endeavor and the epitome of human worth (Engell, 1981). The romantics' notion of what they called the "creative imagination" is associated with an expressivist conception of art, as opposed to the mimetic or didactic conceptions that had been more common in previous centuries in the West or the objectivist conceptions that came to prominence with 20th-century modernism (the latter involving a focus on the artwork itself rather than its message, audience, or inspiration; see Abrams, 1953).

In the romantic view, aesthetic experience requires achieving several things: a sense of unity between self and world, temporary escape from the self-conscious ego and consequent liberation of the vital organic forces of instinct and emotion (e.g., "the spontaneous overflow of powerful feelings," Wordsworth, 1800/1957, p. 321), and a sloughing off of conventional schemata of perception and understanding. These optimal conditions for aesthetic experience were generally seen as characteristic of early childhood; to experience them was, therefore, to return to an earlier and more primitive condition of grace.[3]

The glorification of the primitive and the instinctual is especially clear in Wordsworth (1977), who tended to presuppose a polarity between nature, understood as signifying all that is instinctual, emotional, and spontaneous, and art, understood in the special sense of signifying what is studied and deliberate, the product of self-conscious intellectual control. Although Wordsworth did not reject altogether any role for the ego, secondary process, or more mature psyche, he usually relegated these to a subordinate and inferior plane (Abrams, 1984, p. 126). In Wordsworth's *The Prelude,* conscious revision is described as "the very littleness of life ... relapses from one interior life that lives in all things" (p. 165).

Coleridge (1907) subjected Wordsworth's polarizing of nature and art to a sustained critique. Coleridge, who was profoundly influenced by such German writers as Schiller (1966), spoke not of an alternation but of an intimate integration of psychological processes that are more and less primitive, more and less controlled. In this way, the natural and the artificial blend into a "higher third" with "an interpenetration of passion and of will, of spontaneous impulse and of voluntary purpose" (Coleridge, 1907, p. 50).[4] Coleridge argued that one can no longer oppose nature to art or to mind

[3]The following paragraphs overlap somewhat with Sass (1994b), which contains a more extensive discussion of the romantic assumptions inherent in psychoanalytic theories of creativity and art.

[4]Emotion itself cannot, for example, be conceived of as a mere passive outburst, according to Coleridge (1907). To be aesthetically useful, it has to be "voluntarily encouraged and kept up for the sake of that pleasure" that derives from the creation of "forms and figures of speech" (p. 50).

once one understands nature itself in an appropriately organicist fashion, as a domain not merely of blind or mechanical forces but of spirit and purpose. Coleridge nevertheless argued that the greatest poetry "still subordinates art to nature" (p. 12). He may have rejected Wordsworth's tendency to treat mind and purpose as antinatural. Yet, like Wordsworth and virtually all the romantics, he was acutely aware of the devitalizing effects of self-consciousness and self-constraint: Like a tree that grows purposively but unconsciously, creative thoughts and perceptions needed to germinate spontaneously, without the deadening intrusion of rational, critical, or distancing self-awareness (Abrams, 1953, p. 205). Coleridge (1907) also considered a certain Dionysian element to be a sine qua non for creative expression; he agreed with Wordsworth that poetry "does always imply passion" (p. 56) and that all successful figures of speech had to be based in emotional states.

In his attitude toward childhood, Coleridge (1907) resembled Wordsworth (1977) and many other romantics. The proper goal of art, in Coleridge's view, is

> To give the charm of novelty to things of every day, and to excite a feeling analogous to the supernatural, by awakening the mind's attention from the lethargy of custom, and directing it to the loveliness and the wonders of the world before us. (p. 6)

Both Wordsworth and Coleridge saw childhood as the time when such conditions were fulfilled and maturation as alienation from this state of grace. Both poets glorified childhood for its freshness of sensation and also for its greater sense of union, both within the self, where intellect and emotion were not yet sundered, and between the self and the world, where a quasimystical sense of participation prevailed. According to this romantic view, art recreates the original oneness from which maturation is a falling away.

Romanticist notions of creativity and the arts remain influential, not only in contemporary psychoanalysis, psychology, and psychiatry but also, more broadly, in the public mind and in more traditional and mainstream areas of artistic and literary endeavor. Accordingly, the most prevalent views of artistic experience and expression continue to emphasize the central role of developmentally primitive, irrational, and impassioned modes of experience. The creative core of aesthetic creation and perception is widely assumed to involve a regression or shift backward or downward to forms of consciousness having one or more of several key qualities: ready access to emotional, instinctual, and sensorially concrete modes of experience; a heightened sense of fusion between both self and world and signifier and signified; and freedom from the rationality, conventional rules, and intellectual categories of everyday or scientific modes of awareness. In a classic formulation of this vision of creativity, not just in art but in all fields, Koestler (1967) spoke of the

> Temporary relinquishing of conscious controls [that] liberates the mind from certain constraints which are necessary to maintain the disciplined routines of thoughts but may become an impediment to the creative leap; at the same time other types of ideation on more primitive levels of mental organization are brought into activity. The first part of this sentence indicates an act of abdication, the second an act of promotion. (p. 169)[5]

According to the psychoanalyst Kris (1964), "ego regression (primitivization of ego functions)," which requires "relaxation ... of ego functions" and involves "a greater proximity to the id" (pp. 253, 312), is a necessity for any sort of creative or aesthetic experience. In similar fashion, the aesthetician Ehrenzweig (1967), who combined psychoanalytic ego psychology with Kleinian object-relations theory, believed creativity to be "closely related to the chaos of the primary process" (p. 35). Writers in the tradition of psychoanalytic object-relations theory stress the reevocation in aesthetic experience, whether of creation or of appreciation, of states of quasimystical union rooted in the symbiotic phase of infancy or else of the somewhat more mature forms of symbolic connectedness characteristic of transitional objects (e.g., Bollas, 1978; Fuller, 1980; Milner, 1978; Spitz, 1985).[6]

In emphasizing the primitive, the instinctual, or the spontaneous, most psychoanalytic writers do not deny that more advanced, mature, or rational forms of consciousness also play a role in the production and appreciation of art. Even classical psychoanalysis recognizes that the creation of a work of art (like that of a dream) must include secondary elaboration, the unconscious but ego-dominated process whereby raw in-

[5]Jamison (1993) quoted a very similar passage from Koestler on pages 103 and 104 of her book.

[6]According to the psychoanalyst Rose (1980), the "'source' of aesthetic form arises in the fluid boundaries of the child's primary narcissism, now autonomously flexible in the adult;" the artist is a person who "keeps resampling the early undifferentiated stage of psychological development" (pp. 15, 92).

stinctual fantasies are, partially in the interest of disguise, recoded and given a semblance of rationality. Similarly, Kris (1964) emphasized the necessity that aesthetic regression be "in the service of the ego," and spoke of "a shift in psychic level, consisting in the fluctuation of functional regression and control" (pp. 253–254). Still, most theorists do associate the truly inspirational, productive, or generational element of the aesthetic process with regression to more primitive layers of consciousness, whereas they see more mature, secondary-process modes as serving the subordinate functions of selection, elaboration, or formal smoothing. Whenever symbols have aesthetic force, wrote Kris, they are evoking the resources of the primary process; although he conceded in one essay that artistic creation may not always derive from inspiration, Kris insisted that all art of high quality will have this kind of regressive source (pp. 59, 255).[7]

Similar views appear to be only slightly less prevalent among psychologists and psychiatrists outside the psychoanalytic tradition. Thus, in a review chapter on "Personality, Situation, and Creativity," Martindale (1989) took the relation between creativity and regression for granted, stating that primary process states of consciousness are a necessary element for all creative activity (see pp. 215, 226). Even the behavioristically inclined psychologist Eysenck (1993) associated creativity with a weakening of "higher centers" and a consequent disinhibition of lower and more primitive functions of the mind and brain (p. 341). The romanticist inflection is especially obvious in Jamison's (1993) eloquent book, *Touched With Fire: Manic-Depressive Illness and the Artistic Temperament,* in which the "tumultuous passions" of Lord Byron are presented as the very paradigm of creative activity. "From virtually all perspectives," wrote Jamison (with considerable exaggeration), "there is agreement that artistic creativity and inspiration involve, indeed, require, a dipping into prerational or irrational sources," an ability to regress to earlier, more primitive levels of mental life to "summon up the depths," and to experience the "sheer force of life" that is inherent in a passionate emotional existence (pp. 103–104, 113, 116; see also p. 52).

To Jamison (1993), the seasonal cycling of manic–depressive illness suggests heightened affinity with the periodicities of the natural world that brings the artist "closer to the fundamental pulse of life" (p. 129; compare Abrams, 1984, pp. 126ff). She defended an organicist–vitalist vision of creative imagination while espousing Wordsworthian ideals of reunion with nature as the route to creativity and a heightened sense of life. Without denying the contribution of more mature or nonregressive modes of consciousness, such theories stress, as the productive or specifically aesthetic aspect, those psychological processes that derive from and resonate with key characteristics of the young child (viz., emotional and instinctual vitality and immediacy, freedom from rational and realistic constraints and categories, or lack of differentiation from objects and other persons).

It is important to recognize that despite their prominence, such conceptions of aesthetics are by no means universal or inevitable; indeed, they are largely the product of a particular historical epoch, an epoch whose influence on the less avant-garde areas of contemporary culture is, however, still profound enough to make its assumptions seem virtually self-evident, thus invisible. The regression view does apply rather well to a great deal of art from the last two centuries or more, much of which actually inspired, or was inspired by, the organicist and expressivist ethos of romanticism or closely related postromanticist trends. However, to conclude that the regression view is adequate as a general theory of art or of creativity in all its forms betrays a lack of historical perspective. Preromantic, neoclassical aesthetics, for instance, was far more rationalistic in important respects, stressing the importance of rules and advocating a "pleasingness" based on the achievement or perception of verisimilitude in accordance with certain ideal standards of harmony, proportion, and rational order. Irrationality, spontaneity, the passions, and a sense of union with the ambient world have, in fact, been far less central in most of the conceptions of aesthetic experience that have been dominant both before and after romanticism (Abrams, 1953; Becker, 2000–2001).

Modernism and Postmodernism

For over 100 years, many of the most influential and innovative artists, writers, and critics have been sharply

[7]Some later psychoanalytic theorists, such as Noy (1978, pp. 743–744), have portrayed creative consciousness as a more intimate synthesis, a "new entity" in which primary and secondary, or instinctual–affective and rational–realistic, processes would operate simultaneously. Still, for Noy (1984/1985), "the most interesting ability of the creative individual [is] the ability to enrich his secondary-process cognition with techniques and strategies derived from the primary process" (p. 430).

critical of the organicism, personalism, and emotivism central to the romantics, with their valuing of nature, emotion, and spontaneity over calculation and self-consciousness and their yearning to overcome the Cartesian division of subject from object. Neither Baudelaire nor Mallarme, the key protomodernists of the 19th century, considered spontaneous, irrational processes of free fantasy to be the key to artistic creativity. Baudelaire emphasized instead the role of dispassionate deliberation, conscious craft, and an alienated stance; he placed artifice above nature in his hierarchy of aesthetic worth and praised the dandy's "unshakable resolution never to be moved" (Abrams, 1984, p. 135, pp. 109–144). Mallarme called on the poet to cede his initiative to words, that is, to eliminate his own personal and emotional contribution and signature by standing back and letting words clash and interact like objects independent of the poet's intentions: He called for "*la disparition elocutoire du poete, qui cede l'initiative aux mots* [the elocutionary disappearance of the poet, who cedes initiative to the words]" (as cited in Abrams, 1984, p. 138). Both were precursors to the sometimes virulent antiromanticism of T. E. Hulme, Ezra Pound, and Wyndham Lewis, influential formulators of a modernist aesthetic that recoiled from (what they saw as) the mushy emotivism and personalism inherent in the pathetic fallacy of romantic subjectivism, which Hulme described as "the state of slush in which we have the misfortune to live" (as cited in Bate, 1952, p. 561; see also Schwartz, 1985).

It would be naive to take modernist antiromanticism completely at face value or to deny all continuity between these two periods (see Kermode, 1971; Rajan, 1980). Still, there seems to be a fairly sharp difference between romantic yearnings for unity with the world, heightened emotional arousal, and intense personal engagement and the modernist preference for isolation, coolness, and detachment (see Abrams, 1984, pp. 109–144). Some of the psychological processes that can be involved in these modernist developments are especially clear in the writings of the formalist critics who were allied with the Russian futurist movement. Shklovsky defined art as "defamiliarization," and the Czech formalist critics spoke of "deautomatization" (Jameson, 1972, pp. 50–51). They all saw the essential role of art as to overcome the numbing of perception that occurs with habituation. Unlike the romantics, however, most modernists did not associate this renewal with a return to early childhood; they advocated instead the adopting of a highly detached, often fragmentingly analytic or microscopic perspective on the world. The latter involved a stripping away of all normal affective, practical, or cultural associations of objects, which come to be viewed instead in terms of their mere existence or abstract geometrical form or to take on a curious and tantalizing, pseudo-allegorical quality in which meanings seem to be suggested yet can never be attained (Sass, 1992, pp. 62–67).[8] An early illustration of some of these trends can be found in the weirdly precise, yet disconcerting cityscapes painted by the protosurrealist artist Giorgio de Chirico. De Chirico himself brilliantly described the mood state and worldview that inspired his paintings and is evoked in the viewing of them:

> Day is breaking. This is the hour of the enigma. ... One bright winter afternoon I found myself in the courtyard of the palace at Versailles. Everything looked at me with a strange and questioning glance. I saw then that every angle of the palace, every column, every window had a soul that was an enigma. ... And then more than ever I felt that everything was inevitably there, but for no reason and without any meaning. ... Above all a great sensitivity is needed. One must picture everything in the world as an enigma. ... To live in the world as if in an immense museum of strangeness. (as cited in Jean, 1980, pp. 5–6, 8–9; discussed in Sass, 1992, chap. 2)

Antiromanticism is, if anything, even more prominent in so-called postmodernist art and theory. Such thinkers as Jacques Derrida and Paul de Man and such artists as Marcel Duchamp (a major precursor of postmodernism) and Andy Warhol (perhaps the key postmodernist figure in the visual arts) seem to have banished every vestige of romanticism, rejecting any aspiration toward the ideals of authenticity or unity of the self, passionate spontaneity, intense personal engagement, or immediacy in one's contact with the world. "I want to be a machine," said Warhol (as cited in Hughes, 1984, p. 48). Many of his works, such as the silk-screened photographs of the aftermath of automobile accidents and other disasters, have a deliberately flat, derealized, and affectless quality. In line with modernist trends, these artists and critics tend to view forms of alienation or ironic detachment, often accom-

[8]Many instances of this perceptual stance may have something in common with what Prentky (1989) described as the "C-type" attentional style (i.e., concrete type, a potentially misleading label), a style that involves constriction of the attentional field and that is commonly associated with schizoid-like symptomatology, including blunted or flat affect or withdrawal (see p. 263).

panied by intense self-consciousness or a kind of relativistic speculation, as the key element of significant aesthetic achievement. Included among the targets of the postmodern critique is, in fact, the very notion of creativity itself, a notion that in its prevalent, postromantic incarnations, is criticized for overemphasizing the notions of spontaneity, originality, and individual genius.

Madness and Modernism: Affinities Between 20th-Century Culture and the Schizophrenia Spectrum

I have focused on differing notions of creativity. To address the possible relation between creativity and the schizophrenia spectrum, it is necessary to consider as well some differing conceptions of the latter forms of psychopathology.

Some influential views of schizophrenia and related disorders, prominent in most schools of psychoanalysis as well as in radical antipsychiatry, have seen these disorders as involving regression to a primitive and essentially Dionysian state, to infantile forms of irrationality and symbiotic union or an overwhelming by the polymorphous passions of the id (Sass, 1992, pp. 1–23).[9] (Schizoid and schizotypal individuals have been seen as having a special propensity for or vulnerability to such regression.) Given such a view, those who assume the romantic view of the creative process may well expect schizophrenia to undermine the capacity for formal shaping or editorial pruning (secondary-process consolidation) but, at the same time, to facilitate the more central, inspirational moments of creative work because the latter supposedly require more primitive, chaotic, and affect-ridden forms of consciousness. It is this primitivist or Dionysian view of schizophrenia that has, in fact, been adopted by most theorists who emphasize the potentially creative aspects of this psychiatric condition.

The primitivist or Dionysian vision of schizophrenia has never had universal acceptance, however, and, in recent years, has been receding in influence—with good reason. Although such a vision of madness may apply to certain phases of hypomania or manic psychosis, it utterly fails to capture the distinctive features or overall qualitative "feel" of either schizoid, schizotypal, or schizophrenic existence. The most salient features of these latter conditions are not, in fact, overwhelming by the passions or a recovery of primal unity but an almost opposite set of characteristics: flattened or peculiar affect, apathy, withdrawal, or seeming indifference to real-world events, a general sense of inner disharmony or discordance, what the psychiatrist Eugene Minkowski aptly termed *loss of vital contact with reality,* and, finally, delusions and hallucinations with an ineffable yet distinctive quality of bizarreness (see Parnas & Bovet, 1991; Sass, 1992, 1994a).

In mainstream American and British psychiatry, most of these just-mentioned features are closely bound up with the so-called negative symptoms, a set of features, including alogia or poverty of speech (decline in the fluency and productivity of thought and speech), avolition–apathy, flattened affect, and anhedonia, that have increasingly come to be seen as defining features of schizophrenic disorder. These so-called negative symptoms are frequently understood in quantitative rather than qualitative terms, as defect or deficit states involving a straightforward loss of higher or more complex psychological processes or capacities that occurs in the course of a dementing process fundamentally akin to senile dementia. Such a defect or deficit, conceived in this way, would indeed seem incompatible with imaginative production or sophisticated forms of mental life, so it is not surprising to find that those who adopt such neo-Kraepelinian views are inclined to deny the creative potential of schizophrenic individuals. However, it is important to realize that rejecting the Dionysian and primitivist visions of schizophrenia need not force one to adopt this purely deficit view. Indeed, there are serious grounds for doubting the adequacy of concepts and distinctions on which the neo-Kraepelinian, deficit view is based.

Various critics (Parnas & Bovet, 1994; Sass, 2000) have questioned the aptness of what may be termed the purely negative, deficit-oriented understanding of negative symptoms. As they have pointed out, the positive–negative distinction actually plays rather uncritically (and nondialectically) on commonsense notions of presence and absence and increase and decrease and often involves the assumption that the absence or infrequency of some overt normal behavior must derive

[9]This view, common in psychoanalysis, was also held by J. Hughlings Jackson, the 19th-century neurologist who has had a profound influence on psychoanalysis, neurology, and psychiatry (Sass, 1992, pp. 377–382).

from some dearth or deficit within the person, when in fact these symptoms can often mask psychological processes of a rather complex and sometimes at least quasi-willful sort (see also McGlashan, 1982).

It is true that as a general rule, schizophrenics tend to perform more poorly, often more slowly, than normal individuals on a wide variety of tests of cognitive functioning; this, however, is not always the case; on some tests their performances can be superior (Chadwick, 1997; Sass, 1992, p. 415). Also, as Bleuler (1950) noted, it is all too easy to make the mistake of assuming ignorance or incapacity when one is really encountering indifference, negativism, or reluctance to think, which can make patients profess ignorance or give random answers. The mistakes schizophrenics make (unlike those of patients with organic dementia) do not, in fact, closely correlate with the difficulty of the task: A patient who fails a simple problem of subtraction will, a moment later, solve a much more complex arithmetic problem with ease (Bleuler, 1950, p. 72). Also, "whenever the patient has an earnest aspiration, he shows himself capable of making exceptionally sharp-witted and complex deductions to achieve his desired ends" (Blueler, 1950, p. 77).[10]

The German phenomenological psychiatrist Blankenburg (1971/1991) devoted an important volume to the analysis of what would now be termed *negative-symptom schizophrenics.* He argued that the central feature of their mode of experience is a loss of the sense of the taken-for-granted background of natural evidence, of obviousness or self-evidence, that guides the action and experience of normal individuals. Although in one sense a loss or deficit, this often leads to a hypertrophy of attempts to cope in a self-reflexive and intellectual fashion. In two books, *The Paradoxes of Delusion: Wittgenstein, Schreber, and the Schizophrenic Mind* (Sass, 1994a) and *Madness and Modernism: Insanity in the Light of Modern Art, Literature, and Thought* (Sass, 1992), I addressed this set of issues in some detail, in a way that illuminates their relevance for issues of aesthetics, creativity, and imagination.

In *Madness and Modernism* (Sass, 1992), I argued that the anomalous and often dysfunctional experience and actions of persons in the schizophrenia spectrum are not, in fact, best understood as either primitivity or dementia. They are better seen as manifestations or consequences of a pervasive alienation or detachment from the lived body, the emotions, and the social and practical world that is combined with types of introversion involving hyperintense and often dysfunctional forms of self-consciousness. Similar forms of alienation and hyperreflexivity are also characteristic of the modernist and postmodernist sensibility, where they have been extensively studied. I argued that central phenomena of schizophrenia can best be grasped by comparison with these analogous cultural expressions. (For my purposes, the postmodernist style and sensibility is best seen as a further development and, in some respects, an exacerbation of the hyperreflexivity and alienation central to the modernist art of the early 20th century. See Sass, 1992, pp. 29, 417–418, for more extensive discussion of the relation between modernism and postmodernism.)

There are seven interrelated features of the modernist and postmodernist stance that closely parallel the modes of experience and expression typical of schizophrenia-spectrum individuals (Sass, 1992, pp. 28–39); all can be seen as manifestations of hyperre*flexivity* and alienation:

1. *An adversarial stance:* This is a tendency to defy authority, to flout or ignore convention, and, in general, to go against the grain of natural habit. Schizophrenics have been described as manifesting a devious perversity and as adopting the path of most resistance, traits more than slightly reminiscent of what has been termed the *adversary culture of modernism,* where the only constant is revolution itself, the constant injunction to be different or to "make it new" (in Ezra Pound's famous phrase; quotations in Sass, 1992, pp. 30, 110).

2. *Perspectivism and relativism:* This sometimes results in a disconcerting or dizzying effect as one perspective collapses rapidly into the next. What is particularly characteristic of modernism and postmodernism is a shifting or fusion not of objects but of perspectives; this is akin to what has been called the *fluidity, slippage,* or *contaminatory quality* of schizophrenic thinking and perception, a tendency that can be distinguished from the combining of objects of perception or thought that is more characteristic of patients with affective disorders (see Holzman, Shenton, & Solovay, 1986; Sass, 1992, pp. 119–147).

3. *A certain fragmentation and passivization of the ego:* This is a loss of the self's sense of unity and con-

[10]This paragraph is taken from Sass (1992, p. 24).

trol and of its capacity for voluntary action or effective interaction with the objective world. Analogous phenomena occur in many of Schneider's first-rank symptoms of schizophrenia (Mellor, 1970) and may also be implicated in the apathy and withdrawal so often found in schizophrenia.

4. *Loss of the "worldhood of the world":* This is a phenomenon that manifests itself in two distinct ways. The external world may come to seem devoid of value and significance for the observer, a sentiment expressed in Sartre's (1964) *Nausea,* Camus's (1953) *The Stranger,* and various works by Robbe-Grillet (1965). Alternatively, the world may seem subjectivized and unreal, as exemplified in Woolf's (1919/1984) image of separate human consciousnesses as mutually isolated canopies of light or in Bradley's statement that the whole world can be "regarded as an existence which appears in a soul" (as cited in T. S. Eliot's "The Wasteland") and hence is "peculiar and private to that soul" (Eliot, 1934, p. 74; Sass, 1992, p. 280). Schizophrenics, too, can lose the sense of the meaningfulness of the world, as when visual objects shed their aura of familiarity or practical valence and stand forth as what one patient called "geometric cubes without meaning" (Sechehaye, 1970, p. 33). In their more chronic or withdrawn periods, they may experience the world as private to themselves, even as depending on themselves for its very existence. As one patient put it: "The world must be represented or the world will disappear" (Jaspers, 1963, p. 296; see Sass, 1992, pp. 268–323; Sass, 1994a).

5. *Rejection or loss of the sense of temporal flow or narrative unity:* This is in favor of more static or timeless ways of organizing the world, the latter involving what the critic Frank (1968) termed the *spatial form* found in many works of modern art and literature. Similar transformations of lived time or narrative flow in schizophrenia were described by Minkowski (1927), who spoke of the "morbid geometrism" characteristic of schizophrenic experience and expression.

6. *Forms of intense self-reference:* These forms foreground the formal structures or underlying presuppositions of thought, action, or expression, usually at the expense of more normal worldly commitments and concerns. The central impulse of modern art, wrote the art critic Greenberg (1973), is "the intensification, almost the exacerbation of [the] self-critical tendency that began with the philosopher Kant," a cultural tendency "to turn around and question [one's] own foundations" (p. 67). Analogous tendencies are manifest in the hyperreflexivity, self-questioning, and often dysfunctional intellectualizing of schizophrenia (see Blankenburg, 1991; Sass, 1992).

7. *Extreme and pervasive detachment or emotional distancing:* This is sometimes accompanied by a pervasive, often disconcerting kind of irony. It is exemplified in modern art by the all-encompassing meta-irony of Marcel Duchamp or the "umour" of Jacques Vache, who was a key influence on Andre Breton and surrealism (Sass, 1992, pp. 35–36, 421). Similar tendencies can underlie the flatness and incongruity of affect found in schizophrenics, who will often manifest a peculiar facetiousness, antagonism, or mockery, and who may be prone to a kind of laughter that suggests a sense of being set apart from, or above, all normal forms of human interaction (Blankenburg, 1991, p. 181; Sass, 1992, pp. 108–115).

The aforementioned are seven parallels or affinities, pertaining, in each case, to characteristics that are fairly distinctive of schizophrenia or the schizophrenia spectrum and that would be far less common among affective disorder patients. The existence of these parallels may help to explain an observation made by Jaspers (1963, p. 733; 1977, p. 200), namely, that a remarkable number of schizophrenics have had a significant influence on Western culture since around 1800, whereas hardly any such individuals seem to have been of comparable importance in earlier centuries.

Explanations of Schizophrenia

So far I have remained on a descriptive level, listing affinities in the structure or formal aspects of consciousness and expression in the domains of madness and modernism. If we examine some prominent hypotheses that attempt to explain the special nature of schizophrenic or schizophrenia-like consciousness, whether from cognitive psychology or neurobiology, these too may seem to suggest a particularly close affinity with the modernist or postmodernist sensibility.

One influential neurobiological approach to schizophrenia is the *hypofrontality hypothesis,* the idea that schizophrenic signs and symptoms reflect or derive from a lowered activation of certain parts of the prefrontal cortex. Originally, hypofrontality was interpreted in ways consistent with the views of the influential neurologists J. Hughlings Jackson and Kurt Goldstein, that is, as indicating a decline of higher intellectual capacities and also of inhibitory functions along with a concomitant release of lower functions associated with affect, instinct, and archaic memory and as being associated with a general decline of higher functions involving the capacity for abstraction (Goldberg, Weinberger, Berman, Pliskin, & Podd, 1987; Weinberger, Berman, & Zec, 1986). However, more recently, the main proponents of the hypofrontality hypothesis describe the pattern of brain activation rather differently (Weinberger & Lipska, 1995): as being associated (both as cause and as consequence) with an inability to engage effectively in controlled, sustained, and self-monitored forms of practical activity coordinated with external cues, possibly in conjunction with disturbances of working memory, or with a predilection for withdrawal from such activity. (The latter propensity or inability could, incidentally, be associated with exaggerated tendencies toward ideational speculation, the latter being manifest in hyperactivation of some of the posterior lobes; see Sass, 1992, pp. 388–390.) Such a pattern could be seen as the neurobiological equivalent of the propensity for extreme detachment and withdrawal that is so characteristic of modernism, in which it is personified in the poet Valery's (1973) imaginary character and alter-ego Monsieur Teste (literally, Mr. Head), a personage Valery described as a "monster of isolation and peculiar knowledge" (p. 30), an "eternal observer" (p. 119), a "severed head" (p. 110), and a "mystic and physicist of self-awareness, pure and applied" (Sass, 1992, p. 260).

Another prominent hypothesis postulates dysfunction or attenuation of the neurobiologically based feedback system that allows a person to recognize that a given thought or action was performed willfully or intentionally (Frith & Done, 1988). This offers a very direct way of accounting for the typically schizophrenic self-disturbances captured in Schneider's (Mellor, 1970) first-rank symptoms of schizophrenia, including the experience of thought insertion and the sense that one's own actions or sensations are not under one's own intentional control but are somehow imposed on one from without. Attenuation of such feedback may also help to bring on the disengaged and observational states of mind that the poet Mallarme and other writers of an antihumanist persuasion have considered to be necessary for true poetic inspiration, for creating what Mallarme (1951) described as the work of art that "in its complete purity implies the disappearance of the poet's oratorical presence," in which the independent clash of words replaces "that respiration [of the poet] perceptible in the old lyrical aspiration or the enthusiastic personal direction of the sentence" (p. 366; Sass, 1992, p. 198).

Among the most prominent neurocognitive hypotheses concerning schizophrenia are a family of closely related theories that focus on the perception of novel stimuli and the use of past experience for the categorization and control of ongoing cognitive–perceptual processing. All of these theories postulate abnormalities of frontal as well as temporal lobes of the brain (especially the hippocampus and related areas) or of tempero-limbic connections between these areas. The deficit or anomaly of schizophrenic consciousness at issue has been described variously as a difficulty with "probability prognosis" (Polyakov, 1969; Sass, 1992, p. 127), as a dysfunction of the (hippocampally based) "comparator" system (Gray, Feldon, Rawlins, Hemsley, & Smith, 1991), or as a defect of "working memory" (Goldman-Rakic, 1991). Disturbance of probability prognosis or of the comparator system affects one's ability to register or assess the degree of expectedness of a given stimulus and would result in a tendency to respond to old or trivial stimuli as if they were new and startling. Disturbance of working memory could have similar effects; this factor also seems well suited to explaining the schizophrenic tendency to shift or drift between different frameworks or orientations toward thought and experience (Sass, 1992, pp. 129–134), given that a difficulty in holding information online for current processing would undermine one's ability to maintain a steady set or framework of understanding. The slippage of context that results from a less stable working memory may have some affinities with the kaleidoscopic shifting of perspective that occurs in some modernist and postmodernist art.

An altered functioning of working memory, probability prognosis, or the comparator system does not constitute a mere deficit of cognitive functioning; it can also confer advantages. As the research of the Russian psychologist Polyakov and his coworkers have shown, the schizophrenic person's failure to let his or her thinking be channeled by habitual expectations can actually result in superior performance on certain cognitive tasks because it makes such a person more open to unconventional ideas and creative solutions

(Ostwald & Zavarin, 1980, p. 83; Polyakov, 1969, pp. 376–382; Sass, 1992, p. 127).[11] In addition, this may give the schizophrenic a special affinity for the aesthetic of radical innovation and discontinuity that is characteristic of modernist and postmodernist art, an aesthetic illustrated by the peculiar juxtaposition in the line from Lautreamont (from *Les Chants de Maldoror*) so beloved by the surrealists: "beautiful as the chance encounter, on a dissecting table, of a sewing machine and an umbrella" (Short, 1980, p. 74), or by the startling shift that jolts the reader at the start of Eliot's (1934) "Love Song of J. Alfred Prufrock," where the evening is described as being spread out across the sky "like a patient etherised upon a table" (p. 11).

Each of these three cognitive hypotheses (disturbance of working memory, comparator system, or probability prognosis) can also provide a way of accounting for the distinctive combination of passivity and activity in what may be termed the *modernist stare,* the perceptual stance in which a person desists from applying normal, action-oriented perceptual schemata to experience even as he or she adopts a highly focused (and in this sense active) mode of hyperconcentration that transforms the world into what the influential protosurrealist, de Chirico, once described as "a vast museum of strangeness" (Sass, 1992, pp. 43–74). When actions (and action-oriented perceptions) are frequently performed, they tend to become automatized. This leads to a numbing of perception, to a form of categorical perception in which recognition is so dominant that it precludes any possibility of revelation. To overcome this numbing, it is necessary to destroy not memory itself but all the ways memory usually provides an implicit framework, an omnipresent, constantly updated set of expectations or schemata that channel and domesticate our perceiving. Interestingly enough, de Chirico, who was himself a markedly schizoid individual, emphasized precisely this aspect of memory in a description of a (quintessentially surrealist) frame of mind that he associated with both creativity and madness. He wrote of Schopenhauer's definition of the madman as:

> A person who has lost his memory. It is an apt definition because, in fact, that which constitutes the logic of our normal acts and our normal life is a continuous rosary of recollections of relationships between things and ourselves and vice versa.
>
> ... But let us suppose that for a moment, for reasons that remain unexplainable and quite beyond my will, the thread of this series is broken. Who knows how I might see the seated man, the cage, the paintings, the bookcase! ...
>
> The scene, however, would not be changed; it is I who would see it from a different angle. Here we meet the metaphysical aspect of things ... which can be seen only by rare individuals in moments of clairvoyance or metaphysical abstraction, just as certain bodies that exist within matter which cannot be penetrated by the sun's rays, appear only under the power of artificial light, under X-ray for example. (Chipp, 1968, p. 450)

Evaluating Recent Research: Diagnostic Issues

In the last two sections, I consider some recent research findings mentioned at the outset of my article, work that demonstrates a strikingly high correlation between mood disorders and various indexes of creative potential or achievement, along with a surprisingly low correlation of creativity with schizophrenic conditions. I devote my remarks to the most widely read and influential recent interpretation of this research, Jamison's (1993) *Touched With Fire: Manic–Depressive Illness and the Artistic Temperament.* Jamison's book is not primarily concerned with the creativity–schizophrenia connection, but in it she draws strong conclusions not only in favor of an affective disorder–creativity association but also against any association between schizophrenia and creativity: "As we shall see, virtually all of the psychosis in creative individuals is manic–depressive rather than schizophrenic in nature" (p. 60). Her conclusion is highly dependent on some unstated and controversial assumptions about the nature of both psychopathology and creativity. In the next (and final) section, I address the relevance of romanticism, modernism, and postmodernism. In this section, I examine Jamison's deployment of certain diagnostic or nosological concepts.

In *Touched With Fire,* Jamison (1993) said little about the ambiguities or controversies pertaining to the differential diagnosis of disorders in the schizophrenia as opposed to the affective spectrum. Because her book is directed to a broad and largely nonprofessional audience, avoidance of such apparently technical issues is under-

[11] This affinity may also be understood in a neo-Bleulerian, associationistic fashion (on creativity, see Eysenck, 1993; on schizophrenia, see Spitzer, 1993, regarding the tendency toward distant association in schizophrenic persons). I am dubious, however, about the ability of these essentially associationistic accounts really to capture the relevant phenomena.

standable. Still, this does have a seriously misleading effect. It obscures the extent to which her conclusions and inferences derive not from empirical findings alone but from definitions and conceptual presuppositions that are far from being universally accepted. The first of these assumptions is Jamison's implicit acceptance of a neo-Kraepelinian view of schizophrenia as a "dementing illness" akin to Alzheimer's disease (see p. 96).

Given current knowledge (and given a certain fluidity in definitions of schizophrenia), such a view can certainly be defended, but it is by no means established or even generally accepted. The assumption of inevitable, progressive decline is contradicted by the long-term outcome studies of Harding (Harding, Zubin, & Strauss, 1988), Bleuler (1978), Ciompi (1980), and others, whereas the assumption of an essentially irrational condition involving dementia-like deficits in higher cognitive functions is countered by a considerable amount of research as well as close clinical observation (Chadwick, 1997; Cutting, 1985; Sass, 1992). It is obvious that a reader who unwittingly accepts this neo-Kraepelinian portrayal as simple fact will be primed to accept the denial of creative potential to schizophrenics and, perhaps, also to those who resemble them (residents of the schizophrenia spectrum of disorders). At the limit, in fact, such a conception generates a near tautology: It may be assumed that if someone is creative, he or she cannot (ipso facto), be schizophrenic or, at the very least, must be creative entirely in spite of his or her schizophrenia.

The second nosological assumption I criticize is Jamison's (1993) adoption of an exceedingly wide notion of affective psychoses and an excessively narrow definition of schizophrenia, along with neglect of the important concept of the schizophrenia spectrum.

Oddly enough in a book of this nature, Jamison (1993) completely ignored the intermediary category of schizoaffective illness and also failed to mention either schizoid personality or the contemporary concept of schizotypal personality disorder, which most experts view as a *forme fruste* of schizophrenia (the same is true of Jamison's, 1990, chapter on creativity and eminence in Goodwin & Jamison, 1990, pp. 332–368).[12] Jamison seemed, in fact, to accept something very close to the extreme position (influentially stated by Pope & Lipinski, 1978, 1980) that tends to deny or downplay the existence of any distinctively schizophrenic symptoms and considers almost any sign of mania or depression (in nonorganic, psychotic conditions) to imply a purely affective diagnosis. Such a view has been attacked by critics who dispute the Kraepelinian dichotomy of schizophrenia versus affective psychosis (see Liddle, Carpenter, & Crow, 1994) as well as by critics who have argued that some affective symptoms, particularly depressive phases secondary to psychotic illness, are almost an inevitable accompaniment of schizophrenic disorders (DeLisi, 1990). This position was also contradicted by careful studies that demonstrated distinct patterns of formal thought disorder in schizophrenia as opposed to manic or depressive conditions (Holzman et al., 1986),[13] and studies that have shown certain kinds of hallucinations and delusions, the so-called first-rank symptoms, to be more characteristic (although not pathognomonic) of schizophrenia (Hoenig, 1984; O'Grady, 1990; Sass, 1992, p. 492).

The extremism of Jamison's (1993) diagnostic approach is apparent in her treatment of the playwright August Strindberg. She was correct to dispute the previous writers who have diagnosed him as schizophrenic (p. 60), but Jamison stated without qualification that Strindberg suffered from affective psychosis (pp. 112, 234, 340), not mentioning the possibility of schizoaffective illness, a diagnosis that more adequately accounts for some schizophrenia-like features in Strindberg's clinical presentation (see Jaspers, 1977). Even stranger is her unexplained categorization of both Friedrich Holderlin (p. 267) and Antonin Artaud (pp. 60, 248, 267) as having suffered from affective psychoses. A schizoaffective diagnosis could perhaps be defended in both these cases (although I think it rather dubious in the case of Artaud). A purely affective diagnosis is not, however, consistent either with

[12]The index of Jamison's (1993) *Touched With Fire* contains entries neither for *schizoaffective illness* nor for *schizotypal* or *schizoid personality disorder*. I found no references to these disorders either in this book or in her chapter on creativity in *Manic–Depressive Illness* (Jamison, 1990).

[13]Jamison (1993) criticized the traditional belief that certain forms of thinking or speaking are distinctive of schizophrenia (p. 59). In *Touched With Fire* (e.g., p. 107), she cited work such as that of Holzman et al. (1986) but did not mention that these researchers did find certain qualities and features that appeared to be quite specific to schizophrenic as opposed to manic or normal cognition, namely, certain forms of fluid or contaminatory thinking or perceiving. (The latter point is acknowledged in Jamison, 1990, p. 251.) On the creative potential of these typically schizophrenic types of thought disorder, see Sass (1992), chapters 4 and 5.

the largely unremitting course of illness or with the distinctly schizotypal or schizophrenia-like symptomatic presentation of these writers (regarding Holderlin, see Stierlin, 1977; regarding Artaud, see Sass, 1996). Jamison's inclination to treat the presence of affective symptoms as ruling in an affective diagnosis (rather than, say, treating schizophrenia-like features as tending to militate against such a diagnosis or, at least, against a purely affective as opposed to schizoaffective diagnosis) clearly has the effect of increasing the apparent overlap of creative tendencies and affective conditions.

As I noted earlier, Jamison (1993) made no mention of personality disorders in the schizophrenia spectrum, such as schizotypal disorder as defined in the recent editions of the *Diagnostic and Statistical Manual of Mental Disorders* (e.g., American Psychiatric Association, 1994) or the (admittedly broader) Bleulerian concept of the schizoid or the Kretschmerian concept of the schizothymic type. It is well known that such persons can have prominent depressive symptoms as well. The cases of Franz Kafka and Charles Baudelaire are instructive. If one reads either the writings or the biography of these writers in the light of Kretschmer's (1925) eloquent description of the *schizothymic* personality type, one can hardly doubt that both writers do fall into the schizoid or schizothymic category (a *schizothyme* is a person with mild schizoid traits; Sass, 1992, pp. 79–88). Both suffered from significant periods of depression, and doubtless their creative productivity and general aesthetic orientation was potentiated and otherwise channeled by their periods of affective disturbance. However, it is also clear that central features of their aesthetic sensibilities and creative productions (not to mention their depression itself, which is not unconnected with their schizoid isolation) were bound up with aspects of their schizothymic temperament and schizoid set of defenses (e.g., with the paradoxical combination of hypersensitivity and coldness or of yearning and disdain for intimate contact, as well as with sheer unconventionality of perspective, that are characteristic of such personalities).

In one study of nearly 300 world-famous men, schizoid, schizotypal, and paranoid dispositions were quite common (Post, 1994; also see Chadwick, 1997, pp. 15–16). A number of studies have demonstrated certain similarities in the cognitive styles of creative individuals and of schizophrenics (Hasenfus & Magaro, 1976; Prentky, 1980), for example, in the ability to imagine nonstandard or divergent uses for a common object such as a brick (Keefe & Magaro, 1980; Sass, 1992, pp. 124–134).

In her discussion of creative individuals, Jamison (1993) concentrated almost exclusively on depressive and manic features; she totally ignored the schizoid character and schizotypal cognitive style of certain individuals and dismissed the schizophrenia-like features of their psychotic or near-psychotic periods. Obviously, it is no easy task to weigh the relative contributions of these different aspects of an individual's temperament and psychological functioning. Clearly, however, there is no reason to associate a person's creativity entirely with affective tendencies rather than with underlying character traits or cognitive propensities that, in some instances, have a schizotypal or schizophrenia-like quality.

Now let us turn from issues of diagnosis to the conceptions of creativity that are implicit in Jamison's perspective.

Evaluating Recent Research: Conceptions of Creativity

As I noted before, a striking feature of the romantic conception of creativity is the glorification of the artist or poet as the epitome of the creative imagination. Artistic creativity was especially admired by the romantics because, unlike apparently more cerebral activities such as physics or philosophy, it so clearly evokes emotional reactions and demands an intensely personal form of engagement that overcomes any polarizing of participant from object. To the extent that artistic pursuits do indeed fit this characterization, persons with cyclothymic tendencies or manic–depressive traits may well be expected to be overrepresented in artistic pursuits, especially as compared with persons with schizophrenia or schizotypal characteristics.

The argument for the affective–creativity connection does appear to be strongest for the creative arts (and perhaps especially for literature; see Post, 1994, p. 31), which is the main focus of Jamison's (1993) book. By now it should be clear, however, that we cannot assume artistic creativity to be a homogeneous psychological capacity or process that transcends differing cultures, epochs, styles, or media. It is significant that Jamison's sample of literary figures (e.g., p. 292, note 30; Jamison, 1990, pp. 342–346) is dominated by persons from the last three centuries who seem to fall into an admittedly broad definition of the romantic tradition, one that includes not only Coleridge, Byron, Shelley, and Blake but also such (in some respects) protoromantic figures as William Cowper (1731–1800), Oliver Goldsmith (1730–1774), Thomas Gray (1716–1771), and Thomas Chatterton (1752–1770) and such writers in a post- or late-romantic tradition as Lord Tennyson, F. Scott Fitzgerald, Delmore Schwartz, John Berryman, and Robert Lowell.

In one study of the occurrence of mood disorders and suicide in poets, Jamison (1993) examined information concerning major British and Irish poets born between 1705 and 1805 (see p. 61), a cohort whose creative productivity overlapped considerably with the period of romanticism, whose heyday was circa 1780 to 1830. One wonders how different the results might have been if there had been more focus on such neoclassical writers as Pope, Addison, or Dryden;[14] on such protomodernist figures as Mallarme and Flaubert; or on some of the key modernist and postmodernist figures whom I mentioned previously (and especially if this were done with the broader definitions of schizophrenia and the schizophrenia spectrum indicated previously). In a careful biographical study, Felix Post (as cited in Chadwick, 1997, pp.15–16) found traits suggestive of schizophrenia-spectrum disposition in W. H. Auden, T. S. Eliot, Gerard Manley Hopkins, Ezra Pound, and James Joyce, to mention only a few English-language writers.[15] It is noteworthy that so few of the major modernist or postmodernist artists, writers, or theorists are included in Jamison's list and that those who are included (e.g., Artaud and Strindberg) actually have traits that would argue for placing them in the schizophrenia spectrum.

It seems dubious to assume that the romantic notion of creative imagination captures creativity in general, even outside the arts. On anecdotal, intuitive, as well as theoretical grounds (and on the basis of a small amount of empirical evidence), there is reason to believe that creativity in certain other fields, including philosophy, physics, and other intellectual fields, and possibly also in architecture and engineering (MacKinnon, 1962; Post, 1994), may sometimes be closely associated with schizoid and schizotypal features, a point consistent with Storr's (1972) discussion of the distinctly schizoid personalities of Descartes, Newton, and Einstein.

We must also recognize the culture-bound nature of the ways in which fields or realms of creative endeavor are defined and distinguished. Actually, in many traditional or so-called primitive cultures, art, science, religion, and philosophy are not distinct realms at all; until fairly recently, they were not so clearly separated in the West. Also, when cultures or epochs do distinguish these domains, they often do so in radically different ways. Some work in modern Western literature or visual art deviates dramatically from romantic ideals or resembles work in certain other fields, such as philosophy or other theoretical endeavors; this is the case with conceptualism and certain Dadaist and absurdist trends in the visual and performing arts as well as in the experimentalist fiction and poetry of the *nouveau roman* or "language poetry" schools. One may expect such work to be associated with temperaments or personality types other than the cyclothymic or the *syntonic* (the latter being Bleuler's, 1922, term for persons characterized by a natural spontaneity and sense of harmonious union with self and world; see Sass, 1992, p. 80). Such a speculation is borne out if one considers the personalities of such persons as Marcel Duchamp, Samuel Beckett, Alfred Jarry, Antonin Artaud, Raymond Roussel, Jean-Pierre Brisset, and Jacques Vache, all of whom demonstrate markedly schizoid or schizotypal or even (in the cases of Artaud and Jarry) schizophrenic characteristics (Sass, 1992).

Although Jamison's (1993) main claim concerned creativity and the artistic temperament, she did hint at an association between mood disorders and creativity in general. At times, she presented findings showing an

[14]Jamison's (1990) reference to "the large number of psychotic or severely disturbed poets in the 18th century," which she found "striking in an era designated as 'The Age of Reason'" (p. 344), could be somewhat misleading, given the predominantly protoromantic qualities of so many of her examples.

[15]On Joyce, see Andreasen (1973). Jamison's (1993) treatment of T. S. Eliot is interesting. She cited his famous line about poetry being "not a turning loose of emotion, but an escape from emotion, … not the expression of personality, but an escape from personality" (pp. 122–123) as an indication of strong affective tendencies, which he was presumably defending against, rather than as indicating a schizoid personality orientation. It is true that Eliot went on to write, just after the previously quoted lines, "but, of course, only those who have personality and emotion know what it means to want to escape these things." However, by no means does this indicate that Eliot did not have strong schizoid tendencies; schizoid (and schizophrenic) individuals often have strong feelings underlying their appearance of distance or control or of flattened affect. Regarding Eliot's sense of marginality, see Gardner (1993, chap. 7). See Sass, (1992, pp. 76–82, 439–440) on the complex, almost paradoxical combinations of hypersensitivity and coldness to be found in schizoid and schizothymic personalities, a theme emphasized by Kretschmer (1925).

association between psychopathology and creativity in other fields, architecture and chemistry, for instance, as being consistent with her hypotheses, although the type of psychopathology was not specified in the relevant studies (Jamison, 1993, pp. 82–85, 48).[16] The evidence for a more general association of creativity with manic–depressive illness in particular is, in fact, quite equivocal. However, as one can see, such an association is liable to seem especially plausible to a person who takes artistic creativity of the romantic sort as a paradigm, an ideal that other creative activities will tend to approximate.

Another point worth noting is the necessary dependence of all such empirical studies on judgments of creativity and the inseparability of such judgments from prevalent social values, attitudes, and conventions. This is obvious when eminence, worldly success, or public endorsement are taken as the criteria of creativity, but studies that use psychological tests of creativity must also rely on someone's judgment of what is a worthy, interesting, or creative response. Even engagement in so-called creative activities in one's spare time are dependent on social judgments of what counts as a creative activity (e.g., Richards et al., 1988). I neither mean to criticize researchers for using these criteria (indeed, it is hard to imagine how empirical researchers could avoid using criteria such as these), nor do I deny the importance or value of being able to produce work that is of interest to a decent proportion of one's fellow human beings. Still, it is important to recall that what is being examined in such studies is not some timeless or intrinsic essence but, rather, an interaction between a given personality and the milieu in which the person finds him or herself. Two key questions must be asked: What is one actually acknowledging when one applies the epithet *creative* to some product? What, specifically, are the psychological processes or capacities required for such a product to be produced? I take the second question first.

I think it is fair to say that in Jamison's (1993) view, the key contributions that affective disturbances make to creative accomplishment pertain to the inspirational moment; thus, she described mania as tending to liberate and quicken associational processes and melancholia as deepening a kind of tragic vision. Like the good postromantic thinker she is, Jamison treated the emotionally charged moments of creative inspiration as the crucial element, associating these with exaggerated mood states. Although Jamison was fully aware of the need to prune and structure inspirational material, she clearly assigned to this a secondary status, ascribing it to the less affectively charged periods of normal or only mildly depressed mood (see p. 98). However, can we really be so sure that it is a superiority of inspirational capacity that accounts for the higher proportion of persons with affective rather than schizophrenic disorders in Jamison's samples?

We should recall, after all, that success depends in large measure on factors extrinsic to the inherent originality or cogency of one's work, including the ability to promote oneself by networking, the ability to share the concerns of one's audience, and perhaps most important, the instinct to deviate just enough but not too much from social expectations and norms. At most of these tasks, schizotypes and certainly schizophrenics may well be at a disadvantage in comparison with normals and perhaps especially in comparison with many persons with affective disorder. (Recent findings showing that persons with multiple schizotypal signs demonstrated a high degree of involvement in creative activities and that this was especially marked on avocational activities, such as poetry writing and sophisticated photography, may be relevant; see Kinney et al., 2000–2001; presumably, engaging in avocational pursuits, hobbies done for one's own pleasure, does not require either self-promotion or congruence of perspective with a potential audience.)

It is worth recalling Kuhn's (1970) famous distinction between "normal" and "revolutionary" science. The distinction may have relevance beyond the domain of science alone. The normal scientist, in Kuhn's view, is a person who works within a prevailing cultural paradigm, engaging in the puzzle-solving activity of making and verifying predictions and of resolving anomalies in accord with some widely accepted worldview, model, and set of practices and techniques. The revolutionary scientist is the one who postulates a new paradigm, a radically different framework that changes the prevailing rules of the game so radically as to render it incommensurable with earlier perspectives. Although normal scientific work can certainly be creative (here, of course, there will be important differ-

[16] Jamison (1993) also went on to suggest a more general association between mood disorders and achievement (pp. 86–88). Incidentally, the category "achievement" would seem to be at least as problematic and as context-dependent as that of creativity.

ences of degree), it is surely less profoundly innovative than the revolutionary kind. What is true in science is true as well in literature and the arts; like scientists, creative artists also differ in the degree to which they adopt and work creatively within prevailing stylistic conventions as opposed to shattering these conventions and recasting them anew.

Various writers have questioned Kuhn's (1970) concept of paradigm, and several have disputed his nearly dichotomous way of separating normal from revolutionary science. Few, however, doubt that his distinction does capture something of importance. For our purposes, Kuhn's ideas have two significant implications.

One implication is to remind us of the degree to which much successful creative work, although not perhaps innovativeness of the highest degree, actually relies on considerable conventionality of perspective (viz., the ability to presuppose and work within traditional frameworks of understanding). A second implication is that there will inevitably be many more normal scientists than revolutionary ones; indeed, if we speak of scientists who have had reasonably successful careers (and if we accept Kuhn's [1970] narrative of long periods of normal science punctuated by more brief-lived crises and sudden change), this last point is true virtually by definition. One should expect, then, that in a broad-based sample of so-called creative individuals, especially those who are successful in the eyes of the world, there will nearly always be a predominance of individuals who are conventional in this specific sense; that is, conventional enough to work comfortably, albeit creatively, within standard frameworks, to do the puzzle-solving and controlled innovation inherent in normal science or in normal art. This raises the possibility that what accounts for the higher proportion of persons with a connection to affective than to schizophrenic psychosis might, surprisingly enough, have as much to do with the greater conventionality of the former as with their superior originality or innovativeness per se.

Of relevance is the work, well-known in Europe, of the phenomenologically oriented Heidelberg psychiatrist Tellenbach (1961) on what he called the *Typus Melancholicus* personality orientation or type. As Tellenbach and his student, the psychiatrist Kraus (1977, 1982), argued, many of the persons who have a predisposition to endogenous depression seem, as people, to be extremely preoccupied with and dependent on social norms and social approval and to have little sense of distance or alienation from social roles. In empirical work, Stanghellini and Mundt (1997; Mundt et al., 1997) found this to be especially true of persons with unipolar depression and with the Bipolar II type of illness. Tatossian (1994, p. 300) and Stanghellini (1997, p. 8) argued that a similar norm orientation is characteristic of many manic individuals, who may well be overtly rebellious yet whose manic self-assertion and occasional iconoclasm actually betrays a remarkable preoccupation with and dependence on social roles and expectations (see also the several psychoanalytic references that Jamison [1990, pp. 284, 312–313, 316] cited but whose significance for the psychology of creativity she downplayed; see p. 313; especially Cohen, Baker, Cohen, Fromm-Reichman, & Weigert, 1954). Kretschmer's (1925) conception of the cyclothymic and Bleuler's (1922) of the syntonic type have many affinities with these notions of *Typus Melancholicus* and *Typus Manicus*. The originality of such persons may be highly dependent on the way acute phases of mania or melancholia can heighten one's pattern of perception sufficiently, but without transforming it overly much, so that one may be roused out of a more chronic conventionality of perspective that is a more trait-like feature of one's underlying personality style.

Perhaps mania and melancholia should be seen, then, not as a source of radical innovation so much as of a heightening and subtle transmutation of modes of perception that remain reasonably familiar to the majority of other people in the culture. This would contrast with the situation of the schizothyme or schizotype, whose basic orientation tends to be unconventional or even aconventional.[17] (This contrast corresponds, on the nonpsychotic plane, to that between the understandability of affective delusions and the supposed bizarreness of those characteristic of schizophrenia; Jaspers, 1963.) Another difference is that in the case of the schizotype, the move from eccentricity into psychosis or near-psychosis seems liable to fragment or block rather than to potentiate imaginative productivity, or to move it too far off the rails of the

[17]One may mention as well the creativity that Asperger noted in certain autistic individuals, people endowed with an intelligence that is "scarcely touched by tradition and culture—unconventional, unorthodox, strangely pure and original, akin to the intelligence of true creativity" (as cited in Sacks, 1996, p. 253).

normal human form of life to lead to much in the way of creative production that will be socially acknowledged. (Overtly psychotic phases of mania or melancholia are also unlikely to be productive, especially if we speak of socially acceptable work, but the less persistent nature of these psychotic periods prevents them from having such a devastating effect on overall creative productivity.)

As Blankenburg (1991) argued, a schizophrenic or schizotypal orientation involves detachment from the world of "natural evidence," from all that is socially and practically taken for granted by the members of a given society. Blankenburg pointed out that this has some similarities to the process of "bracketing" in Husserlian phenomenology, the act whereby one withdraws commitment from assumptions that are usually so taken for granted as to remain invisible. Through a detachment that, from a psychological standpoint, has a certain schizoid quality, one gains the capacity to free oneself from the constraining perspectives of normal experience. In this way, two things are made possible: explicit awareness of what usually remains tacit and assumed and an opening up to the possibility of alternative perspectives or frameworks. Storr (1972) argued along related lines. He suggested that the capacity to create a wholly new model of the universe that was demonstrated by such figures as Newton and Einstein (the classical examples of revolutionary scientists in the Kuhnian sense) is itself dependent on an ability to detach from conventional perspectives, an ability that can only be achieved by individuals with a predominantly schizoid orientation (see p. 67).[18]

Bearing all this in mind, I return now to modernism and postmodernism, recalling two features of these movements mentioned previously: first, an intense self-consciousness, especially about the normally presupposed aspects or features of an experiential world, and second, a constant seeking of radically new perspectives. Modernism differs from previous eras of art precisely by its constant demand for innovation, its avant-gardism, if you will. It is as if in much modernism only art that aspires to be revolutionary in a Kuhnian sense is acceptable. "Normal" art may not be considered to be art at all but only kitsch, mere academic painting, middle-brow fiction, or the like. The modernist emphasis on rule-breaking tends, paradoxically enough, to normalize radical innovation; this necessarily calls into question its truly radical nature, thereby to some extent undermining the Kuhnian distinction I have postulated. This is but one of many paradoxical features of modernism, which Paz (1974) aptly referred to as "a bizarre tradition and a tradition of the bizarre" (pp. 1–2, as cited in Sass, 1992, p. 30). Much postmodernist art questions the possibility of real innovativeness, recognizing instead our inevitable belatedness, our inability, as it were, not to be quoting whenever and however we speak.

So it seems that, neither in modernism nor in postmodernism, does the Kuhnian narrative truly apply: Either we are in the age of constant crisis, of permanent, even institutionalized, revolution (modernism), or else we are in an age of permanent self-consciousness and ironic mockery in which no single paradigm can provide a structure or background against which normal creativity may take place (postmodernism). Both these orientations are ones for which schizoid, schizotypal, and schizophrenic individuals may seem to have a special affinity and where they would seem to have a better chance of achieving some kind of recognition or acceptance. I do not mean to imply that persons in the schizophrenia spectrum or those with a schizothymic disposition will necessarily be more numerous in certain creative populations than are persons in the affective spectrum or with a cyclothymic disposition; the aforementioned advantages of those in the affective realm (practicality, ability to network, residual conventionality of perspective, etc.) may still be decisive. This does imply, however, that successfully creative schizophrenics, schizotypes, and schizothymes may at least be more common in the modernist and postmodernist periods or contexts than they are in romanticism and postromanticism and that the relative advantage of persons of the affective type of disposition will at least be lessened in the former contexts. (Obviously, the arguments I offer are largely theoretical in nature; to establish whether such predictions hold true would require empirical work that goes beyond the admittedly selective and anecdotal evidence I have presented in this article.)

It would be difficult, in any case, to deny the profound influence on 20th-century modernism and post-

[18]See also Kretschmer (1925) on the "predominance of schizothymes [viz., persons with mild schizoid traits] among philosophers, rigid systematizers, and metaphysicians" (p. 245). Kretschmer described such persons as having a "preference for rigid construction, for formalism, the taste for the intangible and unreal" (p. 245).

modernism and its accompanying sensibility that has been exerted by such probable schizophrenics (or, possibly, schizoaffectives) as the poet Friedrich Holderlin, the writer and man of the theater Antonin Artaud, and the dancer Vaslav Nijinsky; by such probable schizoaffectives as August Strindberg and Gerard de Nerval; by such severely schizotypal (or possibly, schizophrenic) persons as Alfred Jarry and Raymond Roussel; as well as by many individuals who appear to be of a markedly schizoid or schizothymic temperament including Baudelaire, Kafka, Joyce, Beckett, Nietzsche, Wittgenstein, de Chirico, Salvador Dali, Marcel Duchamp, and Warhol (on Wittgenstein, see Ogilvie, 2000–2001; Sass, 1994a, in press). These writers, philosophers, and artists are (for better or worse) responsible for encouraging some of the most profound innovations of modern art and of modern consciousness, including a rejection of traditional narrative and naturalistic representation in fiction, painting, and the theater; an overturning of standard notions of beauty and the art object; and a revision of widely held notions about the essential unity of the individual ego or self. In none of these instances of innovation can the aesthetic or philosophical contribution in question be said to be a simple consequence of personal characteristics of the author or artist; many other factors are obviously involved, including larger cultural trends that transcend factors of individual personality. Yet, it would be equally naive to think that these innovations occurred entirely in spite of these personal tendencies: After all, in each case, the distinctive contribution does in fact resonate with or reflect one or another aspect of what can be termed the creator's schizoid or schizotypal propensities.

References

Abrams, M. H. (1953). *The mirror and the lamp: Romantic theory and the critical tradition.* New York: Norton.

Abrams, M. H. (1971). *Natural supernaturalism.* New York: Norton.

Abrams, M. H. (1984). *The correspondent breeze: Essays on English romanticism.* New York: Norton.

American Psychiatric Association. (1994). *Diagnostic and statistical manual of mental disorders* (4th ed.). Washington, DC: Author.

Andreasen, N. C. (1973). James Joyce: A portrait of the artist as a schizoid. *Journal of the American Medical Association, 224,* 67–71.

Andreasen, N. C. (1987). Creativity and mental illness: Prevalence rates in writers and their first-degree relatives. *American Journal of Psychiatry, 144,* 1288–1292.

Andreasen, N. C., & Glick, I. D. (1988). Bipolar affective disorder and creativity: Implications and clinical management. *Comprehensive Psychiatry, 29,* 207–217.

Andreasen, N. C., & Powers, P. (1974). Overinclusive thinking in mania and schizophrenia. *British Journal of Psychiatry, 125,* 452–456.

Andreasen, N. C., & Powers, P. (1975). Creativity and psychosis: An examination of conceptual style. *Archives of General Psychiatry, 32,* 70–73.

Bate, W. J. (Ed.). (1952). *Criticism: The major texts.* New York: Harcourt Brace.

Becker, G. (2000–2001). The association of creativity and psychopathology: Its cultural–historical origins. *Creativity Research Journal, 13,* 45–53.

Blankenburg, W. (1991). *La Perte de L'Evidence Naturelle: Une Contribution a la Psychopatholgie des schizophrenies pacuisymptomatiques* [The loss of natural self-evidence: A contribution to the study of symptom-poor schizophrenics] (J.-M. Azorin & Y. Totoyan, Trans.). Paris: Presses Universitaires de France. (Original work published 1971)

Bleuler, E. (1922). Die probleme der schizoidie und der syntonie [The problem of schiziod-ness and of syntony]. *Zeitschrift fur die Gesamte Neurologie und Psychiatrie, 78,* 373–399.

Bleuler, E. (1950). *Dementia praecox or the group of schizophrenia* (J. Zinkin, Trans.). New York: International Universities Press.

Bleuler, M. (1978). *The schizophrenic disorders: Long-term patient and family studies.* New Haven, CT: Yale University Press.

Bollas, C. (1978). The aesthetic moment and the search for transformation. *The Annual of Psychoanalysis, 6,* 385–394.

Camus, A. (1953). *The stranger.* New York: Knopf.

Chadwick, P. K. (1997). *Schizophrenia: The positive perspective.* London: Routledge.

Chipp, H. B. (Ed.). (1968). *Theories of modern art.* Berkeley: University of California Press.

Ciompi, L. (1980). The natural history of schizophrenia in the long term. *British Journal of Psychiatry, 136,* 413–420.

Cohen, M. B., Baker, G., Cohen, R. A., Fromm-Reichman, F., & Weigert, E .V. (1954). An intensive study of twelve cases of manic–depressive psychosis. *Psychiatry, 17,* 103–137.

Coleridge, S. T. (1907). *Biographia literaria* (Vols. 1 & 2). Oxford, England: Clarendon.

Cutting, J. (1985). *The psychology of schizophrenia.* Edinburgh, England: Churchill.

DeLisi, L. E. (Ed.). (1990). *Depression in schizophrenia.* Washington, DC: American Psychiatric Press.

Ehrenzweig, A. (1967). *The hidden order of art.* Berkeley: University of California Press.

Eliot, T. S. (1934). *Selected poems.* New York: Harcourt, Brace, & World.

Engell, J. (1981) *The creative imagination: Enlightenment to romanticism.* Cambridge, MA: Harvard University Press.

Eysenck, H. (1993). Creativity and personality: Suggestions for a theory. *Psychological Inquiry, 4,* 147–178, 238–246.

Foucault, M. (1972). *Historie de la folie a l'age classique* [Madness and civilization]. Paris: Gallimard.

Frank, J. (1968). Spatial form in modern literature. In J. Frank (Ed.), *The widening gyre: Crisis and mastery in modern literature* (pp. 3–62). Bloomington: Indiana University Press.

Frith, C. D., & Done, D. J. (1988). Toward a neuropsychology of schizophrenia. *British Journal of Psychiatry, 153,* 437–443.

Fuller, P. (1980). *Art and psychoanalysis.* London: Writers and Readers Publishing Cooperative.

Gardner, H. (1993). *Creating minds.* New York: Basic Books.

Goldberg, T. E., Weinberger, D. R., Berman, K. F., Pliskin, N. H., & Podd, M. H. (1987). Further evidence for dementia of the prefrontal type in schizophrenia. *Archives of General Psychiatry, 44,* 1008–1014.

Goldman-Rakic, P. S. (1991). Prefrontal cortical dysfunction in schizophrenia: The relevance of working memory. In B. J. Carroll & J. E. Barrett (Eds.), *Psychopathology and the brain* (pp. 1–24). New York: Raven.

Goodwin, F. K., & Jamison, K. R. (Eds.). (1990). *Manic-depressive illness.* New York: Oxford University Press.

Gray, J. A., Feldon, J., Rawlins, J. N. P., Hemsley, D. R., & Smith, A. D. (1991). The neuropsychology of schizophrenia. *Behavioral and Brain Sciences, 14,* 1–84.

Greenberg, C. (1973). Modernist painting. In G. Battcock (Ed.), *The new art: A critical anthology* (Rev. ed., pp. 66–77). New York: Dutton.

Harding, C., Zubin, J., & Strauss, J. (1988). Chronicity in schizophrenia: Fact, partial fact, or artifact? *Hospital and Community Psychiatry, 38,* 477–486.

Hasenfus, N., & Magaro, P. (1976). Creativity and schizophrenia: An equality of empirical constructs? *British Journal of Psychiatry, 129,* 346–349.

Hoenig, J. (1984). Schneider's first rank symptoms and the tabulators. *Comprehensive Psychiatry, 25,* 77–87.

Holzman, P., Shenton, M. E., & Solovay, M. R. (1986). Quality of thought disorder in differential diagnosis. *Schizophrenia Bulletin, 12,* 360–372.

Hughes, R. (1984). The rise of Andy Warhol. In B. Wallis (Ed.), *Art after modernism: Rethinking representation* (pp. 45–58). New York: New Museum of Contemporary Art/David Godine.

Jameson, F. (1972). *The prison-house of language: A critical account of structuralism and Russian formalism.* Princeton, NJ: Princeton University Press.

Jamison, K. R. (1989). Mood disorders and patterns of creativity in British writers and artists. *Psychiatry, 52,* 125–134.

Jamison, K. R. (1990). Manic–depressive illness, creativity, and leadership. In F. K. Goodwin & K. R. Jamison (Eds.), *Manic–depressive illness* (pp. 332–368). New York: Oxford University Press.

Jamison, K. (1993). *Touched with fire: Manic–depressive illness and the artistic temperament.* New York: Free Press.

Jaspers, K. (1963). *General psychopathology* (J. Hoenig & M. W. Hamilton, Trans.). Chicago: University of Chicago Press.

Jaspers, K. (1977). *Strindberg and Van Gogh.* Tucson: University of Arizona Press.

Jean, M. (Ed.). (1980). *The autobiography of surrealism.* New York: Viking.

Keefe, J. A., & Magaro, P. A. (1980). Creativity and schizophrenia: An equivalence of cognitive processing? *Journal of Abnormal Psychology, 89,* 390–398.

Kermode, F. (1971). *Romantic image.* London: Fontana.

Kinney, D. K., Richards, R., Lowing, P. A., LeBlanc, D., Zimbalist, M. E., & Harlan, P. (2000–2001). Creativity in offspring of schizophrenic and control parents: An adoption study. *Creativity Research Journal, 13,* 17–25.

Koestler, A. (1967). *The act of creation.* New York: Dell.

Kraus, A. (1977). *Sozialverhalten und psychose manisch-depressiver* [Social behavior and manic-depressive psychosis]. Stuttgart, Germany: Enke.

Kraus, A. (1982). Identity and psychosis of the manic–depressive. In A. J. De Koning & F. A. Jenner (Eds.), *Phenomenology and psychiatry* (pp. 201–216). London: Academic.

Kretschmer, E. (1925). *Physique and character* (W. J. H. Sprott, Trans.). New York: Harcourt Brace.

Kris, E. (1964). *Psychoanalytic explorations in art.* New York: Schocken.

Kuhn, T. (1970). *The structure of scientific revolutions* (2nd ed.). Chicago: University of Chicago Press.

Liddle, P., Carpenter, W. T., & Crow, T. (1994). Syndromes of schizophrenia: Classic literature. *British Journal of Psychiatry, 165,* 721–727.

MacKinnon, D. W. (1962). The personality correlates of creativity: A study of American architects. In G. S. Nielsen (Ed.), *Proceedings of the XIV International Congress of Applied Psychology* (Vol. 2, pp. 11–39). Copenhagen, Denmark: Munksgaard.

Mallarme, S. (1951). *Crise de vers* [Crisis of verse]. Paris: Editions de la Pleiade.

Martindale, C. (1989). Personality, situation, and creativity. In J. A. Glover, R. R. Ronning, & C. R. Reynolds (Eds.), *Handbook of creativity* (pp. 211–232). New York: Plenum.

Martindale, C. (1993). Psychoticism, degeneration, and creativity. *Psychological Inquiry, 4,* 209–211.

McGlashan, T. (1982). Aphanasis: The syndrome of pseudo-depression in schizophrenia. *Schizophrenia Bulletin, 8,* 118–134.

Mellor, C. S. (1970). First rank symptoms of schizophrenia. *British Journal of Psychiatry, 117,* 16–18

Milner, M. (1978). *On not being able to paint.* New York: International Universities Press.

Minkowski, E. (1927). *La schizophrenie* [Schizophrenia]. Paris: Payot.

Mundt, C., Backenstrass, M., Kronmuller K. T., Fiedler, P., Kraus, A., & Stanghellini, G. (1997). Personality and endogenous/major depression: An empirical approach to Typus Melancholicus: Vol. 2. Validation of Typus Melancholicus core-properties by personality inventory scales. *Psychopathology, 30,* 130–139.

Noy, P. (1978). Insight and creativity. *Journal of the American Psychoanalytic Association, 26,* 717–748.

Noy, P. (1984–1985). Originality and creativity. *Annual of Psychoanalysis, 12–13,* 421–448.

Ogilvie, J. (2000–2001). On self-conceiving: Philosophical yearnings in a schizophrenic context. *Creativity Research Journal, 13,* 87–94.

O'Grady, J. (1990). The prevalence and diagnostic significance of Schneiderian first-rank symptoms in a random sample of acute psychiatric in-patients. *British Journal of Psychiatry, 156,* 496–500.

Ostwald, P., & Zavarin, V. (1980). Studies of language and schizophrenia in the USSR. In R. W. Rieber (Ed.), *Applied psycholinguistics and mental health* (pp. 69–92). New York: Plenum.

Parnas, J., & Bovet, P. (1991). Autism in schizophrenia revisited. *Comprehensive Psychiatry, 32,* 7–21.

Parnas, J., & Bovet, P. (1994). Negative/positive symptoms of schizophrenia: Clinical and conceptual issues. *Nordic Journal of Psychiatry, 48*(Suppl. 31), 5–14.

Paz, O. (1974). *Children of the mire: Modern poetry from romanticism to the avant-garde.* Cambridge, MA: Harvard University Press.

Polyakov, U. F. (1969). The experimental investigation of cognitive functioning in schizophrenia. In M. Cole & I. Maltzman (Eds.), *A handbook of contemporary Soviet psychology* (pp. 370–386). New York: Basic Books.

Pope, H. G., & Lipinski, J. F. (1978). Diagnosis in schizophrenia and manic–depressive illness: A reassessment of the specificity of "schizophrenic" symptoms in the light of current research. *Archives of General Psychiatry, 35,* 811–828.

Pope, H. G., & Lipinski, J. F. (1980). "Schizoaffective disorder": An invalid diagnosis? A comparison of schizoaffective disorder, schizophrenia, and affective disorder. *American Journal of Psychiatry, 137,* 921–927.

Post, F. (1994). Creativity and psychopathology: A study of 291 world-famous men. *British Journal of Psychiatry, 165,* 22–34.

Prentky, R. A. (1980). *Creativity and psychopathology: A neurocognitive perspective.* New York: Praeger.

Prentky, R. A. (1989). Creativity and psychopathology: Gambolling at the seat of madness. In J. A. Glover, R. R. Ronning, & C. R. Reynolds (Eds.), *Handbook of creativity: Assessment, research, and theory* (pp. 243–269). New York: Plenum.

Rajan, T. (1980). *Dark interpreter: The discourse of romanticism.* Ithaca, NY: Cornell University Press.

Richards, R. (1981). Relationships between creativity and psychopathology. *Genetic Psychology Monographs, 103,* 261–324.

Richards, R. (1993). Everyday creativity, eminent creativity, and psychopathology. *Psychological Inquiry, 4,* 212–217.

Richards, R. (1998). Everyday creativity. In H. S. Friedman (Ed.), *Encyclopedia of mental health* (pp. 619–633). San Diego, CA: Academic.

Richards, R., & Kinney, D. K. (1990). Mood swings and creativity. *Creativity Research Journal, 3,* 202–217.

Richards, R., Kinney, D. K., Lunde, I., Benet, M., & Merzel, A. P. C. (1988). Creativity in manic–depressives, cyclothmes, their normal relatives, and control subjects. *Journal of Abnormal Psychology, 97,* 281–288.

Robbe-Grillet, A. (1965). *For a new novel* (R. Howard, Trans.). New York: Grove.

Rose, G. (1980). *The power of form: A psychoanalytic approach to aesthetic form.* New York: International Universities Press.

Sacks, O. (1996). *An anthropologist on Mars: Seven paradoxical tales.* New York: Vintage.

Sartre, J. P. (1964). *Nausea* (L. Alexander, Trans.). New York: New Directions.

Sass, L. (1992). *Madness and modernism: Insanity in the light of modern art, literature, and thought.* New York: Basic Books.

Sass, L. (1994a). *The paradoxes of delusion: Wittgenstein, Schreber, and the schizophrenic mind.* Ithaca, NY: Cornell University Press.

Sass, L. (1994b). Psychoanalysis, romanticism, and the nature of aesthetic consciousness—With reflections on modernism and postmodernism. In J. B. Franklin & B. Kaplan (Eds.), *Development and the arts: Critical perspectives* (pp. 31–56). Hillsdale, NJ: Lawrence Erlbaum Associates, Inc.

Sass, L. (1996). "The catastrophes of heaven": Modernism, primitivism, and the madness of Antonin Artaud. *Modernism/Modernity, 3,* 73–91.

Sass, L. (2000). Schizophrenia, self-experience, and the so-called "negative symptoms" (Reflections on hyperreflexivity). In D. Zahavi (Ed.), *Exploring the self: Philosophical and psychopathological perspectives on self-experience* (pp. 149–184). Philadelphia: Benjamin.

Sass, L. (in press). "Deep disquietudes": Reflections on Wittgenstein as anti-philosopher. In J. Klagge (Ed.), *Ludwig Wittgenstein: The man and the philosophy.* Cambridge, England: Cambridge University Press.

Schiller, F. von. (1966). *Naïve and sentimental poetry and On the sublime.* New York: Ungar.

Schuldberg, D. (1990). Schizotypal and hypomanic traits, creativity, and psychological health. *Creativity Research Journal, 3,* 218–230.

Schwartz, S. (1985). *The matrix of modernism: Pound, Eliot, and early 20th-century thought.* Princeton, NJ: Princeton University Press.

Sechehaye, M. (Ed.). (1970). *Autobiography of a schizophrenic girl.* New York: New American Library.

Short, R. (1980). *Dada and surrealism.* London: John Calmann & Cooper Limited.

Spitz, E. (1985). *Art and psyche: A study in psychoanalysis and aesthetics.* New Haven, CT: Yale University Press.

Spitzer, M. (1993). Associative semantic network dysfunction in thought-disordered schizophrenic patients: Direct evidence from indirect semantic priming. *Biological Psychiatry, 34,* 864–877.

Stanghellini, G. (1997). For an anthropology of vulnerability. *Psychopathology, 30,* 1–11.

Stanghellini, G., & Mundt, C. (1997). Personality and endogenous/major depression: An empirical approach to Typus Melancholicus: 1. Theoretical issues. *Psychopathology, 30,* 119–129.

Stierlin, H. (1977). *Lyrical creativity and schizophrenic psychosis in Friedrich Holderlin's fate. Psychoanalysis and family therapy: Collected papers.* New York: Aronson.

Storr, A. (1972). *The dynamics of creation.* New York: Atheneum.

Tatossian, A. (1994). La subjectivite [Subjectivity]. In D. Widlocher (Ed.), *Traite de psychopathologie* (pp. 253–318). Paris: Presses Universitaires de France.

Tellenbach, H. (1961). *Melancholie.* Berlin: Springer.

Valery, P. (1973). *Monsieur Teste* (J. Matthews, Trans.). Princeton, NJ: Princeton University Press.

Weinberger, D., Berman, K. F., & Zec, R. F. (1986). Physiologic dysfunction of dorsolateral prefrontal cortex in schizophrenia: I. Regional cerebral blood flow evidence. *Archives of General Psychiatry, 43,* 114–124.

Weinberger, D., & Lipska, B. K. (1995). Cortical maldevelopment, anti-psychotic drugs, and schizophrenia: A search for common ground. *Schizophrenia Research, 16,* 87–110.

Wittgenstein, L. (1953). *Philosophical investigations* (G. E. M. Anscombe, Trans.). Oxford, England: Blackwell.

Woolf, V. (1984). Modern fiction. In M. A. Leaska (Ed.), *The Virginia Woolf reader* (pp. 283–291). San Diego, CA: Harcourt Brace Jovanovich. (Original work published 1919)

Wordsworth, W. (1957). Preface to the second edition of the lyrical ballads. In D. Perkins (Ed.), *English romantic writers* (pp. 320–333). New York: Harcourt, Brace, & World. (Original work published 1800)

Wordsworth, W. (1977). *The prelude, 1798–1799.* Ithaca, NY: Cornell University Press.

Creativity Research Journal
2000–2001, Vol. 13, No. 1, 75–76

COMMENT

Reply to Louis A. Sass: "Schizophrenia, Modernism, and the 'Creative Imagination'"

Kay Redfield Jamison
The Johns Hopkins School of Medicine

Sass (2000–2001) raises important issues in his discussion of schizophrenia, affective disorders, and creativity. Although rightfully stressing the complexity of diagnostic categories and the definition of creativity, however, he misrepresents my views and the views of many other researchers. I briefly discuss just a few of these.

Of course the concept of creativity is complex, difficult to define and study empirically, and to some extent, it is time and culture bound. No one would dispute this. Certainly I do not.

Sass (2000–2001) acknowledges from the start that no one

> Can ignore the empirical findings of the last 15 or 20 years … [that] have demonstrated a strikingly high correlation between affective disorders or propensities and various indexes of creative potential or achievement, along with an often surprisingly low association of creativity with schizophrenic conditions. (p. 55)

He then, for the most part, ignores these empirical findings, which are, in more than 20 studies, highly consistent in showing a disproportionate rate of mood disorders in highly creative and artistic individuals.

Sass (2000–2001) states that he is concerned that this research will be, and has been used, "to support a purely deficit view of schizophrenia, a condescending, sometimes denigrating attitude" (p. 56). This is unwarranted. Just because research does not demonstrate a link between schizophrenia and creativity does not mean that the researchers who conduct the studies denigrate schizophrenia.

Sass (2000–2001) is correct in saying that schizophrenia was not covered in detail in my book *Touched With Fire: Manic–Depressive Illness and the Artistic Temperament* (Jamison, 1993). My focus was instead on mood disorders and their affective, cognitive, perceptual, and energy links with artistic creativity. There have been great many books written about schizophrenia and the arts and society, including Sass's (1992) *Madness and Modernism: Insanity in the Light of Modern Art, Literature, and Thought,* which, in turn, dealt very little with affective disorders.

Although I did not discuss diagnostic issues in detail in *Touched With Fire* (Jamison, 1993), I have written extensively about them elsewhere. In our medical textbook, *Manic–Depressive Illness,* Fred Goodwin and I (Goodwin & Jamison, 1990) discussed at great length the differential diagnosis between manic–depressive illness, schizophrenia, personality disorders, schizoaffective disorders, and the schizophrenia–affective spectrum. To characterize my understanding and writing on psychopathology as an "extreme position" and one that "considers almost any sign of mania or depression … to imply a purely affective diagnosis" (Sass, 2000–2001, p. 66) completely misrepresents my academic work and clinical thinking.

I neither deny the possible benefits of schizophrenia to the individuals affected, to their first-degree relatives, nor to society. I discussed this briefly in *Touched*

Correspondence and requests for reprints should be sent to Kay Redfield Jamison, Johns Hopkins Hospital, Meyer Building 3–181, 600 North Wolfe Street, Baltimore, MD 21287–7381.

With Fire (Jamison, 1993) and cite studies that discuss the issue in greater detail. More recently, I wrote about this in a book about suicide, *Night Falls Fast* (Jamison, 1999).

I am, of course, aware of affective symptoms in schizophrenia (and in most forms of psychopathology, for that matter) and have written and lectured extensively about the clinical dangers, especially suicide, associated with the depressive symptoms of schizophrenia.

I do not focus primarily on the role of affective illness in the "inspirational moment." On the contrary, I write in detail about the complex reconciliation of opposite mood states, the importance of normal as well as abnormal moods and cognitive styles, the necessity for rational thought and iron discipline, and the critical role of introspection and world weariness.

Sass (2000–2001) quarrels about the diagnosis of 3 individuals from the more than 200 I presented in *Touched With Fire* and states that the "extremism of Jamison's (1993) diagnostic approach is apparent in her treatment of the playwright August Strindberg" (p. 66). "Extremism" is rather extreme. I did classify Strindberg as manic–depressive, based on his symptoms, the natural course of his illness, and his family history. Although it can be argued that he was "schizoaffective," his clinical course was consistent with a diagnosis of schizoaffective, manic (rather than depressive) type. This has been shown to be more closely associated with manic–depression than with schizophrenia.

References

Goodwin, F. K., & Jamison, K. R. (1990). *Manic-depressive illness.* New York: Oxford University Press.

Jamison, K. (1993). *Touched with fire: Manic–depressive illness and the artistic temperament.* New York: Free Press.

Jamison, K. R. (1999). *Night falls fast: Understanding suicide.* New York: Knopf.

Sass, L. (1992). *Madness and modernism: Insanity in the light of modern art, literature, and thought.* New York: Basic Books.

Sass, L. A. (2000–2001). Schizophrenia, modernism, and the "creative imagination": On creativity and psychopathology. *Creativity Research Journal, 13,* 55–74.

Creativity Research Journal
2000–2001, Vol. 13, No. 1, 77–85

REJOINDER

Romanticism, Creativity, and the Ambiguities of Psychiatric Diagnosis: Rejoinder to Kay Redfield Jamison

Louis A. Sass
Rutgers—The State University

I would like to stress at the outset that there is much that I am inclined to accept and much that I admire in Jamison's writings on creativity. Also, it should be noted that my critique approaches her work somewhat obliquely: I focus on issues that are peripheral to her own primary interests, and I address not only her overt arguments and claims but also the implications that these can easily be taken to have. It is possible that I should have stressed these points more in my original article. In my article, I was concerned with what may be termed the *collateral damage* that can be done, largely inadvertently, to the image and the self-understanding of schizophrenia-spectrum patients in the course of a vigorous pursuit of the affective–creativity connection.

As I said, there is much to appreciate in Jamison's writings on creativity and psychopathology. I had hoped to have a substantial dialogue with her.[1] Due to the fact that she was unable to accept the invitation to participate in the original symposium, I made a point of soliciting her reflections on my article. As it is, however, her response strikes me as missing the point of my argument. In some places, Jamison (2000–2001) interprets my remarks in an overly literal way. In others, she refers to her personal beliefs or professional background in ways that do not seem pertinent to the published work that had to be the focus of my article. Overall, she does not confront the substance of my critique.

I certainly do not question Jamison's psychiatric knowledge, her expertise, or her fundamental good will toward suffering individuals. I had assumed, however, that the focus would be on what she has written on the psychopathology–creativity relation; that is, on the evidence, arguments, and claims contained in *Touched With Fire: Manic–Depressive Illness and the Artistic Temperament* (Jamison, 1993), her chapter in *Manic–Depressive Illness* (Jamison, 1990), and on the implications these may seem to have. Jamison's (2000–2001) reply is very brief. Unfortunately, this forces me to respond at some length to reply to her assertions of misrepresentation and also to attempt to clarify a number of issues that are central to the creativity and psychopathology debates.

As I emphasize in my article (Sass, 2000–2001), I do not deny the results of the empirical studies, many of them methodologically rigorous, that as stated in my first paragraph, have indeed "demonstrated a strikingly high correlation between affective disorders or propensities and various indexes of creative potential or achievement, along with an often surprisingly low association of creativity with schizophrenic conditions" (Sass, 2000–2001, p. 55).[2] Jamison (along with

Correspondence and requests for reprints should be sent to Louis A. Sass, Rutgers—The State University, GSAPP–Busch Campus, 152 Frelinghuysen Road, Piscataway, NJ 08854–8085. E-mail: lsass@rci.rutgers.edu.

[1]I am grateful to James Walkup, David Schuldberg, and Ruth Richards for helpful comments on a draft of this rejoinder.

[2]Another relevant line from the end of my article (Sass, 2000–2001) is "I do not mean to imply that persons in the schizophrenia spectrum or those with a schizothymic disposition will necessarily be more numerous in certain creative populations than are persons in the affective spectrum or with a cyclothymic disposition" (p. 71).

Schuldberg and others) is certainly correct to criticize the past tendency to associate creativity only or primarily with schizophrenic forms of pathology. (I may note as well that I do not dispute and am inclined to accept much of what Jamison says about the likely nature of creative processes in mood-disordered individuals.) My article, however, is an attempt to put some of the recent empirical findings into a larger theoretical context, a context that, I argue, shows that these studies do not necessarily demonstrate all that they have been or may easily be taken to show regarding the creativity or creative potential of persons in the schizophrenia spectrum.

In my article (Sass, 2000–2001), I do object to Jamison's (1993) characterization of schizophrenia in purely negative terms. (Her only clinical characterizations of schizophrenia in *Touched With Fire* describe it as a "dementing illness" akin to Alzheimer's disease; see pp. 74, 96.) I also object to a failure to appreciate the existence or relevance of specific kinds of creativity that are associated with distancing or self-consciousness, a kind of creativity prominent in modernist and postmodernist literature and art and probably also in scholarly or intellectual fields that require abstract and critical thinking, such as philosophy and physics (on the latter point, see Post, 1994, and Storr, 1972, regarding "thinkers").[3] I agree that persons who merit a schizophrenic diagnosis are seldom successfully creative, at least in the eyes of the world. However, this does not hold for the schizophrenia spectrum of conditions, nor should one assume that there is nothing at least potentially creative about the thinking of many persons with schizophrenia itself. The lack of successful creative accomplishment may well be due to factors that are distinct from the presence of creativity or creative potential itself, including poor health and the limited social networks of many people with schizophrenia, as well as their relative lack of interest in (or competence for) interpersonal or narcissistic display.

In my article (Sass, 2000–2001), I make a series of arguments:

[3]One may also question the appropriateness of the rather Dionysian and individualistic models deriving from romanticism for understanding the kinds of creativity central to producing a great deal of non-Western art (e.g., think of the serenity and traditionalism of Chinese or Japanese landscape painting; thanks to James Walkup for this point).

1. A closer, more critical, and more historically informed look at the concept of creativity may lead one to question the universality of the essentially romanticist account of creativity that is offered by Jamison (1993) and so many other psychologists and psychiatrists. (This is not to deny, however, that such an account may indeed be applicable to many instances or forms of creativity.)

2. A more careful and wide-ranging consideration of diagnostic issues and diagnostic possibilities makes one realize that the apparent creative superiority of manic–depressive psychosis over schizophrenia cannot be taken to imply a similar superiority of the affective spectrum over the schizophrenic spectrum (I do not claim the reverse, however).

3. Finally, an understanding of what may be called certain elective affinities between, on the one hand, romanticism and manic–depressive illnesses, and, on the other, modernism and postmodernism and the schizophrenia spectrum, may lead one to expect that

> Successfully creative schizophrenics, schizotypes, and schizothymes may at least be more common in the modernist and postmodernist periods or contexts than they are in romanticism and postromanticism and that the relative advantage of persons of the affective type of disposition will at least be lessened in the former contexts. (Sass, 2000–2001, p. 71)

In her reply, Jamison (2000–2001) does not really address any of these key points.

In one of her comments, Jamison (2000–2001) states that I question only 3 out of more than 200 diagnoses in her samples (actually, it is 6: in addition to Hölderlin, Strindberg, and Artaud, I mention T. S. Eliot, Baudelaire, and Nerval). Is this meant to be an example of how I supposedly "ignore" the empirical studies? However, Jamison appears to have missed my main point. My primary argument on this issue is not that her diagnoses of the presence of mood disorder are in general incorrect; indeed, I accept that they are probably correct for the most part (albeit possibly incomplete). What I suggest, however, is that this finding is attributable, at least in part, to a kind of cultural sampling bias, namely, the prominence in her samples of writers who fall into a broadly defined concept of the romantic tradition. If I focus attention on the aforementioned 6 writers, it is because, at least to my knowledge, they are (with the exception of Faulkner and Virginia Woolf) the only persons in her samples who have been considered to be central examples of a modernist or postmodernist sensibility and style. In her reply, Jamison says nothing to dispute my observation that the literary–artistic periods from which her samples of creative individuals are drawn overlap largely with the period of romanticism (broadly defined, as I admit) and that the earlier and more recent figures whom she cites in support of her argument are mostly proto- or postromantic in spirit.

Let us turn now to Strindberg, the only case specifically mentioned in Jamison's (2000–2001) reply. There are two issues here, the first pertaining to Strindberg, his probable diagnosis, and the diagnoses of several other writers and artists; the second pertains to the general conception of diagnosis or the underlying attitude toward diagnostic issues and controversies that is implicit in Jamison's remarks. It is worth dwelling on these more general diagnostic issues; a grasp of their ambiguities is critical to understanding certain key complexities inherent in studying the creativity–psychopathology relation.

In my own discussion of Strindberg (Sass, 2000–2001), I acknowledge that previous researchers had probably been wrong in diagnosing him simply as schizophrenic, given the nature and prominence of the affective features, and I suggest he is probably best seen as schizoaffective. In her book, Jamison (1993) offered Strindberg without qualification as an example of affective disorder; now she concedes that he may well have been schizoaffective. What, then, of Hölderlin, Artaud, or Nerval (persons whose schizotypal or schizophrenia-like qualities are, if anything, even more prominent than are those of Strindberg)?[4] Will Jamison now acknowledge that these three were schizoaffective as well? What of the distinctly schizoid qualities of Baudelaire and T. S. Eliot? A fair number of other writers and artists whom she presents as being mood disordered may, if carefully considered, turn out to fall as well into some part of the schizophrenia spectrum. This seems especially likely in the cases of J. M. R. Lenz, Richard Dadd, Ernest Josephson, and Ralph Blakelock. At least the last three seem to have demonstrated persistent thought disorder in the context of a chronic, unremitting illness that lacked the cyclical quality characteristic of manic–depressive illness.[5]

Jamison (2000–2001) states that Strindberg would have to be considered to have schizoaffective illness of the manic type. Does she mean what (in the *Diagnostic and Statistical Manual of Mental Disorders,* 4th ed. [*DSM–IV*]; American Psychiatric Association, 1994) is called *schizoaffective disorder, bipolar type?* (There are two subtypes of schizoaffective disorder in the *DSM–IV,* the bipolar type and the depressive type.) If so, she is certainly correct, given that the presence of any manic or mixed manic with depressive signs or symptoms is criterial for this subtype. However, this should not be taken to imply that manic or hypomanic characteristics, or affective ones, were the dominant features of Strindberg's personality or in their contribution to his creative functioning.

In a comprehensive article, the psychiatrist Anderson (1971) presented considerable evidence for a significant depressive component in Strindberg's personality and illness. He mentioned the "occurrence

[4]On both Hölderlin and Strindberg, see Jaspers (1922/1977). On the nature of Strindberg's personality as well as his esthetic innovations, see Sprinchorn (1982). The innovations in question involved forms of radical relativism and a fragmenting of the ego, central characteristics both of modernism and postmodernism and of schizophrenia-spectrum illnesses.

[5]J. M. R. Lenz (listed on p. 268 of Jamison's, 1993, book) is a writer whom Bleuler (1950, p. 160, note 28) and many others have considered to have clear schizophrenic traits. With regard to Dadd, Blakelock, and Josephson, I am relying on the research of Robert Sommer, a professor in the departments of both psychology and art at the University of Southern California–Davis, who has written on all three (Motley & Sommer, 1999; Sommer & Cassandro, 2000; Sommer & Sommer, 2000). Sommer cited the following sources of biographical information: Allderidge (1974, 1993), Greysmith (1973; regarding Dadd), Davidson (1996; regarding Blakelock), and Blomberg (1964; regarding Josephson).

In a letter sent to me, R. Sommer (personal communication, September 1999) wrote:

> Reading biographies of these artists [Dadd, Blakelock, Josephson] made it clear to me (consistent with hospital diagnoses) that these artists had schizophrenia/dementia praecox. There was long-term thought disorder, no trace of cyclicity with periods of normality in between, etc. It was with some amazement that I came across Kay Jamison's listing of these artists, and many others, as having an affective disorder. This diagnosis is not only in her book *Touched With Fire,* but it is on Internet sites concerned with mood disorders. When I read these diagnoses, I was very puzzled. Either I have been teaching error in my abnormal psychology class for decades and continue to teach error, or something is wrong with Dr. Jamison's diagnostic criteria. One possibility is that Jamison sees creativity linked to hypomania, so if an artist is creative, ergo the individual must have a mood disorder.

of depressive phases … frequently recurring suicidal trends, and the dominating sense of guilt" (p. 114). More important in this context, however, are indicators of a schizophrenia-spectrum condition. As Anderson (1971), Jaspers (1977), and Sprinchorn (1982) noted, Strindberg's personality was characterized both by extreme hypersensitivity and by a tendency toward coldness, detachment, and a sense of superiority to others, a paradoxical combination of traits characteristic of the schizoid personality type ("I am hard as ice, and yet so full of feeling that I am almost sentimental," wrote Strindberg of himself [Kretschmer, 1925, p. 157]). Strindberg manifested, both in his personality and in his art, a tendency toward a kind of extreme relativism and self-detachment that, I have argued, is characteristic both of modernism and of the schizoid or schizophrenia-like temperament (Jaspers, 1922/1977, pp. 84–85 and passim; Sprinchorn, 1982, pp. 298–300 and passim; Sass, 1992, chaps. 3, 4, and 5). Anderson, at least, also thought that Jaspers and Storch (1921) may have been correct in believing that Strindberg suffered from an atypical schizophrenic or schizophrenia-like illness, possibly of the kind that Kretschmer (1974) associated with "sensitive delusions of reference" and that has more recently been termed "schizophrenia with premorbid inferiority feelings" (Kendler & Hays, 1982).

Jamison (2000–2001) writes in her reply that the diagnosis of schizoaffective, manic type, "has been shown to be more closely associated with manic–depression than with schizophrenia" (p. 76). This is not false. However, if one is familiar with the history of psychiatric diagnoses in this century or with contemporary debates, it is difficult to be satisfied with a blanket statement of this kind. The fact is that we do not currently have—indeed, it is possible that we shall never have (unless they are imposed by fiat)—simple or definitive answers concerning issues about the differential diagnosis of schizophrenia, manic–depressive or major affective illness, and schizoaffective disorder. Some experts see schizophrenia and major affective illness as existing on a continuum that runs through various schizoaffective types; others emphasize the distinctness of schizophrenia and manic–depression and doubt the very existence of schizoaffective illness. Some are inclined to deny the distinction altogether, perhaps taking a neo-Kretschmerian view that ascribes the apparent differences in the psychotic manifestations to underlying differences of personality or temperament. (For a recent discussion of these issues, see Crow, 1998, and Kendler, Karkowski, & Walsh, 1998; on the ambiguities of the schizophrenia concept and the inappropriateness of seeking a single "correct" definition, see Janzarik, as cited in Hoenig, 1983, p. 555.) Over 50 years ago, Jaspers (1946/1963) noted the controversy between those, like Bleuler, who emphasized the nature of the initial symptomatic presentation and others (e.g., Kraepelin) who emphasized course of illness: "Thus for many years," he wrote, "the border between manic–depressive insanity and dementia praecox has vacillated considerably without anything new emerging" (p. 567).

Some of the reasons for the persistence of these diagnostic controversies are nicely laid out in Kendler's (1990) important article, "Toward a Scientific Psychiatric Nosology: Strengths and Limitations." As Kendler noted, there are various criteria that can be used for the validation of a psychiatric diagnosis, including not only the cross-sectional symptomatic presentation and the long-term course but also specific drug responsivity and family history, among others. As Kendler pointed out, there is no reason to assume in advance that these different criteria will necessarily eventually agree. Just as likely is the possibility that these criteria represent distinct perspectives on diagnosis that may never really converge. Furthermore, the question of which is the correct criterion may have no single answer. To answer it, one would first have to determine one's criterion for selecting the "correct" criterion; this is not a purely empirical question but one that is essentially theoretical and debatable in nature. Kendler's primary examples, by the way, were schizoaffective illness, schizotypal personality disorder, and mood-incongruent psychotic depression (which has been considered to be a type of both schizophrenia and mood disorder).

What, then, of the question of whether we should align schizoaffective illness or schizoaffective illness of the manic type more closely with schizophrenia or with affective illness? The reality is that the answer to this question will depend on which criterion or criteria we choose. The best available research on what is often considered to be the most important aspect of cross-sectional symptomatic presentation, formal thought disorder, actually suggests that schizoaffective psychosis in general is more similar to schizophrenia than to affective psychosis and that this is especially true of schizoaffective–

manic patients (Shenton, Solovay, & Holzman, 1987). On the acceptability of defining a disease according to presenting symptoms rather than purported etiology, see Scadding (1990), and on the affinities of schizoaffective and schizophreniform disorders with schizophrenia, see Kendler, Spitzer, and Williams (1989, p. 958). I accept, however, that according to other, equally important criteria, such as clinical course of illness, which Jamison (2000–2001) cites as her criterion for diagnosing Strindberg, it may well be closer to bipolar illness (as Pope, Lipinski, Cohen, & Axelrod, 1980, argued).

In her first remark, Jamison (2000–2001) acknowledges the problematic nature of the concept of creativity, noting that it is time and culture bound: "No one would dispute this," she writes. "Certainly I do not." What is relevant, however, is the concept of creativity that is presented in her writings, both explicitly and implicitly. Anyone who reads *Touched With Fire* (Jamison, 1993) or the relevant chapter in *Manic–Depressive Illness* (Jamison, 1990) will find that a basically romanticist portrayal of creative process, conventional among psychologists writing on creativity (Sass, 1998), is presented there as if it captured the essence of creativity in general. (The romanticist spirit that permeates Jamison's [1993] arguments is apparent in her book's title, chapter headings, and quoted mottoes, as well as in her choice of Byron for chapter-length treatment.) Although Jamison (1993) did mention the quite different, classical views that preceded romanticism and protoromanticism, she quickly dismissed these as a temporary aberration from what she presented as an overwhelming consensus that must surely converge on the truth:

> The eighteenth century witnessed a sharp change in attitude; balance and rational thought, rather than "inspiration" and emotional extremes, were seen as the primary components of genius. This comparatively brief period, which associated moderation with genius, was almost completely reversed by the nineteenth-century Romantics, who once again emphasized not only the melancholic side, but also the more spontaneous, inspired, and swept-by-the-muses quality of genius. (Jamison, 1993, p. 52)

There is no reference whatsoever to modernism or postmodernism or to the possible relevance of any of the antiromantic viewpoints that actually came to dominate the more innovative esthetic movements starting early in the 20th century and that may suggest a somewhat different view of creativity or the possibility of different kinds of creativity.[6] (For an excellent, highly focused discussion of these issues, including some remarks on the relations among modernism, romanticism, and classicism, see Levenson, 1984.)

In her fourth point, Jamison (2000–2001) suggests that it is unfair to fault her for not dealing in more detail with schizophrenia because her book has the perfectly legitimate goal of studying mood disorders and creativity.[7] In my article (Sass, 2000–2001), I did, of course, acknowledge that schizophrenia was not Jamison's main focus. However, given the nature of her argument, it is impossible to ignore the implications for schizophrenia and the schizophrenia spectrum; one is dealing with it whether one likes it or not, if not explicitly then implicitly. The difference between schizophrenia and major affective illness, whether conceived as a continuum or a dichotomy, has long been central to our diagnostic system and general nosological conceptualizations. Given this background and the way Jamison (1993) frames her argument, it would be natural for a reader to assume that

[6]My own esthetic and cultural preferences are of little importance. I will say, however, that neither in this article nor elsewhere am I trying to champion any particular form either of psychopathology or of art. In *Madness and Modernism: Insanity in the Light of Modern Art, Literature, and Thought* (Sass, 1992), I described my main goal:

> To reinterpret schizophrenia and certain closely related forms of pathology (the so-called schizophrenia spectrum of illnesses …); to show, using the affinities with modernism, that much of what has been passed off as primitive or deteriorated is far more complex and interesting—and self-aware—than is usually acknowledged. (p. 9)

Also, as I hinted at the end of *Madness and Modernism* (pp. 343), my own preferences are not for the more extremely antiromantic forms of modernism or postmodernism (e.g., Ezra Pound, Marcel Duchamp, Andy Warhol) but rather for those forms of modernism—I call them *postromantic*—that actually retain a certain allegiance to the romantic tradition and some of its critical oppositions (e.g., Wallace Stevens, Virginia Woolf).

[7]In her reply, Jamison (2000–2001) notes that in my book *Madness and Modernism* (Sass, 1992), I dealt extensively with schizophrenia but said little about the affective disorders. It is worth noting that *Touched With Fire* (Jamison, 1993) and *Madness and Modernism* are very different kinds of books; they aim at different goals and adopt quite different methods. In fact, I did discuss affective illnesses at key points in my argument. I frequently described, for example, the difference between the more vibrant qualities of paradigmatic cases of affective disorder and the hyperreflexive and alienated qualities of schizophrenia.

there must be an inverse relation between demonstrating the creative potential of manic–depressive illness and that of schizophrenia. Jamison herself clearly stated that "virtually all of the psychosis in creative individuals is manic–depressive rather than schizophrenic in nature" (Jamison, 1993, p. 60). She set up the opposition on the second page of her book: "Having previously focused on the relationship between creativity and 'schizophrenia' (often misdiagnosed manic–depressive illness) or diffuse notions of psychopathology, these researchers have left largely unexamined the specific role of mood disorders in creative work" (pp. 3–4).

Jamison (2000–2001) acknowledges that she did not discuss diagnostic issues in detail in *Touched With Fire* but points out that she has written about such issues elsewhere. She notes as well that she has written and lectured on the implications of affective symptoms in schizophrenia. I always assumed that Jamison was well informed about these matters. The issue, however, is whether this plays a role in her analysis of the creativity–psychopathology connection. In fact, I cannot locate a single mention of the schizotypal, schizoid, or schizoaffective diagnoses at any point in *Touched With Fire* or *Manic–Depressive Illness* (1993). There is no evidence that she has considered the ways in which issues of differential as well as possible dual diagnosis may weaken or qualify her general interpretation and argument concerning the creativity/mood-disorder relation.

In my article (Sass, 2000–2001), I state that Jamison's (1993) approach was reminiscent of what is now considered an extreme approach, advocated by Pope and Lipinski (1978), that "considers almost any sign of mania or depression ... to imply a purely affective diagnosis" (p. 66). Jamison (2000–2001) denies that she adopts an extreme position regarding differential diagnosis of schizophrenia and affective disorder. I was not attempting, however, to characterize the diagnostic position that Jamison explicitly adopts or may readily acknowledge but rather the only diagnostic position that would be consistent with—that would in fact justify—what appears to be her actual diagnostic practice in her book and chapter (Jamison, 1990, 1993). The diagnostic practice in her book (Jamison, 1993) demonstrates a propensity to consider the presence of significant signs of mood disorder to be the decisive diagnostic criterion, whereas schizophrenia-like signs and symptoms appear to be accorded little, if any, significance in differential diagnosis.

Jamison (1993, pp. 59–60) listed a number of diagnostic criteria that she claimed can no longer be considered indicators of schizophrenia because they are also present in manic–depressive illness. The only symptomatic criteria for differential diagnosis that she endorsed are ones that would tend to rule in manic–depressive illness and, in her view, to rule out schizophrenia. This is precisely what Pope and Lipinski (1978) claimed in their influential and controversial article: "Most so-called schizophrenic symptoms, taken alone and in cross section, have remarkably little, if any demonstrated validity in determining diagnosis" (p. 811). Whereas "some affective symptoms tentatively appear to possess some specificity in differential diagnosis," they wrote, "'schizophrenic' symptoms" are largely "nonspecific" and, in fact, "almost unusable for many research purposes" (p. 826). Unless Jamison adopts a position like that of Pope and Lipinski, then she is bound, it seems to me, to consider in some detail the possibility that the schizophrenia-like clinical features of a number of the artists and writers whom she discusses might indicate an Axis I or Axis II diagnosis in the schizophrenia spectrum, if not schizophrenia then perhaps schizophreniform disorder, schizoaffective disorder, or schizotypal or schizoid personality. At least in the cases of Strindberg, Artaud, Hölderlin, Nerval, and Baudelaire, she does not seem to have done this. (The clinical features I am thinking of include the characteristically schizophrenic or schizotypal types of thought disorder described by Holzman, Shenton, & Solovay, 1986; the prominence of Schneiderian first-rank symptoms [Hoenig, 1984]; the lack of syntony characteristic of schizophrenic "autism" [Parnas & Bovet, 1991]; prominent hyperreflexivity and alienation [Sass, 1992]; the "praecox feeling" [Rümke, 1941/1990]; and indicators of schizoid personality [Sass, 1992, chap. 3].)

In my article (Sass, 2000–2001), I write, "in Jamison's (1993) view, the key contributions that affective disturbances make to creative accomplishment pertain to the inspirational moment; thus she describes mania as tending to liberate and quicken associational processes and melancholia as deepening a kind of tragic vision" (p. 69). Jamison (2000–2001) retorts that she does not, in fact, "focus primarily on the role of affective illness in the 'inspirational moment'" (p. 76).

Readers will have to peruse her important, fourth chapter (Jamison, 1993), called "Their Life a Storm

Whereon They Ride," to judge for themselves whether my characterization is accurate or exaggerated in a significant way. Jamison wrote: "In looking at changes associated with extreme mood states that might be related to artistic creativity, especially changes in emotion and thinking, it is perhaps helpful to first discuss *the pivotal issue of 'inspiration'* [italics added]" (p. 103). A number of pages later, she stated, with apparent approval, that "a passionate emotional makeup is thought by many to be an integral part of the artistic temperament" (p. 116), going on to quote the poet and essayist George Edward Woodberry:

> The sign of the poet, then, is that by passion he enters into life more than other men. That is his gift—the power to live. … [Poets] have been singularly creatures of passion. They lived before they sang. Emotion is the condition of their existence; passion is the element of their being. (as cited in Jamison, 1993, p. 116)

It is certainly true that for Jamison, as for most psychologists writing on creativity, both the inspirational element and the capacity for distance, discipline, and editorial control are necessary features of creative activity and that neither one, taken alone, constitutes a sufficient feature. In my article (2000–2001), I acknowledge that Jamison is "fully aware of the need to prune and structure inspirational materials" (p. 69), but I say that she assigns this a secondary status. As Jamison (1993) herself noted, at least some of the creative advantage that cyclothymia or manic–depression provides has to do with the fact that in contrast with schizophrenics, such persons have periods of relative normalcy during which they may gather themselves, recollect in tranquility, and negotiate with the social world. We could think of this as an intrinsic feature of manic–depressive illness, or else we could think of it as a period when the illness is no longer present. When I described Jamison as associating the affective illness primarily with the "inspirational moment," I was thinking in the latter way; that is, I was conceptualizing the periods of normalcy as remissions from, rather than as part of, the illness itself.

On reflection, however, my formulations (Sass, 2000–2001) do underplay the emphasis that Jamison (1993) placed on the crucial role of "rational thought and iron discipline" in mood-disordered persons, a feature that, as she noted (p. 98), is associated with the prominence of obsessional traits in such persons. In her book and chapter (Jamison, 1990, 1993), she emphasized the rationality, self-discipline, and perfectionism characteristic of the underlying personality types common in affective disorders. There is probably a great deal of truth in what she said on this point. However, a different (although nonconflicting) perspective on the underlying personality or character type, one that invokes traits that may seem more tenuously related to the valued core of creativity or the capacity for creative work, was offered by the German psychiatric research on *Typus Melancholicus* mentioned in my article. This work suggests the important motivating role played by certain conventionalistic and perhaps narcissistic factors (viz., by the unusually strong need for social approval and approbation that also seems to be characteristic of many persons with mood disorders).

Post's (1994, p. 27) study of 291 world-famous men is of relevance. Post found that the incidence of Cluster B personality disorders (antisocial, narcissistic, borderline, and histrionic) was much higher in creative writers (novelists and playwrights) than in thinkers or intellectuals: 40% versus 14%, respectively. Just the reverse was found with Cluster A personality disorders (viz., the paranoid, schizoid, and schizotypal types): 20% of thinkers versus only 4% of creative writers. Although Cluster A is more closely associated with the schizophrenia spectrum than with the affective spectrum, the reverse is probably the case with Cluster B. This is consistent with a claim I made in my article (Sass, 2000–2001): One would be especially likely to find characteristics of the (broadly defined) schizophrenia spectrum in philosophers and other abstract thinkers as well as in creative writers and visual artists who are drawn to conceptualism and other postmodernist movements. Incidentally, all of the creative groups whom Post studied had a high incidence of Cluster C disorders, which include the obsessive–compulsive, dependent, and avoidant personality disorders; this was particularly true of those in the arts. More distinctive of creative writers and artists (and of politicians), however, was the presence of Cluster B characteristics. This suggests a point that Jamison (1993) did not stress: the important motivating role in creative activity that may be played by an intense need for interpersonal response and interaction, nurturance, admiration, or a sense of superiority, traits that are especially salient in the histrionic, borderline, narcissistic, and antisocial personalities of Cluster B.

Jamison (2000–2001) protests my statement (Sass, 2000–2001) that the research on creativity and mood disorders that she discusses "can be used, indeed to some extent already has been used, to support a purely deficit view of schizophrenia, a condescending, sometimes denigrating attitude" (Sass, 2000–2001, p. 56). In reply, she writes that "just because research does not demonstrate a link between schizophrenia and creativity does not mean that the researchers who conduct the studies denigrate schizophrenia" (Jamison, 2000–2001, p. 75). Of course not. I was not trying to fathom the hearts and souls or to describe the intentions of the actual people who conduct this or that research study but, rather, to describe the general impact of their findings and of the interpretations they give. One would have to be naive to think that general views about the supposed underlying nature of a psychopathological condition, particularly if these concern intelligence, creativity, or other loaded and highly valued qualities, do not have an important influence on how such persons are seen as well as treated by other human beings, professional or otherwise. One would have to be living in a different mental health environment than the one I have observed over the past 2 decades to deny that the now-dominant neo-Kraepelinian deficit models of the illness that Jamison (1993) explicitly endorsed in *Touched With Fire* (by characterizing schizophrenia as a "dementing illness" akin to Alzheimer's disease; pp. 74, 96) do in fact foster a rather negative view of the capacities and worth of individuals with schizophrenia.[8] (I should note, however, that, in one important passage in her most recent book, *Night Falls Fast: Understanding Suicide* [Jamison, 1999, pp. 178–179], Jamison acknowledged that schizophrenic traits may, in milder form and under certain circumstances, have some positive potential: that of fostering watchfulness, novelty of thought, and attentiveness to possible danger. This certainly suggests a more nuanced view of schizophrenia and the schizophrenia spectrum than is apparent in *Touched With Fire.*)

Jamison's (1993) eloquent book does an admirable job of showing the potential advantages that are perhaps inextricably associated with the painful and debilitating ravages of manic-depressive illness. It is unfortunate that readers of *Touched With Fire* (Jamison, 1993) and her chapter in *Manic–Depressive Illness* (Jamison, 1990) are likely to be left with the impression that there are few such redeeming aspects to schizophrenia.

[8]The recent tendency to put less emphasis on "positive symptoms," certain hallucinations and delusions, in favor of symptoms frequently seen as more closely related to Bleuler's (1950) fundamental symptoms of schizophrenia, has caused some writers to say that psychiatry is now in a kind of neo-Bleulerian period (e.g., Maj, 1989). In a sense, this is certainly true. We must realize, however, that there is something very Kraepelinian about this contemporary neo-Bleulerianism, given that the key symptoms in question, the so-called negative symptoms, are generally understood in a largely defect- and deficit-oriented way, that is, as indicating a loss or decline of quintessentially rational and human faculties (e.g., the *DSM–IV* refers to "diminution or absence of affect" and to an apparent "diminution of thoughts"; American Psychiatric Association, 1994, pp. 276–277). For a critique of the concept of negative symptoms, see Sass (2000). The current focus on the "dementia" of schizophrenia contrasts with Bleuler's (1950) strong emphasis on the importance of appreciating the distinctness of the schizophrenic intellectual abnormalities, which are so very different from those of organic or senile dementia (pp. 71–90).

References

Allderidge, P. (1974). *The late Richard Dadd.* London: Tate Gallery.

Allderidge, P. (1993). *Richard Dadd.* Mujinkan, Japan: Reiko Koyanagi.

American Psychiatric Association. (1994). *Diagnostic and statistical manual of mental disorders* (4th ed.). Washington, DC: Author.

Anderson, E. W. (1971). Strindberg's illness. *Psychological Medicine, 1,* 104–117.

Bleuler, E. (1950). *Dementia praecox or the group of schizophrenias* (J. Zinkin, Trans.). New York: International Universities Press.

Blomberg, E. (1964). *Drawings and painting by Ernst Josephson, 1851–1906.* Portland, OR: Portland Art Museum.

Crow, T. J. (1998). From Kraepelin to Kretschmer leavened by Schneider. *Archives of General Psychiatry, 55,* 502–504.

Davidson, A. A. (1996). *Ralph Albert Blakelock.* University Park: Pennsylvania State University Press.

Greysmith, D. (1973). *Richard Dadd.* New York: Macmillan.

Hoenig, J. (1983). The concept of schizophrenia: Kraepelin, Bleuler, Schneider. *British Journal of Psychiatry, 142,* 547–556.

Hoenig, J. (1984). Schneider's first rank symptoms and the tabulators. *Comprehensive Psychiatry, 25,* 77–87.

Holzman, P. S., Shenton, M. E., & Solovay, M. R. (1986). Quality of thought disorder in differential diagnosis. *Schizophrenia Bulletin, 12,* 360–372.

Jamison, K. R. (1990). Manic–depressive illness, creativity, and leadership. In F. K. Goodwin & K. R. Jamison (Eds.), *Manic–depressive illness* (pp. 332–367). New York: Oxford University Press.

Jamison, K. R. (1993). *Touched with fire: Manic–depressive illness and the artistic temperament.* New York: Free Press.

Jamison, K. R. (1999). *Night falls fast: Understanding suicide.* New York: Knopf.

Jamison, K. R. (2000–2001). Reply to Louis A. Sass: "Schizophrenia, modernism, and the creative imagination." *Creativity Research Journal, 13,* 75–76.

Jaspers, K. (1963). *General psychopathology* (J. Hoenig & M. W. Hamilton, Trans.). Chicago: University of Chicago Press. (Original work published 1946)

Jaspers, K. (1977). *Strindberg and Van Gogh* (O. Grunow & D. Woloshin, Trans.). Tucson: University of Arizona Press. (Original work published 1922)

Kendler, K. (1990). Toward a scientific psychiatric nosology: Strengths and limitations. *Archives of General Psychiatry, 47,* 969–973.

Kendler, K., & Hays, P. (1982). Schizophrenia with premorbid inferiority feelings. *Archives of General Psychiatry, 39,* 643–647.

Kendler, K., Karkowski, L. M., & Walsh, D. (1998). The structure of psychosis: Latent class analysis of probands from the Roscommon family study. *Archives of General Psychiatry, 55,* 492–499.

Kendler, K., Spitzer, R., & Williams, J. B. W. (1989). Psychotic disorders in *DSM–III–R. American Journal of Psychiatry, 146,* 953–962.

Kretschmer, E. (1925). *Physique and character* (W. J. H. Sprott, Trans.). New York: Harcourt Brace.

Kretschmer, E. (1974). The sensitive delusion of reference. In S. R. Hirsch & M. Shepherd (Eds.), *Themes and variations in European psychiatry: An anthology* (pp. 153–195). Charlottesville: University Press of Virginia.

Levenson, M. H. (1984). *A genealogy of modernism: A study of English literary doctrine 1908–1922.* Cambridge, England: Cambridge University Press.

Maj, M. (1989). Nosology of schizophrenia and "schizophrenia spectrum": Return to Bleuler? In M. Cassacchia & A. Rossi (Eds.), *Schizophrenia: A psychological view* (pp. 17–30). Dordrecht, The Netherlands: Kluwer.

Motley, J. C., & Sommer, R. (1999). A content analysis of Richard Dadd's art. *The Arts in Psychotherapy, 26,* 295–301.

Parnas, J., & Bovet, P. (1991). Autism in schizophrenia revisited. *Comprehensive Psychiatry, 32,* 7–21.

Pope, H. G., & Lipinski, J. F. (1978). Diagnosis in schizophrenia and manic–depressive illness. *Archives of General Psychiatry, 35,* 811–828.

Pope, H. G., Lipinski, J. F., Cohen, B. M., & Axelrod, D. T. (1980). Schizoaffective disorder: An invalid diagnosis? A comparison of schizoaffective disorder, schizophrenia, and affective disorder. *American Journal of Psychiatry, 137,* 921–927.

Post, F. (1994). Creativity and psychopathology: A study of 291 world-famous men. *British Journal of Psychiatry, 165,* 22–34.

Rumke, H. C. (1990). The nuclear symptom of schizophrenia and the praecox-feeling. *History of Psychiatry, 1,* 331–341. (Original work published 1941)

Sass, L. (1992). *Madness and modernism: Insanity in the light of modern art, literature, and thought.* New York: Basic Books.

Sass, L. (1998). Psychoanalysis, romanticism, and the nature of esthetic consciousness—With reflections on modernism and postmodernism. *Psychoanalytic Review, 85,* 717–746.

Sass, L. (2000). Schizophrenia, self-experience, and the so-called "negative symptoms" (Reflections on hyperreflexivity). In D. Zahavi (Ed.), *Exploring the self: Philosophical and psychopathological perspectives on self-experience* (pp. 149–184). Philadelphia: Benjamin.

Sass, L. A. (2000–2001). Schizophrenia, modernism, and the "creative imagination": On creativity and psychopathology. *Creativity Research Journal, 13,* 55–74.

Scadding, J. G. (1990). The semantic problems of psychiatry. *Psychological Medicine, 20,* 243–248.

Shenton, M. E., Solovay, M. R., & Holzman, P. (1987). Comparative studies of thought disorder: II. Schizoaffective disorder. *Archives of General Psychiatry, 44,* 21–30.

Sommer, R., & Cassandro, V. J. (2000). Perceived psychopathology in a painter's work (on the painter R. A. Blakelock). *Psychiatric Quarterly, 71,* 153–164.

Sommer, R., & Sommer, B. A. (2000). Ernst Josephson's art before and after a breakdown. *The Arts in Psychotherapy, 27,* 165–170.

Sprinchorn, E. (1982). *Strindberg as dramatist.* New Haven, CT: Yale University Press.

Storch, A. (1921). *August Strindberg im Lichte seiner Selbstbiographie* [August Strindberg in light of his autobiography]. Munich, Germany: Bergmann.

Storr, A. (1972). *The dynamics of creation.* New York: Atheneum.

Creativity Research Journal
2000–2001, Vol. 13, No. 1, 87–94

On Self-Conceiving: Philosophical Yearnings in a Schizophrenic Context

James Ogilvie
North Central Bronx Hospital, Bronx, New York

ABSTRACT: My focus in this article is on creativity within a schizophrenic context. I argue that it is characteristic of schizophrenic experience to be particularly concerned with the question of creativity. Such a view of schizophrenia opens a perspective on certain philosophical yearnings as they are revealed within schizophrenic states. The later period work of Wittgenstein (e.g., 1953, 1967) provides a vehicle for exploring the philosophical dimensions of schizophrenic experience. Wittgenstein's work is well suited to this purpose as it centrally concerns itself with the living out, the "instantiation," of philosophical positions. As such, it provides a view from inside on the schizophrenic situation and, thereby, an entryway into a more empathic understanding of schizophrenic experience. Wittgenstein's analysis of the traps into which one can fall in doing philosophy offers clues to the nature of schizophrenic conflict around coming into being. I make reference to his discussions of solipsism and of the (schizophrenic) attempt to experience the "because."

My focus in this article is on creativity within a schizophrenic context. I argue that it is characteristic of schizophrenic experience to be particularly concerned with the question and, indeed, the very possibility of creativity. This is a result of the way in which schizophrenic creative production both emerges from and seeks to address the ontological insecurity characteristic of schizophrenic modes of being. Such a view of schizophrenia will open a perspective on certain philosophical yearnings as they are revealed within schizophrenic states. The later period work of Wittgenstein (e.g., 1953, 1967) provides a vehicle for exploring the philosophical dimensions of schizophrenic experience.

Aspects of Schizophrenic Engagement

Consider the patient, Mr. D., a man in his mid-20s, who told me of his previous hospitalization in a nearby state psychiatric facility. He recounted how for several months he had refused to speak to anyone. His therapist described him as "mute, isolative, seeming internally pre-occupied." What was the subject of his absorption?

> For that time I worked real hard. It was exhausting. I would sit in the corner of the day room. You see I would be busy, working inside my body. I would travel in my body, checking the machinery. You know, the organs, the liver, heart all that. ... For what reason you ask? ... To make sure they were all working right. If they weren't I would work on them. ... And I am now nearly done. They are almost all ready. ... For what? So I can emerge of course. Emerge as The Master, what I know myself to be. Master, you ask? Yes, master of the universe! Yes, as my breath is the wind, my tears the rain, my semen the snow.

Several aspects of Mr. D.'s experience are of particular interest. Notice the sense of being far from life, apart; this combined with a keen focus on the mechanism of coming into being, on agency. Notice, too, the sense of a link between emergence into life and self-dissolution.

Correspondence and requests for reprints should be sent to James Ogilvie, Lincoln Building, 60 East 42nd Street, Room 610, New York, NY 10165.

The sense of apartness, of standing outside life, which was suggested in Mr. D.'s delusional construction, is frequently evident in schizophrenic experience. It has been seen as an aspect of schizophrenic autism. Bleuler (1911/1950) spoke of the "pathological predominance of the inner life" in schizophrenic individuals:

> The most severe schizophrenics, who have no more contact with the outside world, live in a world of their own. They have encased themselves with their desires and wishes (which they consider fulfilled) or occupy themselves with the trials and tribulations of their persecutory ideas; they have cut themselves off as much as possible from any contact with the external world.
>
> This detachment from reality, together with the relative and absolute predominance of the inner life, we term autism. (p. 63)

Minkowski (1933/1970) described "the loss of vital contact with reality" as characteristic of schizophrenia. As pointed out by Parnas and Bovet (1991), Minkowski's approach extended the sense of schizophrenic autism beyond Bleuler's definition, with its "predominance of a withdrawal element" (Parnas & Bovet, 1991, p. 14). Influenced by the philosopher Henri Bergson, Minkowski saw schizophrenic autism less in terms of introversion and more as a matter of being out of touch with

> The depths, with the very essence of our personality, in which it links with the world around us. This world is not just a collection of external stimuli, of atoms, forces and energy. It is a moving stream that envelops us at all points and constitutes the milieu without which we would not know how to live. (Minkowski, 1927/1987, p. 191)

Extending Minkowski's conceptualization, Bovet and Parnas sought to link "delusion formation to the autistic predisposition," which they regarded as "the elementary phenotypic expression of the vulnerability to schizophrenia." Autism is "viewed as a defective preconceptual (i.e., before language) attunement to the world" (Bovet & Parnas, 1993, p. 579).

Wittgenstein Brings Us Inside Schizophrenic Experience

My central theme in this article is that we may view Wittgenstein's later period philosophical work as bringing us inside schizophrenic experience. In particular, he brings us inside with regard to the aforementioned issue, the issue of being inside or outside life. In so doing, his work can be enlisted to help us give this issue a philosophical place and a clinical home as well.

Consider this passage from Wittgenstein (1967):

> "Only the intended picture reaches up to reality like a yardstick. Looked at from outside, there it is, lifeless and isolated."—It is as if at first we looked at a picture so as to enter into it and the objects in it surrounded us like real ones; and then we stepped back, and were now outside it; we saw the frame, and the picture was a painted surface. In this way, when we intend, we are surrounded by our intention's *pictures,* and we are inside them. But when we step outside intention, they are mere patches on a canvas, without life and of no interest to us. When we intend, we exist in the space of intention, among the pictures (shadows) of intention, as well as with real things. Let us imagine we are sitting in a darkened cinema and entering into the film. Now the lights are turned on, though the film continues on the screen. But suddenly we are outside it and see it as movements of light and dark patches on a screen. (§ 233)
>
> And now it seems to us as if intending could not be any process at all, of any kind whatsoever.—For what we are dissatisfied with here is the grammar of *process,* not the specific kind of process.—It could be said: we should call any process "dead" in this sense. (§ 236)

To begin to get a sense of Wittgenstein's relevance for schizophrenic experience, notice the kinship with Mr. D.'s delusional concern. Consider the similar focus on being inside or out and on the movement between these. Notice, too, how attention is being given to the agency of such a shift, the vehicle of its coming about, as in Mr. D.'s concern with the means to his emergence. Wittgenstein's interlocutor invokes the intention, the act of meaning, as the imagined necessary vehicle to traverse the imagined gap between self and world: "Only the intended picture reaches up to reality like a yardstick." The movement into reality is crucial, and notice that as with Mr. D., we are drawn to the idea of movement via a certain connection, one that has a quality of necessity or ineluctability to it.

Consider also the question of whether one's experience, one's world, is alive or dead. Can we sense how this question finds expression in Mr. D.'s self-description, how it may take the form: "Am I alive or dead?" May we be able to see a kinship between the assumptions made in a schizophrenic attempt to "bring oneself alive" and the philosopher's assumptions regarding the conditions needed for meaningful reference to the world?

To see the relevance of Wittgenstein's later period philosophical work to an understanding of creativity in a schizophrenic context, it is important to bear in mind the overall context of ontological insecurity within which schizophrenic experience occurs and to which it gives profound expression. Laing (1959), among others, spoke to the fundamental ontological questioning that can accompany schizophrenic modes. In *The Divided Self: An Existential Study in Sanity and Madness,* he wrote:

> If the individual cannot take the realness, aliveness, autonomy and identity of himself and others for granted, then he has to become absorbed in contriving ways of trying to be real, of keeping himself or others alive, of preserving his identity, in efforts, as he will often put it, to prevent himself losing his self. (pp. 42–43)

Within schizophrenic experience we can often see the in-life manifestation of Wittgenstein's dilemma cited previously, where the light has come up and one feels far away from the flow of life. In so being apart, that which one confronts may appear strange or dead, a thing, rather than a live entity, in or through which, we may say, one could be expressed. One is, oneself, in question. Wittgenstein's philosophical investigations hold the promise of being particularly relevant to schizophrenic experience as he explored the place of our concern with such fundamental, usually taken for granted, conditions of everyday "going on being." Moreover, he regarded his investigations as clinical in nature, as, in effect, diagnosing how we become entrapped in our schizophrenic–philosophical pursuits and how we may free ourselves. "What is your aim in philosophy?—To show the fly the way out of the fly-bottle" (Wittgenstein, 1953, § 309). The potential relevance of Wittgenstein's work to the treatment of schizophrenia, given the schizophrenic entrapment in an autistic stance, is further suggested when we note that Wittgenstein likened the "fly to be liberated" to the solipsist, the one who "flutters and flutters in the flyglass, strikes against the walls, flutters further. How can he be brought to rest" (Wittgenstein, 1971, p. 256)?

Sass on Wittgenstein and Schizophrenia

In Mr. D.'s experience, we see an example of that to which Sass (1994) drew our attention with the idea of schizophrenic *hyperreflexivity.* Schizophrenia, Sass argued, tends to be misleadingly thought of as the "overcoming of reason" by primordial passions. Rather, it may better be regarded as a "self-deceiving condition ... generated within rationality itself rather than by the loss of rationality" (p. 12). Wittgenstein's later period work is taken to be relevant to the understanding of schizophrenic experience given his concern with the existential contexts of philosophical dilemmas:

> The parallels between Wittgenstein and Schreber reveal not a primitive or Dionysian condition but something akin to Wittgenstein's notion of a disease of the intellect, born at the highest pitches of self-consciousness and alienation. Madness, in this view, is the endpoint of the trajectory consciousness follows when it separates from the body and the passions, and from the social and practical world, and turns in upon itself; it is what might be called the mind's perverse self-apotheosis. (Sass, 1994, p. 12)

Sass's (1994) basic thesis is that madness may be regarded as a heightening rather than dimming of conscious awareness, an alienation not from reason but from the emotions, instincts, and the body: "Philosophical abstractions may, oddly enough, be the most apt way of capturing the actual feel of such a [schizophrenic] world" (p. 10). I want to take this a step further, investigating the extent to which it is not just in their being abstract that philosophical issues evoke schizophrenic worlds but by virtue of the extent to which they are both concerned with foundational matters, including being creatively engaged with the very notion of creativity itself.

One feature of Mr. D.'s delusion that is of particular interest has to do with the way in which he focused on normally taken-for-granted conditions of action, for example, that the physical–mechanical preconditions of movement are intact. In discussing two other cases of schizophrenic preoccupation with a mechanized self-world, Sass (1992) linked schizophrenic hyperreflexivity with an awareness of what is normally implicit:

> If Natalija's influencing-machine delusion represents the lived body turned inside out and contemplated at a remove, Lang's "strata" involve an analogous externalization—a projection outward of the usually implicit phenomena of inner speech and dialogue. In the apt vocabulary of the philosopher Samuel Alexander, each tends to "contemplate" experiences or psychological processes that would normally be inhabited (lived through) or "enjoyed." And such tendencies are hardly likely to confirm a sense of self: the formula of exigent intro-

> spection is not "I think therefore I am" but "It thinks and therefore I am not." (p. 232)

In marking out these two modes—contemplation and enjoyment—Sass (1992) enlisted the notions of the third- and first-person perspectives in his description of schizophrenic experience. Furthermore, he suggested how the adoption of a third-person position is related to an attenuation of a sense of self within schizophrenia.

Sass (1992) saw this objectification of the normally implicit conditions of experience as a consequence of the hyperreflexivity that characterizes schizophrenia. Wittgenstein, I contend, placed us inside this "investigation," where the possibility of movement between third-person and first-person perspectives becomes of in-life concern. Can Wittgenstein provide us with a view from inside on the engagement in the philosophical questions around issues of coming into being, on the relation between thought and action which we can see as being of in-life concern within schizophrenic experience? Can we use Wittgenstein's work to illuminate the ways in which we may regard schizophrenic creative production as being concerned with the conditions of creativity, of coming into being?

I show that what Wittgenstein "diagnosed" is the dilemma that arises when one attempts to capture from one perspective what cannot be so seen, so captured. This has particular relevance for schizophrenic attempts to be, as I describe it, "present at creation" in the context of seeking to bring oneself into being. I show how Wittgenstein brings us inside a moment that is characteristic of the creative process. He brings us inside a moment that can become of greater concern within schizophrenic experience, as there it cannot so easily be taken for granted.

Schizophrenic Concern With the Implicit

Next is a clinical example that highlights a schizophrenic concern with the implicit and with its revelation and gives a sense of its place in the context of a concern with agency, with emergence.

A patient, Mr. P., spoke of the movie *Black Hole.* He recalled a scene involving "a spaceship, like a living room, with people around smoking." He reported that he had only seen 20 min of this movie years ago while in the local state hospital, but that it has stayed with him. Mr. P. described how a crisis of some sort arose in the film, leading to the lights in the spaceship being extinguished, thereby revealing the illuminated control panels. "There were dials along all the walls of the room. They hadn't been visible before and now they were everywhere." A terror arose in him as he became aware that he "didn't know if they would remember how to work them." He would have to wake the captain, who was in suspended animation. The captain, he recalled, coughed a few times before arousing.

Compare this passage from Wittgenstein (1953):

> The machine as symbolizing its action: the action of a machine—I might say at first—seems to be there in it from the start. What does that mean?—If we know the machine, everything else, that is its movement seems already to be completely determined. (§ 193)

In speaking of the machine that appears to symbolize itself, Wittgenstein (1953) portrayed key elements of the relation to mechanization that we saw in Mr. D.'s delusion and with Mr. P. He captured the sense that one is carried along, guided by a hidden machine. Also suggested is the question of whether one can "get it right," if one can master the now revealed mechanism. Toward what end would such mastery tend? Application of Wittgenstein's analysis would suggest, for one, that it would tend toward ineluctable movement, toward a situation where, we may say, one "could not but" move, could not but, for example, emerge as Master. Sass (1994) described how a schizophrenic person may lose the sense of initiating his own actions. We may ask: How would you react to such a loss? Perhaps with an absorption in the idea of an apparatus that may ineluctably lead to action as result.

How is it that we are misled here? As Wittgenstein (1953) put it

> We do say: "Now I can go on, I mean I know the formula," as we say "I can walk, I mean I have time" ... that is when we are contrasting *this* condition for walking with others. But here we must be on our guard against thinking that there is some *totality* of conditions corresponding to the nature of each case (e.g., for a person's walking) so that, as it were, he *could not but* walk if they were all fulfilled. (§ 183)
>
> We have got onto slippery ice where there is no friction and so in a certain sense the conditions are ideal, but also, just because of that, we are unable to walk. We want to walk: so we need *friction*. Back to the rough ground! (§ 107)

What is involved in seeking to hold to the slippery ice? Think, for example, of the fervid search, often seen within schizophrenia, for number connections. What seems from outside to be coincidental is regarded within schizophrenic experience as pregnant with meaning, as that which could give birth to or express something of highest significance. We notice a characteristic clinging to certainty within schizophrenic states and the accompanying, ever-growing dread, the sense of emptiness at the center. We sense an attempt to make certain, to make what cannot be so made.

Notice how we see again a shift in perspective in Wittgenstein's (1953) aforementioned remarks. We have the point of view from inside a situation, going on in so far as one factor, among others, is concerned. We have the tempting elision to the "could not but" standpoint that appears to offer the security of inevitable movement but that actually no longer serves to distinguish anything, rendering itself thereby empty, delusional. We want to walk, but suddenly the ground is icy beneath us, too slippery to give us the traction we need. How are we to find our way back to the rough ground?

On the Grammar of Agency and the Experience of the "Because"

The aforementioned remarks regarding "could not but" are intended to help us begin to see how, in Wittgenstein's (1953) terms, aspects of the "grammar" of agency can become the locus of concern in schizophrenic experience; that is, they may illuminate how the everyday logical and existential features of agency, normally assumed, can become of pressing importance or can stand out sharply in the glare of schizophrenic doubt and concomitant hyperreflexivity.

Consider Wittgenstein (1953) on the experience of the because. He presented the grammatical context of that which can become of pressing in-life concern within schizophrenic experience. The discussion that I have in mind focuses on the phenomenon of "being guided" (§ 172–§ 176). Among the actions that we would be inclined to consider are ones where we are being guided; there are a variety of everyday voluntary activities such as "walking along a field track, simply following it" (§ 172). Wittgenstein asked us to imagine a situation in which we are copying "some arbitrary doodle," allowing ourselves to be guided by it. In what, he asked, does the guidance consist? He noted how easily we are able to carry out this request, how "*while* I am being guided everything is quite simple, I notice nothing *special*" (§ 175). The situation is dramatically different, however, when I attempt to say what it was that characterized my being guided in making the copy:

> But afterwards, when I ask myself what it was that happened, it seems to have been something indescribable. *Afterwards* no description satisfies me. It's as if I couldn't believe that I merely looked, made such and such a face, and drew a line. (§ 175)

Why do such phenomena as looking in a certain way and making a certain face not seem to be enough? What else is there for which we are looking? Wittgenstein's (1953) answer follows:

> When I look back on the experience I have the feeling that what is essential about it is an "experience of being influenced," of a connection—as opposed to a mere simultaneity of phenomena: but at the same time I should not be willing to call any experienced phenomenon the "experience of being influenced." (This contains the germ of the idea that the will is not a *phenomenon*.) I should like to say I had experienced the "*because*," and yet I do not want to call any phenomenon the "experience of the because." (§ 176)

When I look back on the experience of being guided, I am inclined to say that there must be something more going on than that I just made a certain face and drew a line in a certain way. The "something more" that I seek is something that may serve to connect my drawing a line in a certain way with the original line that guided me. It is not as though my drawing the line happened merely simultaneously with my being aware of the line to be copied. It was not as though I, so to speak, just found myself drawing the line as I did; no, rather, I experienced the influence of the original. Under its influence, I drew the line. Here I am active. It did not just happen that I drew the line as I did. I had a reason for so drawing it.

At a related juncture, when considering the phenomenon of reading, Wittgenstein (1953) spoke in the following way of what it is that we are attempting to capture when we talk of influence: "For when I speak of the experiences of being influenced, of causal connection, of being guided, that is really meant to imply that I as it were feel the movement of the lever which connects seeing the letters with speaking" (§ 170). I cannot find any experience that is the experience of being influenced, but we want to insist, I certainly was influenced. In a cryptic passage from this section, Wittgenstein remarked that "you would like to say:

'And it just is a *particular* inner experience.' (And that is, of course, to add nothing)." He then suggested: "This is connected with the problem of the nature of intention, of willing" (§ 174). What did he see here? What is this connection?

As is characteristic of Wittgenstein's work, we find several interwoven strands of thought in these passages. It is also typical that the phenomenon of the crossing of lines of thought, of ways of seeing, is central to the content of what is being suggested. I would like to draw attention to the way in which two distinct vantage points on experience manifest themselves in the passages under consideration.

Recall that while copying the line "I notice nothing special;" only afterward am I unable to be satisfied with any description of what happened. There is a sense, we may say, in which in my subsequent thinking about what happened I stand "outside" that which interests me. Speaking intuitively, there is a sense in which while being guided I am "absorbed" in what I am doing. I am focused on the matter at hand; I am not reflecting on what is taking place in doing whatever it is that I am doing. Notice also that there is a sense in which while being guided I am not concerned with "how things are," am not making any claims about "the way things are." The situation is different when I am looking back on what happened, attempting, as it were, to see the process of being influenced. I am reflecting on the way things occurred; I am looking to be in a position to make some statement about the way things are.

Now consider a passage in which the limits of a third-person perspective are presented in a context that is strikingly evocative of a schizophrenic state:

> Writing is certainly a voluntary movement, and yet an automatic one. And of course there is no question of a feeling of each movement in writing. One feels something, but could not possibly analyze the feeling. One's hand writes; it does not write because one wills, but one wills what it writes.
>
> One does not watch it in astonishment or with interest while writing; does not think "What will it write now?" But not because one had a wish it should write that. For that it writes what I want might very well throw me into astonishment. (Wittgenstein, 1967, § 586)

Just intuitively, notice the psychotic "feel" of, for example, being astonished that my hand does what I want it to do. Something important is being suggested. Think about the uncanny kinship between schizophrenic experience and similar states that Wittgenstein (1967) evoked, such as the astonishment at the movement of one's hand.

One may say, indeed, there is something quite astonishing about my hand doing what I will it to!

What is involved when so seeing may be a certain picture of the act of will and its consequent. We are in the territory of and can understand a reason for wanting to say with Wittgenstein's (1953) interlocutor: The will "cannot be allowed to stop anywhere short of the action" (§ 615). The kinship with schizophrenic experience is suggestive. What we have, in effect, is an example of bringing a third-person perspective right into experience. We can sense the estrangement of such a vantage point, but also the insight it may open.

One's hand writes; it does not write because one wills, but one wills what it writes.

We could put it this way: We are looking around within the space of such astonishment, seeking to walk within this neighborhood. We see the import of the idea of grammar; that is, rather than speaking with Sass (1994) of a consequence of hyperreflexivity, we are looking for its address, for the contexts within which such a hyperreflexive stance is adopted. From a Wittgensteinian perspective, a grammatical understanding would, of course, include a familiarity with the consequences of such a hyperreflexive stance, among which we would expect to find the vitiation of a solid sense of self.

On Seeking the Will as Phenomenon

To return to the shift in perspective that we saw in the "experience of the because" passage, can we see this as both sought and feared within schizophrenic experience? Can we sense a sought movement from being outside, apart, to a going on, a being within life? Consider the longing and terror contained within this moment. We may speak of a wish to remain "present at creation" as a means of seeking to negotiate this moment, a wish to stand apart from the process of one's own coming into being.

To see why this is often the case, I approach this moment from another direction, considering how psychodynamic determinants of a schizophrenic position may intersect with the schizophrenic concern with such core foundational conditions of going on. I have been looking at the relation between hyperreflexivity and a sense of agency, where it is not as though the hyperreflexivity simply results in the vitiation of a sense of agency. Rather we are seeking an awareness of the extent to which schizophrenic hyperreflexivity may also be an integral aspect of the search for such a sense. Consider, for example, how Mr. D.'s reflexive stance toward his own internal organs, described at the outset of this article, may be regarded as an instantiation of the dilemma Wittgenstein presented in his discussion of the yearning to experience the because. Just as in the situation described by Wittgenstein, Mr. D. seeks, as it were, to remain present at the moment of emergence, to grasp from a third-person perspective that which is regarded as being capable of carrying him ineluctably into the world. Such a desperate clinging to a third-person stance serves an essential if ultimately impossible purpose: to ward off the feared dissolving of self in the inevitable loss of the third-person perspective that characterizes the immediacy of everyday agency. Are we witnessing a desperate attempt to defend against the threat posed by the immediacy characteristic of everyday human agency, everyday going on? Think of the often encountered poignant delusions of implosive disintegration or shattering expansion that we see within schizophrenic worlds. Can we see such experiences as that which is defended against, yet ultimately engendered, by the schizophrenic attempt at objectified self-creation?

The will, as Wittgenstein (1953) put it, is "not a phenomenon" (§ 176). It cannot be grasped from a third-person perspective. Within schizophrenic experience, we can see an in-life coming up against the limits of such an attempt.

Recall where we began, with a description of schizophrenic autism. With his analysis of philosophical solipsism, Wittgenstein (1953) offered us a framework for understanding the schizophrenic entrapment that results from the attempt to remain "present at creation." Consider the well-known passage from Wittgenstein's (1953) *Philosophical Investigations* that preceded his description of the liberative, freeing the fly, intent of his work:

> How does the philosophical problem about mental processes and states and about behaviorism arise?—The first step is the one that altogether escapes notice. We talk of processes and states and leave their nature undecided. Sometime perhaps we shall know more about them—we think. But that is just what commits us to a particular way of looking at the matter. For we have a definite concept of what it means to learn to know a process better. (The decisive movement in the conjuring trick has been made, and it was the very one that we thought quite innocent.)—And now the analogy which was to make us understand our thoughts falls to pieces. So we have to deny the yet uncomprehended process in the yet unexplored medium. And now it looks as if we had denied mental processes. And naturally we don't want to deny them.
>
> What is your aim in philosophy?—To show the fly the way out of the fly-bottle. (§ 308–309)

Within schizophrenic experience we can see what we may term the *instantiation* of the aforementioned conjuring trick that entraps the philosopher. We can see the assumption of internal processes, in the context of schizophrenic hyperreflexivity, as a step in the ultimately further entrapping attempt to find the vehicle of movement, of emergence, of one's self-creation. This is an attempt that is bound to fail as it seeks to capture that which cannot be so grasped, inevitably resulting in solipsistic self-containedness. The immediacy that characterizes creative expression cannot be so caught. The will is not a phenomenon.

Clinical Implications

In a famous remark, describing the philosopher's yearning for the "visual room" of his unique inner world, Wittgenstein (1953) strikingly described the coming into being of the solipsist's entrapment. This passage also vividly presents the coming into being of a schizophrenic state:

> "But when I imagine something, or even actually *see* objects, I have *got* something which my neighbor has not."—I understand you. You want to look about you and say: "At any rate only I have got THIS."—What are these words for? They serve no purpose.—Can one not add: "There is here no question of a 'seeing'—and therefore none of a 'having'—nor of a subject, nor therefore of 'I' either"? Might I not ask: In what sense have you *got* what you are talking about and saying that only you have got it? Do you possess it? You do not even *see* it. Must you really say that no one has got it? And this too is clear: if as a matter of logic you exclude other people's having something, it loses its sense to say that you have it.
>
> But what is the thing you are speaking of? It is true I said that I knew within myself what you meant. But that meant that I knew how one thinks to conceive this object, to see it, to make one's looking and pointing mean it. I know how one stares ahead and looks about in this case—and the rest. I think we can say: you are talking (if, for example, you are sitting in a room) of the "visual room." The "visual room" is the one that has no owner. I can as little own it as I can walk about it, or look at it, or point to it. Inasmuch as it cannot be any one else's it is not mine either. ...

> Think of a picture of a landscape, an imaginary landscape with a house in it.—Someone asks "Whose house is that?"—The answer, by the way, might be "It belongs to the farmer who is sitting on the bench in front of it." But then he cannot for example enter his house. (§ 398)

Think of schizophrenic delusional worlds. Can we see the kinship with the dilemma facing the farmer in the imaginary landscape? Think of Mr. D., who sought to enter his body so that he may emerge a Master, or Mr. P., who experienced a sudden sense of apartness from the guiding, controlling machine. We tend to think that they cannot enter our world, as they are lost in theirs. However, we sense how it may be that they cannot enter theirs either. This opens the possibility of a therapeutic meeting, a meeting "from the inside," around this metalevel dilemma. Can we see "if only yours, then not yours" as opening a liberative (therapeutic) road here? To enter theirs they would have to enter ours. How can we make this awareness come to life clinically?

In describing our temptation in doing philosophy, Wittgenstein (1953) spoke of our longing for a kind of purity. In a metaphor that is quite evocative of a schizophrenic world he spoke of our yearning for a "crystalline" purity. This he regarded as a "preconceived idea" that "can only be removed by our turning our whole examination round" (§ 108). Why do we have this yearning? Think of the way in which we have noticed the "coming up against a gap," the coming up against an apartness from being in the world that we long and fear to bridge. Our problem may be described this way: We speak of the sense of a gap here, yet the movement across this gap needs to also involve a turn, a change in perspective, so that we no longer stand outside ourselves but each see through our own eyes. From a clinical standpoint, we must evoke this first-person perspective. This is what the solipsist seeks as well but in a futile, self-entrapping manner.

In Wittgenstein's (1953) words, "the axis of reference of our examination must be rotated, but about the fixed point of our real need" (§ 108). Recall our discussion of the experience of the because. This is Wittgenstein's clinical intervention: "'But being guided is surely a particular experience!'—The answer to this is: you are now *thinking* of a particular experience of being guided" (§ 173).

We can see the return to the "rough ground." We are looking right at what is taking place as a means of facilitating a turnabout. Now the question arises concerning what's going on around, in the neighborhood of, this particular experience. We will ask such questions rather than those that would seek conditions such that we "could not but walk."

"You are now thinking." See this as a therapeutic intervention. Think of what this move may accomplish. It gives a context, one that invokes you, your so thinking. It invokes that which, when sought from a third-person perspective, can only lead to the solipsist's entrapment. Wittgenstein (1953, § 121) described his philosophy as being "first order," not metalevel. (Hence, he is able to bring us inside schizophrenic experience.) There is no metalevel place for us to stand, no place for us to be "present at creation," but then why should we think we really need one?

References

Bleuler, E. (1950). *Dementia praecox or the group of schizophrenias* (J. Zinkin, Trans.). New York: International Universities Press. (Original work published in 1911)

Bovet, P., & Parnas, J. (1993). Schizophrenic delusions: A phenomenological approach. *Schizophrenia Bulletin, 19,* 579–597.

Laing, R. D. (1959). *The divided self: An existential study in sanity and madness.* Baltimore: Penguin.

Minkowski, E. (1970). *Lived time: Phenomenological and psychopathological studies* (N. Metzel, Trans.). Evanston, IL: Northwestern University Press. (Original work published 1933)

Minkowski, E. (1987). *La schizophrenie.* In J. Cutting & M. Shepard (Eds. & Trans.), *The clinical roots of the schizophrenia concept* (pp. 188–212). Cambridge, England: Cambridge University Press. (Original work published 1927)

Parnas, J., & Bovet, P. (1991). Autism in schizophrenia revisited. *Comprehensive Psychiatry, 32,* 7–21.

Sass, L. (1992). *Madness and modernism: Insanity in the light of modern art, literature, and thought.* New York: Basic Books.

Sass, L. (1994). *The paradoxes of delusion: Wittgenstein, Schreber, and the schizophrenic mind.* Ithaca, NY: Cornell University Press.

Wittgenstein, L. (1953). *Philosophical investigations* (G. E. M. Anscombe, Ed. & Trans., & R. Rhees, Ed.). Oxford, England: Basil Blackwell.

Wittgenstein, L. (1967). *Zettel* (G. E. M. Anscombe, Ed. & Trans., & G. H. von Wright, Ed.). Berkeley: University of California Press.

Wittgenstein, L. (1971). Notes for lectures on "private experience." In O. R. Jones (Ed.), *The private language argument* (pp. 232–275). New York: St. Martin's.

Creativity Research Journal
2000–2001, Vol. 13, No. 1, 95–104

Mental Illness and Roots of Genius

R. A. Prentky
Justice Resource Institute, Bridgewater, Massachusetts

ABSTRACT: In earlier writings, I addressed presumptive similarities between creative cognition and deviant cognition that reflect a predisposition to psychosis (e.g., Prentky, 1980, 1989). I proposed that certain biologically conceived cognitive styles that are peculiar to extraordinary creativity possess common biological ancestry with certain cognitive styles that are associated with a predisposition to major mental illness. In this article, I revisit some of the assumptions made in the neurocognitive model set forth in my earlier writings. In particular, I suggest that the normal range of input regulation is distorted by imbalances in hemispheric activity, resulting in 2 very different data-processing strategies that enhance or facilitate creative solutions to problems. Due to the fact that these imbalances are often associated with genetic predispositions to mental illness, there is a greater-than-chance probability that highly creative individuals may evidence signs or symptoms of mental illness. In addition, I address the question of whether creativity possesses a uniquely consanguineous relation to affective disorders or to a broader range of afflictions. I conclude with a plea for an empirical strategy that addresses the seemingly intractable methodological problems associated with research on creativity.

Since the days of Aristotle, there has been a romantic notion that madness is allied with genius. Throughout civilized history, we can trace a remarkable continuity of tales reflecting the symbiosis of genius and madness. The literature inspired by these tales has sought to understand this inscrutable marriage by posing such questions as: Are geniuses divinely inspired? Is genius something that can be cultivated or perhaps harnessed like a beast of draught? If the roots of genius are intrinsic to the human condition, inspired by God, madness, or some other mysterious force, is genius a gift that is inaccessible to the uninspired?

These queries pose several interesting dilemmas: Why should a feature of human behavior so (seemingly) critical to the advancement of the species be restricted to so small a segment of the population? Why would the curse of mental illness be wed to the gift of genius? It certainly would not appear to be adaptive from an evolutionary perspective to yoke mental illness to the extraordinary gifts of highly creative people.

After more than 2,500 years of speculation, we can conclude very little that is definitive. We cannot state with certainty that some genetic contribution enhances creative potential. We cannot state with certainty how creativity can be encouraged, although we undoubtedly can state how it may be discouraged. Despite endless tales and anecdotal reports, some farfetched and some true, relating creativity to mental illness, the idea that one must be slightly mad to be creative is so counterintuitive that it is rejected by most sober-minded scientists.

The crucial question, I would argue, is not whether creativity and mental illness are causally linked but whether a correlative association between presumptive mental illness and creativity in a small, highly selected group of individuals offers us any insight into the mechanics of creativity. Does the proposition, be it true or false, that an unusually high percentage of extraordinarily gifted people were mentally ill help us in any way to comprehend the creative process?

I have proposed elsewhere (Prentky, 1979, 1980, 1989) that the coincidental association between creativity and real emotional turmoil in a parade of remarkable, highly celebrated individuals may provide,

Correspondence and requests for reprints should be sent to R. A. Prentky, Justice Resource Institute, The Massachusetts Treatment Center, Bridgewater, MA 02324.

in a serendipitous fashion, an important key to unlocking one of the secrets of their creativity . It has never been my thesis that mental illness is a prerequisite for creativity. Rather, I have proposed that a fruitful theoretical model for understanding the creative process may be in terms of cognitive style (i.e., mode of information processing) and that a genetic predisposition to certain forms of mental illness may be associated with a cognitive style similar to that which promotes creativity. If there is one feature that characterizes all highly creative people, it is the unique manner in which they apprehend their world (i.e., they see things, experience things, or conclude things that the rest of us do not). One of the Schneiderian first-rank symptoms of psychosis is thought disorder, a distortion in the way that information is assembled, processed, and interpreted. One feature that characterizes all individuals diagnosed as psychotic is a disorder in the processing of information. Thus, a cardinal feature of both creativity and mental illness is an aberration or deviation in the way that information is processed. Highly creative people turn into a distinct and productive asset what mentally disturbed people blindly grope for: the ability to absorb and efficiently process information from the environment. The majority of us seem to find sufficient light in the tunnel to navigate without excessive fumbling, although we are rarely blessed with that sudden illumination that, for a split second, makes everything clear. Severely mentally ill people seem to fall at one of two extremes, a constant blinding illumination or a black-out condition. The obvious parsimony of this analogy is intended only to provide a simple heuristic model for looking at two otherwise unrelated phenomena: creativity and mental illness.

In a delightful article on "Lunatics, Lovers, and Poets: On Madness and Creativity," Behrens (1975) concluded that "the difference between the schizophrenic act and the act of creation is the difference between Don Quixote (as madman) and author Cervantes (as poet). Madmen take metaphors literally, and the difference is one of awareness" (p. 232). Bronowski (1965) referred to the Pythagorean *geistesblitz* as "explosions of a hidden likeness" (p. 19), which the creator fuses two aspects of nature into one. In Behren's terms, Don Quixote's penchant was to see hidden likeness where likeness clearly did not reside. What we seek to understand is neither Quixote's madness nor Sancho Panza's straight vision of reality ("those which appear yonder are not giants, but windmills," as cited in Behrens, 1975, p. 229), but the genius of those who first thought of harnessing the wind on land using the same sails that harness the wind at sea.

A Historical Footnote

Alliances or misalliances between genius and psychosis have been noted in the literature for at least 2,300 years. One of the earliest references dates back to Aristotle's *Problemata* (cited in Ruelle, 1922): "Those who have become eminent in philosophy, politics, poetry, and the arts have all had tendencies toward melancholia." Aristotle may have had his eminent predecessor Socrates in mind. The first case study of genius was written about Socrates in 1836 by the psychiatrist Louis-Francois Lélut (*Du Demon de Socrate* [The Demon of Socrates]). Becker (1978) stated that "Socrates's inclination 'to take the inspirations of his conscience for the voice of a supernatural agent (his demon),' confirmed, in Lélut's opinion, that Socrates suffered from a 'most undeniable form of madness'" (p. 28). Gibson's (1889) observation was similar. He stated that, "Socrates, heathen though he was, was a great philosopher; yet it is credited of him that he acknowledged a tutelary genius or demon, who informed him of coming events and directed—probably in a measure controlled—his behavior" (p. 4).

Despite the often-noted association between *enthousiasmos* (enthusiasm or mania)—demonic possession or melancholia—and genius during antiquity, Greek madness is not equatable to modern notions of insanity. According to Aristotle, the *Homo melancholicus,* depending on humoral balance, could be divinely distinguished or mad. When black bile was not properly counterbalanced by blood, phlegm, and yellow bile, the result was depression and anxiety.

Some 2,000 years after Aristotle, the prevalent conception of genius was that it was allied with degeneracy. This notion was first set forth by Morel, who argued that degeneracy was a state of biological inferiority and that it was inherited. It was conceived that geniuses evolved from the same maladaptive gene pool as the lowliest elements of society, criminals and lunatics. Among many others who supported this degeneracy theory was the Italian criminologist Cesare Lombroso. The first systematic study of the relation between genius and insanity was published by Lombroso in 1864. Over a quarter of a century later,

Lombroso (1891) published his research in book form, concluding that genius was often a "degenerative psychosis of the epileptic group."

As noted, there is a long history of association between exceptional acts (however they were defined) and deviant behavior, ranging from eccentricity to psychosis. It is essential to keep in mind, however, that even informal psychiatric classification is inadvisable and, in most instances, impossible. Writers have had to rely on archival documents, third-person accounts, and anecdotes. Thus, resulting diagnoses, sometimes made several thousand years after the person was alive, are unreliable, imprecise, and certainly not compatible with modern nosology. Occasionally, writers even disagreed as to the mere presence of pathology. Such a case was Michelangelo, who was given a clean bill of health by Lombroso (1910) but was said to be melancholic by Tsanoff (1949).

A quick glance through the roster of those alleged to have been mentally disturbed may well leave one with the distinct impression that everyone who was anyone was afflicted. Current research does not support such a conclusion, and early studies may have been more "afflicted" than the presumptive geniuses they were examining. In Ellis's (1904) well-known study of British geniuses, for example, he found that out of 1,030 names drawn from the *Dictionary of National Biography* (Stephen & Lee, 1885–1900), only 44 (or 4.2%) had a demonstrable mental disorder. Obviously, this percentage would change somewhat if the *Diagnostic and Statistical Manual of Mental Disorders* (American Psychiatric Association, 1994) criteria were applied. To play devil's advocate, one may argue, of course, that the accomplishments of many of the individuals abstracted by Ellis and cited as examples of geniuses were an order of magnitude inferior (less creative, less exceptional, less revolutionary) to the accomplishments of the individuals most often cited as examples of disturbed geniuses.

These matters are, of course, moot. Perhaps the single most significant methodological issue undermining progress in research on creativity is the criterion problem. What creativity is, and what it is not, hangs as the mythical albatross around the neck of scientific research on creativity. The word *creativity* has been associated with everything from the scores of college students on paper-and-pencil measures to the greatest creations and most momentous discoveries in the history of humankind. Because the umbrella of creativity subsumes so diverse a domain of output, we could only rank order degrees of creativity by specifying how creativity was measured. It certainly would appear that the field of creativity could benefit from the uniform application of a single, operationalized construct or a complex, multifaceted construct that has been subjected to taxonomic differentiation.

Research on Cognitive Aspects of Creativity

The domain of research that has provided the most promise for yielding a metatheoretical bridge between mental illness and creativity is cognitive experimental psychopathology. Probably the most well-known area of research that falls within this domain involves convergent and divergent thinking styles. Creativity may derive from either thinking style and may do so with little or no regard to profession (e.g., artists and scientists may be divergent or convergent).

Similarities in cognitive styles between normals and psychotics have been discussed in detail by McConaghy (1960, 1961; McConaghy & Clancy, 1968). McConaghy (1960) distinguished two modes of thinking that reflect predispositions to psychosis. In one case, filtering mechanisms are impaired, thereby permitting the intrusion of irrelevant associations. Thought processes are vague, dominated by intuition. This disorder is said to affect about 10% of the population and may imply vulnerability to schizophrenia. In the other case, the capacity for making logical attributions is enhanced. Thus, once a conclusion is reached, it is adhered to with greater than normal devotion. In this instance, logic has been said to triumph over common sense, a condition that may predispose to paranoia.

McConaghy (1961) referred to the former mode of thinking as *allusive* (considered to be less pejorative than *loose*) and proposed that it may be observed in a wide variety of people, many of whom never become schizophrenic. Allusive thinking is characterized by imprecise (overabstract) and inappropriate speech (similar to overinclusion).

McConaghy's (1961) conceptualizations were based, in good measure, on the work of Pavlov (1955), who also distinguished two personality types. The artistic type, prone to hysterical or manic–depressive reactions, is intense, vivid, and highly responsive to external stimulation. The thinking type, prone to obsessive–compulsive and schizophrenic reactions, is quiet, ruminative, and hypersensitive to excessive stimulation. It was Pavlov's early writing that led McConaghy (1961), Claridge (1972), and others to attribute allusive thinking to weak levels of central nervous system inhibition resulting from low cortical excitability.

There is marked resemblance between the cognitive styles characterizing creative thought that Cattell and his colleagues (Cattell & Butcher, 1968; Cattell & Drevdahl, 1955) sought to define and the psychotic loosening (or tightening) of ideational boundaries that McConaghy (1960) described. In the latter case (McConaghy, 1960), the disorder may be called *overinclusion* or *underinclusion,* and in the former case (Cattell, 1966), the gift is called *creativity.* The presumptive difference among the divergent thinking, loose associations, and irrelevant themes of psychotics and the amazing conceptual leaps, cognitive flexibility, and serendipitous discoveries of creative artists and scientists is one of control. Psychotic thinking is unbridled and capricious, whereas creative thinking is rationally directed and purposeful. In sum, it appears that there is reason to suspect a continuity between normal and pathological thinking, a point convincingly argued by Claridge (1972). Thought disorder is not present or absent but measured dimensionally with numerous shades of gray. Thus, some features of psychotic thinking are also found in the general population, only in less severe or debilitating fashion. The existence of such cognitive styles may facilitate creativity as well as reflect a genetic predisposition to psychosis.

There is sparse, although interesting, evidence that associates the Claridge research with Guilford's research. Claridge, Canter, and Hume (1973) looked at personality variation in monozygotic and dizygotic twins, using an extensive battery of psychophysiological tests. The investigators defined a personality dimension of *psychoticism,* based on a principal components analysis of the psychophysiology data. They discovered, among other things, that psychoticism was related to scores on tests of Guilford's (e.g., 1966, 1968) divergent thinking. Woody and Claridge (1977) administered the Eysenck Personality Questionnaire (EPQ) and tests of divergent and convergent thinking to university students. The association of divergent thinking with psychoticism (on the EPQ) was strongly confirmed, although the hypothesis of an inverse relation between psychoticism and convergent thinking was not.

Over the past several decades, there has been a strong attraction to the concept of divergent thinking as an operational construct for defining creativity. It is a clean, simple concept and can be measured easily with a variety of different tests. Additionally, anecdotal reports seem to suggest that something like divergence captures the essence of creativity. This enthusiasm survives despite Guilford's (1970, 1971) own note of caution, as well as the research, indicating that divergent thinking does not correlate highly with creativity. There are at least three possible explanations: (a) Divergent thinking is only one of several independent cognitive styles that facilitate creativity, (b) divergent thinking interacts with another style (e.g., convergent thinking), or (c) the criteria used to measure creativity failed to capture the intended behavior.

A significant contribution to our understanding of the relation between creativity and information processing comes from the research of Martindale and his colleagues (e.g., Martindale & Armstrong, 1974; Martindale & Hasenfus, 1978; Martindale & Hines, 1975; Martindale, Hines, Mitchell, & Covello, 1984). They accumulated evidence that relates creativity (as measured in college students using the Remote Associates Test and the Alternate Uses Test; cf. Mednick & Mednick, 1967) to low levels of cortical activation, variability in level of activation, and disinhibition. The conclusion drawn by Martindale and Hines (1975) that associated disinhibition with creativity appears to be consistent with expectation. *Disinhibition,* or dehabituation, is the use of a novel stimulus to revive a habituated orientation reaction. It was a phenomenon ascribed by Pavlov (1955) to dissipation of inhibition.

Martindale (1977–1978) hypothesized that primary process cognition is associated with either high or low arousal, whereas the secondary process is associated with medium arousal. In keeping with the classic inverted-U, efficient task performance is optimized at medium levels of arousal, with performance dropping off when arousal is too low or too high. It has been assumed in the past that as task difficulty increases, the optimal level of arousal decreases. This would suggest that low arousal favors creativity. Such a conclusion assumes that creativity has something to do with task complexity. It makes more sense to suppose that in cases where a need for solitude is a prerequisite for creative inspiration, low arousal is facilitatory. As Martindale pointed out, even the often-noted listlessness of creative individuals can be attributed to either high or low arousal. Martindale et al. (1984) hypothesized that creativity involved the use of primary process cognition that would be accompanied by right hemisphere activation. Three studies supported the hypothesis that highly creative students would exhibit greater right hemisphere than left hemisphere activity during creative activity, as measured by the electroencephalogram. It is not possible in this brief article to do justice to Martindale's research; however, the findings from his studies draw support from many quarters, including the literatures on evoked responses, lateralization, and hemispheric deficit and input regulation.

A Neurocognitive Model

At this point, we may fairly conclude that creativity and major mental illness (i.e., psychosis) are not causally related. As Ornstein (1997) commented, "there is a similarity between schizophrenic thought and creative thought, but it is conceptual, not real" (p. 128). The conceptual similarity, according to Ornstein, is that departures from convention may reveal new possibilities. Thus, the crucial question is not whether creativity and mental illness are causally linked but whether our understanding of mental illness offers insight into the creative process. Out of the total pool of, for example, highly creative (e.g., award-winning) writers, if the number who were demonstrably disturbed exceeds the base rate for that disturbance in the general population, the (possibly) coincidental association between creativity and disturbance in those cases invites plausible explanation.

I have, on prior occasions (Prentky, 1980, 1989), been so intrepid (or foolhardy) as to advance a theoretical model based on a neurocognitive view of thought process. I proposed that there is a normally distributed, information processing continuum ranging from extreme constriction to extreme expansion. The overlap between extraordinary creativity and mental illness lies somewhere at the tails of this continuum. Marked deviation toward either extreme results in thought disorder, whereas some hypothetical optimum deviation promotes creativity without high risk of major mental illness. When this optimum deviation slides farther out into one of the tails of the distribution, normality slips into abnormality. The notion of an optimum deviation was implicit in Ornstein's (1997) remark that "it is interesting to note that among the relatives of schizophrenics are many highly creative people, perhaps indicating that a small amount of disorganized thought is very helpful but too much can cause severe problems" (p. 129).

Because creative people "live" farther from the hypothetical norm and, hence, are closer to the fringes of deviation, there may be a higher incidence of psychopathology among this group. This increased incidence of psychopathology would most often be manifested in characterological depression or behavioral eccentricities or perhaps "peculiarities," in Berenbaum's (1995) terminology. Although such eccentricities, depending on their nature, may reflect a genetic predisposition to major mental illness, such a proposition remains in the realm of speculation. The notion that disordered thinking falls along a continuum with normal thinking and that thought disorders are not discrete entities bearing no relation to orderly thinking is, of course, not new. Well over 20 years ago, Harrow and Quinlan (1977) and others expressed such views.

I further proposed that the hypothetical optimum deviation toward constriction or expansion of sensory input defined two distinct profiles, each of which possessed identifiable cognitive, physiological, and clinical characteristics (Prentky, 1980). Each hypothetical profile was intended to capture a unique constellation of characteristics that promoted different forms of creativity.

One profile was labeled *A-type* (abstract). A-type is characterized by extensive scanning that often incorporates much peripheral, extraneous information, erratic mental "threshing" of large amounts of information, and a hyperalertness that facilitates the whole process. Such individuals possess "strong nervous systems" (Gray, 1967) that tend to resist (reduce or dampen) stimulation and habituate to stimuli so rapidly that they often pay little or no attention to prior stimuli. In a task situation, one would expect rapid performance with many errors. It was predicted that the A-type would evidence a weak attentional focus, high distractibility, low input registration, easy attentional shift, and relatively poor (diffuse, broad) selection.

Clinically, one may expect to find affective symptoms, such as lability and depression and, in more severe cases, symptoms of major depression or possibly schizoid symptoms (e.g., solitary, emotionally cold and detached, flat affect, lack of close friends, generally anhedonic). In general, a negative symptom picture, characterized by flat affect, avolition, and anhedonia, would be expected. In the case of psychosis, one again would expect primarily negative symptoms (e.g., flat or negative affect, social withdrawal, anhedonia, lack of motivation, blocking). Negative symptoms tend to be associated with higher right than left hemispheric activity (Gruzelier & Raine, 1994), and overactivation of the right hemisphere or underactivation of the left hemisphere was hypothesized in this case.

A-type creativity is characterized by the accumulation of the widest possible array of information. This smorgasbord of data is then harvested, with a keen eye to uncovering previously unobserved relations. If the search is fruitful, and subsequent input bears out the validity of the observation (or contribution), the discovery (or product) is often relegated to the mystical realm of intuition because no systematic effort immediately preceded it. Robinson and Sabat (1977) metaphorically equated the nervous system to radar. In their terms, the A-type functions in a broad-band "coasting" mode, responding with reduced resolution to a wide variety of input.

The second profile was labeled *C-type* (concrete). C-type is characterized by the tendency to underinclude or constrict the attentional field. Such individuals possess weak nervous systems that tend to augment or magnify stimulation and habituate to stimuli so slowly that they may appear, at the behavioral level, obsessive–compulsive. In a task situation, one would expect slow performance with few errors. It was predicted that C-type individuals would evidence a strong attentional focus, low or normal distractibility, high input registration, and difficult attentional shift.

Clinically, one may expect, in more severe cases, to see schizotypal symptoms (e.g., odd, eccentric, or peculiar behavior, odd or strange beliefs, ideas of reference, odd thinking [metaphorical, overelaborate ideas], acute social anxiety, lack of close friends, constricted affect). In the event of psychosis, one would expect primarily positive symptoms (e.g., hallucinations, delusions, loose associations, bizarre behavior, pressured speech) and a diagnosis of schizophrenia. Positive symptoms, as Gruzelier and Raine (1994) reported, are associated with higher left than right hemispheric activity, supporting the hypothesis that general overactivation of the left hemisphere or underactivation of the right hemisphere characterizes the C-type. Thus, there is a hypothetical optimal hemispheric imbalance that promotes a constructive, task-specific hyperfocus on detail and facilitates problem solving but does not seriously incapacitate or debilitate the individual. A continuum of severity of cognitive deficits was further supported by Raine, Benishay, Lencz, and Scarpa (1997), who reported that schizophrenics, relatives of schizophrenics, and those diagnosed as schizotypal all evidence similar information processing deficits.

C-type creativity is characterized by a microscopic, dissectional focus on the separate constituent elements of a problem. The hypothesized C-type approach to problem solving is to zero in on detail, observing critical relations or unexpected but meaningful anomalies. Again, the "magic" of intuition arises when no logical explanation suffices. I have argued that the fortuitous association between formerly unrelated elements is no less important to C-type than to A-type. In Robinson and Sabat's (1977) terms, the C-type functions under the most band-limited conditions and is thus least variable in response to sequential input.

The cognitive deficits of schizophrenics are consistent with this characterization of C-type. Cutting (1985) noted, for instance, that schizophrenics "concentrate on detail, at the expense of theme" (p. 300). Knight (1984) concluded that schizophrenics show "some deficiency in perceptual schema formation, in automaticity, or in the holistic stage of processing" (p. 120). It was hypothesized that in the "normal" case (i.e., balanced, interhemispheric communication), there is an optimum regulation of input that provides for maximally efficient information processing and, parenthetically, may reduce the likelihood both of psychiatric disorder and extraordinary creativity. As argued, there is also an optimum deviation from this normative regulation of input that increases the likelihood of A-type or C-type cognition whereas still permitting adequate filtering of stimuli. Too much deviation, in the form of extreme abstraction or concretization, may manifest itself as psychotic thought disorder.

Ornstein's Hypothesis

In Ornstein's (1997) latest book, *The Right Mind,* he explored the role of lateralized specialization and interhemispheric communication in schizophrenia. The "split-mind" name associated with the condition of schizophrenia may, after all, apply, not because schizophrenics are split from reality (the popular myth) but because there is a fundamental problem in how the hemispheres communicate (a different type of split). Ornstein proposed that schizophrenics have a right hemisphere deficit, a decrease in the balance of input from the right hemisphere. This condition may come about as a result of "diminished activity of the right hemisphere itself, increased left hemisphere activity, a lack of interhemispheric communication and cooperation, or a mix of all three" (p. 127). Ornstein pointed out that right hemisphere deficits in children have been associated with solitariness, "weirdness," problems with expressing emotions, and interpersonal difficulties in adulthood. Ornstein concluded his brief overview of the literature by noting that "the simplest theory to explain all of the abnormalities is that there is a basic malfunction in deep, subcortical areas that control activity and attention and integrate the functions of the left and right hemispheres" (p. 136).

What Ornstein (1997) proposed would seem to be fundamentally compatible with the neurocognitive model of creativity presented in this article. The C-type is more likely characterized by a right hemisphere deficit (or overactivation of the left hemisphere), resulting in focal attention to detail and a generalized inability to capture the large picture. As Ornstein noted, overactivation of the left hemisphere may result, in extreme cases, "in an overinterpretation of isolated bits of reality, seeing patterns where there are none" (p. 139). In less extreme cases (e.g., less interhemispheric incongruity), this deficit that potentially is so disruptive to normal cognition may facilitate certain types of creativity. Conversely, the A-type is more likely characterized by a left hemisphere deficit (or overactivation of the right hemisphere), resulting in poor attention to detail but a superior ability to grasp complex integrated patterns (i.e., recognize the gestalt).

Creativity and Affective Disorders

A matter of consequential debate is whether creativity possesses a stronger heritable relation to affective disorders than to other forms of major mental illness (principally schizopnrenia). As I noted earlier, the association between melancholia and genius can easily be traced far back into antiquity, and the empirical research of Andreasen and her colleagues (e.g., Andreasen, 1980; Andreasen & Canter, 1974; Andreasen & Powers, 1975) and Jamison and her colleagues (e.g., Goodwin & Jamison, 1990; Jamison, Gerner, & Goodwin, 1979; Jamison, Gerner, Hammen, & Padesky, 1980) certainly supports the observation that if creative writers and poets are afflicted, the disturbance is likely to be expressed through affective symptoms. Indeed, the clinical literature does seem to suggest that a large number of well-known writers, poets, and philosophers were reputed to have some affective disturbance (e.g., Kafka, Rousseau, Coleridge, Johnson, Mill, Poe, Woolf, Crane). That same literature, however, alleges that others (e.g., Byron, Heine, Pascal, Swift, Strindberg, Baudelaire) evidenced symptoms that would be more associated with schizophrenia. It certainly would be foolhardy to accept at face value the reliability of any of these post hoc diagnoses. The important point is that there are no discrete nosological entities or even nosological categories (e.g., affective disorder) that capture all psychiatrically disturbed, highly creative individuals.

Given the current state of knowledge, it seems highly untenable to conclude that creativity has a greater affinity for manic–depressive illness than schizophrenia or vice versa. Psychosis is, without doubt, a highly heterogeneous domain of signs and symptoms. Schizophrenia and manic–depressive illness, the two principle forms of psychosis, are heterogeneous and nosologically complex. As such, it is artless, at best, to suggest that either schizophrenia or manic–depressive illness has a corner on the market of creativity.

There are several possible explanations for the apparently disproportionate number of creative individuals with depressive symptoms. One explanation is the course of symptoms. Although obviously there are substantial individual differences, Gray, Feldon, Rawlins, Hemsley, and Smith (1991) pointed out that "there is a tendency for positive symptoms to decrease and negative symptoms to become more prominent over time" (p. 5). Thus, the negative symptoms associated with A-type (e.g., flat or negative affect, social withdrawal, anhedonia) may have a longer life than the positive symptoms associated with C-type (e.g., bizarre behavior, hallucinations, delusions).

A second explanation is the base rates for different psychiatric disorders, which vary considerably. The general population base rates for schizophrenia and bipolar disorder are generally around 1% to 2% and 0.5% to 1%, respectively. The lifetime rate for major depression in the United States, however, is around 5% and is two to three times higher in Europe, ranging from 9.2% to 16.4% in Italy, France, and Germany (Weissman et al., 1996). Similarly, the general population base rate for schizotypy is about 10% (Lenzenweger & Korfine, 1992). Thus, the latent liabilities, in Meehl's terms, for major depression and for schizotypy are present at a considerably higher frequency in the general population than conditions diagnosable as psychotic (schizophrenia or bipolar illness). In particular, it appears that a predisposing vulnerability to major affective disorder, manifested primarily as depression, may have the highest population base rate of all serious Axis I psychiatric disorders.

When we control for psychosis, however, the affective "advantage" is less clear. That is, if we examined only those creative people who are diagnosable as psychotic, it is not at all clear that most of them would be classified with an affective psychosis. To play devil's advocate, however, one could argue that this argument is begging the question. That is, the critical issue is not a positive history for psychosis but a symptom picture that is predominantly affective.

Genetic and Eugenic Considerations

A dilemma was posed at the beginning of this article: Why should a feature of human behavior that seemingly is so critical to the advancement of the species be restricted to so small a segment of the species? The tendency of the human species is to resist change, both genetically and socioculturally. To let up on the biological brakes that regulate extraordinary creativity may threaten the delicate adaptational balance of the species. This would tend to explain the otherwise inexplicable eruption of creativity at isolated moments in history, each moment being separated by long periods of adjustment. This line of reasoning implies, of course, that there is some biological or genetic underpinning to extraordinary creativity. Darlington (1969) argued, in this regard, that an entire epoch of human inspiration and talent, the golden age of Athens, was attributable to genetics. The forces of heredity alone contrived to initiate (and conclude) that remarkable period of intellectual development. Darlington may have been correct, but it is all speculation. There is no way of determining the influence of Athenian genes independent of the current zeitgeist. Indeed, Pickering (1974) maintained that the achievements of Periclean Athens were attributed to "the peace of mind allowed by good government" and "intellectual freedom and the consequent encouragement to entertain new ideas, and new art forms" (p. 276). In sum, evidence supporting higher rates of illness in the biological parents or offspring of gifted participants may imply a diathesis for that illness and suggest nothing about the (possibly) coincidental appearance of creativity.

My focus has been on the presumed similarities between creative cognition and deviant cognition that reflects a predisposition to psychosis. Preceding discussion presented two lines of argument: In one case that there is a hypothetical genetic basis to extraordinary creativity, and in the other case that there is a genetic basis to, and possibly a selective advantage for, a predisposition to psychosis. If there is a common biological thread linking creativity with forms of major mental illness, such a thread may be cognition. Thus, we may infer that certain biologically conceived cognitive styles that are peculiar to extraordinary creativity possess common biological ancestry with certain cognitive styles that are associated with a predisposition to major mental illness. Although it is not intuitively (or empirically) obvious that there may be a selective advantage for certain forms of psychosis, the concept itself helps to explain another riddle presented at the beginning of this article, namely, how could it be adaptive, from an evolutionary standpoint, to wed the curse of mental illness to the gift of creativity? The outcome of major mental illness remains a curse for the afflicted and cannot be assumed, in any respect, to be adaptive. There are those who have argued, however, that normal individuals who carry the abnormal gene without manifest psychosis do in fact have some selective advantage (e.g., Jarvik & Chadwick, 1973; Jarvik & Deckard, 1977). Thus, although it makes little sense to wed the outcome of mental illness to creativity, it may make sense to wed a predisposition to mental illness (i.e., normal carriers of the aberrant gene) to creativity.

Concluding Comments

I have not proposed that creativity and mental illness coexist harmoniously. As mental illness begins to intrude, creativity typically recedes into the background. In fact, the stress occasionally associated with creativity may help to precipitate a psychiatric breakdown. As Kuhn (1970) observed, there are those who "have undoubtedly been driven to desert science because of their inability to tolerate crisis" (pp. 78–79). As I indicated at the outset, consideration of the relation of mental illness to creativity serves primarily a heuristic purpose. That is, the high incidence of cases in which there is a presumptive co-occurrence of extraordinary creativity and mental illness, may, in keeping with the Persian fable about the three princes of Serendip (Remer, 1965), inform our understanding of the elusive phenomenon that we call creativity.

I have proposed a neurocognitive model for understanding noteworthy creative achievements. The model suggests that the normal range of input regulation is distorted by imbalances in hemispheric activity, resulting in two very different data processing strategies that enhance or facilitate creative solutions to problems. Because these imbalances are often associated with genetic predispositions to mental illness, there is a greater-than-chance probability that highly creative individuals may evidence signs or symptoms associated with mental illness. It should be manifestly evident, however, that the hemispheres of the brain do not operate independently of each other and that neither can do the job, certainly not the optimal job, without the other (Ornstein, 1997). Thus, although some imbalance may favor creativity, cross-talk is, arguably, essential for optimizing creative output.

The model that I described in this article and discussed in more detail elsewhere (Prentky, 1980, 1989) represents, however, nothing more than an unsubstantiated theory. What is vitally important is an empirical strategy that (a) addresses the seemingly intractable methodological problems associated with research on creativity, (b) is guided by theory, (c) precisely defines the domain that qualifies as creativity, (d) identifies and specifies the qualities that differentiate creative from noncreative output, and (e) tests theory-driven hypotheses about how creative individuals differ from their less creative counterparts. In sum, what is needed in research on cognitive deficits that facilitate creativity is the kind of process-oriented strategy (Knight, 1984; Knight & Silverstein, 1998) that has been fruitfully applied to research on cognitive deficits in schizophrenia.

References

American Psychiatric Association. (1994). *Diagnostic and statistical manual of mental disorders* (4th ed.). Washington, DC: Author.

Andreasen, N. J. C. (1980). Mania and creativity. In R. H. Belmaker & H. M. Van Praage (Eds.), *Mania: An evolving concept* (pp. 377–386). New York: Spectrum.

Andreasen, N. J. C., & Canter, A. (1974). The creative writer: Psychiatric symptoms and family history. *Comprehensive Psychiatry, 15,* 123–131.

Andreasen, N. J. C., & Powers, P. S. (1975). Creativity and psychosis: An examination of conceptual style. *Archives of General Psychiatry, 32,* 70–73.

Becker, G. (1978). *The mad genius controversy.* Beverly Hills, CA: Sage.

Behrens, R. R. (1975). Lunatics, lovers, and poets: On madness and creativity. *Journal of Creative Behavior, 9,* 228–232.

Berenbaum, H. (1995). Peculiarities. In C. G. Costello (Ed.), *Personality characteristics of the personality disordered* (pp. 206–241). New York: Wiley.

Bronowski, J. (1965). *Science and human values.* New York: Harper & Row.

Cattell, R. B. (1966). The personality and motivation of the researcher from measurements of contemporaries and from biography. In C. W. Taylor & F. Barrons (Eds.), *Scientific creativity: Its recognition and development* (pp. 119–131). New York: Wiley.

Cattell, R. B., & Butcher, H. J. (1968). *The prediction of achievement and creativity.* Indianapolis, IN: Bobbs-Merrill.

Cattell, R. B., & Drevdahl, J. E. (1955). A comparison of the personality profile of eminent researchers with that of eminent teachers and administrators of the general population. *British Journal of Psychology, 46,* 248–261.

Claridge, G. (1972). The schizophrenias as nervous types. *British Journal of Psychiatry, 121,* 1–17.

Claridge, G., Canter, S., & Hume, W. I. (1973). *Personality differences and biological variations: A study of twins.* Oxford, England: Pergamon.

Cutting, J. (1985). *The psychology of schizophrenia.* London: Churchill.

Darlington, C. D. (1969). *The evolution of man and society.* London: Allen & Unwin.

Ellis, H. (1904). *A study of British genius.* London: Hurst & Blackett.

Gibson, C. (1889). *The characteristics of genius: A popular essay.* London: Walter Scott.

Goodwin, F. K., & Jamison, K. R. (1990). Manic-depressive illness, creativity, and leadership. In F. K. Goodwin & K. R. Jamison (Eds.), *Manic-depressive illness* (pp. 332–367). Oxford, England: Oxford University Press.

Gray, J. A. (1967). Strength of the nervous system, introversion–extraversion, and conditionability and arousal. *Behavior Research and Therapy, 5,* 151–169.

Gray, J. A., Feldon, J., Rawlins, J. N. P., Hemsley, D. R., & Smith, A. D. (1991). The neuropsychology of schizophrenia. *Behavioral and Brain Sciences, 14,* 1–20.

Gruzelier, J., & Raine, A. (1994). Bilateral electrodermal activity and cerebral mechanisms in syndromes of schizophrenia and the schizotypal personality. *International Journal of Psychophysiology, 16,* 1–16.

Guilford, J. P. (1966). Intellectual resources and their values as seen by scientists. In C. W. Taylor & F. Barron (Eds.), *Scientific creativity: Its recognition and development* (pp. 101–114). New York: Wiley.

Guilford, J. P. (1968). *Intelligence, creativity, and their educational implications.* San Diego, CA: Knapp.

Guilford, J. P. (1970). Creativity: Retrospect and prospect. *Journal of Creative Behavior, 4,* 149–168.

Guilford, J. P. (1971). Some misconceptions regarding measurement of creative talents. *Journal of Creative Behavior, 5,* 77–87.

Harrow, M., & Quinlan, D. (1977). Is disordered thinking unique to schizophrenia? *Archives of General Psychiatry, 34,* 15–21.

Jamison, K. R., Gerner, R. H., & Goodwin, F. K. (1979). Patient and physician attitudes toward lithium. *Archives of General Psychiatry, 36,* 866–869.

Jamison, K. R., Gerner, R. H., Hammen, C., & Padesky, C. (1980). Clouds and silver linings: Positive experiences associated with primary affective disorders. *American Journal of Psychiatry, 137,* 198–202.

Jarvik, L. F., & Chadwick, S. B. (1973). Schizophrenia and survival. In M. Hammer, K. Salzinger, & S. Sutton (Eds.), *Psychopathology: Contributions from the social, behavioral sciences* (pp. 57–73). New York: Wiley.

Jarvik, L. F., & Deckard, B. S. (1977). The odyssean personality: A survival advantage for carriers of genes predisposing to schizophrenia? *Neuropsychobiology, 3,* 179–191.

Knight, R. A. (1984). Converging models of cognitive deficit in schizophrenia. In W. D. Spaulding & J. K. Cole (Eds.), *Nebraska symposium on motivation, 1983: Theories of schizophrenia and psychosis* (pp. 93–156). Lincoln: University of Nebraska Press.

Knight, R. A., & Silverstein, S. M. (1998). The role of cognitive psychology in guiding research on cognitive deficits in schizophrenia: A process-oriented approach. In M. Lenzenweger & R. Dworkin (Eds.), *Origins and development of schizophrenia: Advances in experimental psychopathology* (pp. 247–295). Washington, DC: American Psychological Association.

Kuhn, T. S. (1970). *The structure of scientific revolutions.* Chicago: University of Chicago Press.

Lenzenweger, M. F., & Korfine, L. (1992). Confirming the latent structure and base rate of schizotypy: A taxometric analysis. *Journal of Abnormal Psychology, 101,* 567–571.

Lombroso, C. (1891). *The man of genius.* London: Walter Scott.

Lombroso, C. (1910). *The man of genius* (2nd ed.). New York: Scribner's.

Martindale, C. (1977–1978). Creativity, consciousness, and cortical arousal. *Journal of Altered States of Consciousness, 3,* 69–87.

Martindale, C., & Armstrong, J. (1974). The relationship of creativity to cortical activation and its operant control. *Journal of General Psychology, 124,* 311–320.

Martindale, C., & Hasenfus, N. (1978). EEG differences as a function of creativity, stage of the creative process, and effort to be original. *Biological Psychology, 6,* 157–167.

Martindale, C., & Hines, D. (1975). Creativity and cortical activation during creative, intellectual and EEG feedback tasks. *Biological Psychology, 3,* 91–100.

Martindale, C., Hines, D., Mitchell, L., & Covello, E. (1984). EEG alpha asymmetry and creativity. *Personality and Individual Differences, 5,* 77–86.

McConaghy, N. (1960). Modes of abstract thinking and psychosis. *American Journal of Psychiatry, 117,* 106–110.

McConaghy, N. (1961). The measurement of an inhibitory process in human higher nervous activity: Its relation to allusive thinking and fatigue. *American Journal of Psychiatry, 118,* 125–132.

McConaghy, N., & Clancy, M. (1968). Familial relationships of allusive thinking in university students and their parents. *British Journal of Psychiatry, 114,* 1079–1087.

Mednick, S. A., & Mednick, M. T. (1967). *Remote Associates Test: Examiner's manual.* Boston: Houghton Mifflin.

Ornstein, R. (1997). *The right mind.* New York: Harcourt Brace.

Pavlov, I. P. (1955). *Selected works* (S. Belsky, Trans.). Moscow: Foreign Languages.

Pickering, G. (1974). *Creative malady.* New York: Oxford University Press.

Prentky, R. A. (1979). Creativity and psychopathology: A neurocognitive perspective. In B. A. Maher (Ed.), *Progress in experimental personality research* (Vol. 9, pp. 1–39). New York: Academic.

Prentky, R. A. (1980). *Creativity and psychopathology: A neurocognitive perspective.* New York: Praeger.

Prentky, R. A. (1989). Creativity and psychopathology: Gambolling at the seat of madness. In J. A. Glover, R. R. Ronning, & C. R. Reynolds (Eds.), *Handbook of creativity: Assessment, research, and theory* (pp. 243–269). New York: Plenum.

Raine, A., Benishay, D., Lencz, T., & Scarpa, A. (1997). Abnormal orienting in schizotypal personality disorder. *Schizophrenia Bulletin, 23,* 75–82.

Remer, T. G. (1965). *Serendipity and the three princes.* Norman: Oklahoma University Press.

Robinson, D. N., & Sabat, S. R. (1977). Neuroelectric aspects of information processing by the brain. *Neuropsychologia, 15,* 625–641.

Ruelle, C. A. (Ed.). (1922). *Aristotelis quae feruntur problemata physica.* Lipsiae: B. G. Teubneri.

Stephen, L., & Lee, S. (Eds.). (1885–1900). *The dictionary of national biography* (Vol. 1). London: Smith Elder.

Tsanoff, R. A. (1949). *The ways of genius.* New York: Harper & Brothers.

Weissman, M. M., Bland, R. C., Canino, G. J., Faravelli, C., Greenwald, S., Hwu, H.-G., Joyce, P. R., Karam, E. G., Lee, C.-K., Lellouch, J., Lepine, J.-P., Newman, S. C., Rubino-Stipec, M., Wells, E., Wickramaratne, P. J., Wittchen, H.-U., & Yeh, E.-K. (1996). Cross-national epidemiology of major depression and bipolar disorder. *Journal of the American Medical Association, 276,* 293–299.

Woody, E., & Claridge, G. (1977). Psychoticism and thinking. *British Journal of Social and Clinical Psychology, 16,* 241–248.

Creativity Research Journal
2000–2001, Vol. 13, No. 1, 105–110

COMMENT

Creativity and Psychopathology: Categories, Dimensions, and Dynamics

David Schuldberg
The University of Montana

The articles in the previous section (Becker, 2000–2001; Ogilvie, 2000–2001; Prentky, 2000–2001; Sass, 2000–2001) present programmatic arguments regarding the relation between the symptoms of schizophrenia, as well as other mental disorders, and the processes of creativity. In addition, these articles develop important lines of reasoning from Becker's (1978), Prentky's (1980; see also 1979, 1989), and Sass's (1992, 1994) influential books in this field. In this concluding commentary, I address, selectively, some of the issues raised in these articles; I also suggest connections to additional current work. I end by making a case for further consideration of one of my own interests, dynamical systems conceptions of creativity.

Comments on Becker (2000–2001)

Becker (2000–2001) developed some of the ideas in his seminal, important (1978) book, *The Mad Genius Controversy: A Study in the Sociology of Deviance.* A sociological critique such as this one keeps us, as psychologists, honest, representing a tonic to the individualistic, medically focused approaches so familiar to us. It trenchantly calls into question too-facile interpretations of observed correlations between one socially embedded, socially defined phenomenon and another. At the minimum (and it does much more), Becker's (2000–2001) article is a reminder to psychologists to engage in open-systems thinking.

Becker (2000–2001) views deviance in general—and this includes both creativity and madness—in social–functional terms, in the context of the induction of, adherence to, and performance of roles. The characteristics of both madness and genius are presented as self-fulfilling prophecies deriving from expectations tied to particular roles, roles that have served particular ends. In this view, the genius–madness connection emerges as largely artefactual, an only-apparent relation between two phenomena (or really between two facets of the same phenomenon: the artist's self-conception) deriving from the same social demand characteristics.

For example, Becker (2000–2001) raises the likelihood of inadvertent volunteering of symptoms by artists in psychiatric interviews, due to their adoption and enactment of the romantic view of creativity and psychopathology. He also argues that such a romantic position precludes the coexistence, in the same individual, of health and creativity. This romantic position is one that many would now dispute, as there are a variety of new visions of creativity as a component of health (see chapters in Runco & Richards, 1997; see also Rogers's, 1961, formulation).

Becker's (2000–2001) analysis raises some additional questions. First, what is to be said about the genuine suffering of either the artist or the person with severe mental illness? Is there such a thing, or is this all elaborate play acting, albeit perhaps method play acting, with true feeling? This touches on an old question regarding the extent to which psychopathological symptoms are unconscious or involuntary. The difference between a behavioral symptom of mental disor-

Correspondence and requests for reprints should be sent to David Schuldberg, Department of Psychology, The University of Montana, Missoula, MT 59812–1584. E-mail: py_das@selway.umt.edu.

der and merely "bad" or even malingered behavior has classically made reference to the often unsubstantiated status of the symptom as outside of the patient's awareness or control. This position has been famously disputed by Szasz (1974) and others, and of course, involuntary phenomena can be induced socially, as occurs in hypnosis. Becker does leave open, in the last pages of his article, the question of whether the phenomena of creativity and mental disorder may be other than entirely role related.

Sociological approaches to deviance (e.g., labeling theory) share some of the features of postmodernist relativism and skepticism; we can be left wondering whether there is such a thing as real madness or real creativity. (See Sass's, 2000–2001, questioning of Martindale's and others' definitions of creativity, which include notions of utility, at the beginning of his article. Usefulness is a socially embedded construct, and invoking it does not make defining creativity any easier.) Even if these phenomena are genuine, we may wonder whether we can definitively detect and identify them or uncover real linkages between them.

As I read this article (Becker, 2000–2001), I wondered whether the strategy of studying subclinical traits and subeminent creativity may allow researchers to finesse this role-theoretic critique by lessening the effects of role adherence on individuals' self-report. In other words, by taking a methodological approach that embraces dimensional rather than categorical views of both creativity and psychopathological symptoms, might it be possible to study less "dramatic" phenomena that are not explainable as forms of adoption of the full-blown roles?

On the other hand, the phenomena of role adherence and conformity may seem inescapable in any behavior or at any level of measurement. At the level of psychometric assessment of traits and creative functioning, social desirability (Edwards, 1970) does seem potentially to be an important factor in self-report. Walsh, Tomlinson-Kesey, and Klieger (1974) demonstrated that social desirability, defined as "a general explanation for item endorsements in terms of social normative processes" (Walsh, 1990, p. 290) is learned early. Thus, there can be learning and induction of quite small changes in behavior, more microscopic than the behaviors characterizing a full-blown role or syndrome; such learned modes of responding can mask measurable individual characteristics, if these even exist.

Nevertheless, a preliminary examination of some of my own data indicates that a Minnesota Multiphasic Personality Inventory–2 (Butcher, Dahlstrom, Graham, Tellegen, & Kaemmer, 1989) version of Edwards's (1970) Social Desirability scale is virtually uncorrelated with such paper-and-pencil creativity measures as the Revised Art Scale (Welsh & Barron, 1963), the How Do You Think (Davis & Subkoviak, 1975), and Richards's (Richards, Kinney, Lunde, Benet, & Merzel, 1988) Peak and Extent Vocational and Avocational Lifetime creativity ratings. This does lend support to the possibility that studying microscopic processes and less extreme forms of deviance can get around some of the problems Becker (2000–2001) raises. Indeed, we can even think of some psychometric creativity scores as positively desired or social desirable neutral measures of otherwise psychopathological traits. We do need, however, to learn more about the microinduction of microroles or the induction of components of roles (part roles). This is a fruitful line of inquiry for experimental social psychological methods in the study of creativity.

As a final word, I was left, after reading Becker's (2000–2001) article, wondering whether there is ever such a thing as nonconformity. Is every act a performance or role enactment for some audience?

Comments on Sass (2000–2001)

Sass's (2000–2001) article attempts to counter the denigration of schizophrenia inherent in focusing on the disorder as comprising deficits or regression. His approach takes us into contemporary territory in the study of the phenomenology of subjects with schizophrenia, including examining the positive aspects of so-called negative symptoms (see Strauss, Rakfeldt, Harding, & Lieberman, 1989). Current interest in the atypical neuroleptic medications is also related to this reexamination of the scope of schizophrenic phenomenology.

I step aside for the moment and do not engage in addressing whether schizophrenia or the affective disorders are more associated with creative processes and activities, for my own preference is to attempt to catalog the multiple stylistic dimensions that come into play in both genius and madness. (Sass and I are really in accord on this.)

Sass (2000–2001) discusses Kuhnian paradigms and the distinction between the forms of creativity involved in normal and in nonnormal science. Scientific revolutions include a shattering of the conventional, a going beyond even inventive forms of business as usual. This brings up the romantic notion of the iconoclast and the question of whether there is a place for the revolutionary in cultural endeavors. Sass's treatment of these topics goes beyond romanticism to modernist and postmodernist aesthetics. There are, however, aspects of romanticism (e.g., images of the alienated artist) that persist in modernism as well.

For Sass (2000–2001; and this appears to be a point of contrast with Becker, 2000–2001), there are indeed such things as unconventionality and nonconformity, and he associates these more with schizophrenia than with bipolar traits. Sass mentions what he views as the conventionality of bipolar individuals, a characteristic that may be useful during periods of normal science but not, perhaps, for genre busting. Perhaps it takes a person with schizophrenic, schizotypal, or schizoid characteristics to really break a paradigm, to really leave the village.

The modernist metaphors concern fragmentation, calling to mind Wynne and Singer's (1963) fragmented form of schizophrenic thinking. This connects to another important point, namely, that the thought disorder of schizophrenia comes in a variety of forms, including combinatory as well as contaminatory varieties. As I noted elsewhere, this field awaits the definitive research uncovering the overlap among and distinctions between the specific disturbed modes of thought and language characteristic of manic and depressed affective states and positive and negative symptom schizophrenic-like states.

Thought disorder can also be observed and defined in a variety of domains, including association, category formation, set maintenance, use of context, concrete versus abstract thinking, bizarreness, and more. So too, creativity is observed in different forms and across a variety of domains, and it encompasses a number of cognitive processes. For example (see Ludwig, 1995), an ongoing question concerns the distinction between generativity and consolidation as components of creativity. *Generativity* refers to the inspired creation of new forms, genres, or ideas, whereas *consolidation* refers to the more secondary process activities of refinement, editing, polishing, and communicating (see Schuldberg, 1994). Sass (2000–2001) wants to emphasize the special kind of generativity characteristic of persons in the schizophrenia spectrum without, however, devaluing the inspiration of the romantic manic in certain genres or movements. His argument suggests that consolidation, however, may be especially characteristic of the more conventional and socially facile individual with bipolar disorder (or, perhaps, of narcissistic individuals). Finally, Sass discusses the importance of nonnarrative forms and the loss of temporal flow in the modern and postmodern visions, a topic that is discussed in more detail at the end of this commentary.

Comments on Ogilvie (2000–2001)

Ogilvie (2000–2001) turns around the perspective of the preceding two articles and provides a view of the desperately creative activity of the person with schizophrenia from the inside. He uses the philosophy of Wittgenstein (1953/1958) to provide this perspective from the other side of the lens or through the mirror into which we gaze when we see psychopathology as the obverse of "normal" life.

Ogilvie's (2000–2001) focus is on struggles involving everyday life and everyday language as phenomena to be inhabited or enjoyed. The lived-in everyday world is strikingly elusive in madness, and the therapeutic challenge in severe mental illness may be the facilitating of a return to the everyday world and not, as in mystical transcendence, a leaving of it. For example, one of the therapeutic issues that can be raised by medication concerns whether ingesting a substance (particularly a synthetic one) can return one to a "natural" state of presumed health (see Wright, 1994). Ogilvie's description of attempts to embrace the immanence of the mundane has elements of naturalism and perhaps even of primitivism, and in this respect, at least this view of health seeking has some affinities with one kind of romanticism (see Lovejoy, 1948).

Everyday life may be ordinary but not to the mad, who, along with the sick, are sometimes seen as inhabiting a different country, as Sontag (1977) put it, or as operating according to a distinct set of norms (Canguilhem, 1991). For the person with schizophrenia, mundane normality may be something that one must strive to attain. From the point of view of the person with schizophrenia (who is "doing philosophy" because he or she has no choice), philosophy consists of trying to get back inside, not getting outside. This is what one must do when one is already, in the language of jazz, outside or already an outsider.

Thus, the schizophrenic person (not unlike the philosopher Ludwig Wittgenstein) may be doing philosophy to regain the ordinary, seeking creative solutions to foundational matters and the basic problems of being. This puts a new twist on Szasz's (1974) view of mental disorders as "problems in living." These problems are at the same time mundane and foundational. The question becomes: How do I defocus enough to make my world real? Another question could perhaps be: How do I will myself out of bed in the morning (a meditation also considered by William James)? Finally, Ogilvie's (2000–2001) article emphasizes the importance in creativity of the struggle to return "home" (Schuldberg, 1994; see also Suleiman, 1998).

Comments on Prentky (2000–2001)

Prentky (2000–2001) stresses the role of cognitive processes, input regulation, and hemispheric imbalance, as well as the role of biology and ultimately of genetics in the creativity–madness question. He argues in favor of common factors in creativity and psychopathology rather than for a causal relation involving genius and madness. Essentially, he describes what Richards (1981) termed an "indirect, fully-mediated creativity-pathology relationship" (p. 313), what Prentky calls a "correlative association" rather than a causal relation.

Prentky (2000–2001) also argues for the dimensionality of thought disorder, the abnormal thought processes characterizing both schizophrenia and creativity. He mentions a two-way typology of information processing styles, and his article includes what he himself terms possibly "foolhardy" remarks regarding distinctive forms of thinking of constriction and expansion: his A- versus C-types of thinking. I would add that in his 1980 book, Prentky went farther than this and proposed a two-dimensional, four-cell typology. In my opinion, such conjectures are not foolhardy at all. Further study of information processing employing dynamic and systems formulations suggests the need for just such multidimensional models.

This part of Prentky's (2000–2001) article underlines the importance of multifactorial approaches to the genius–madness problem, also raising the possibility of another control or health-related factor or factors in creativity. Multidimensional models need not be limited to different types of thought disorder or affective symptoms; health or competence can also define one or more relevant dimensions. In this context, it is important to mention Barron's (1972) construct of ego strength and his important two-factor model of creativity that includes both schizotypal characteristics and ego strength.

Any consideration of multifactorial models invariably raises the question of how many factors there are, of how many independent variables are required for a parsimonious yet reasonably complete model of creative activity. If bipolar disorder and schizophrenia are separate and both are related to creativity, more than two factors will be required. However, how many specifically affective dimensions are there? How many dimensions are required to capture the phenomenology of bipolar disorder? Of schizophrenia?

Concluding Remarks

As a group, these articles (Becker, 2000–2001; Ogilvie, 2000–2001; Prentky, 2000–2001; Sass, 2000–2001) point toward the importance of considering subtypes, that is different types of thought disorder and of creativity. In addition, the articles emphasize the social embeddedness of the different forms of creativity, as of madness. Judgments of creativity and judgments of madness are both judgments, and they are suspect for that reason, as both Becker and Sass point out.

A consideration of the social construction of creativity and madness also begs for further treatment and development of the role of gender in creative activity (see Battersby, 1990). In this field, it is still somewhat common for people to speak of the great man, leading to the question: What about the great woman?

Dynamics

To conclude, I argue for a dynamical systems approach to understanding the vicissitude of the creative process. If one accepts that there are both cognitive and affective dimensions underlying creative production and that these dimensions are relatively continuous rather than dichotomous, it is a small step to add dynamics to the picture: People are not always the same, and they change with time. An individual can vary over time in affective state, cognitive style, and creative functioning.

If we then add nonlinearity to such a model, something mentioned by Kinney et al. (2000–2001), Richards (2000–2001), and Prentky (2000–2001), we arrive at a nonlinear dynamical systems view of human functioning, and specifically of creativity (see Schuldberg, 1999). A number of these authors suggest that cognitive approaches and affective states have curvilinear (inverted-U, in this case) dose–response relations with creative outcomes. This implies that personal fluctuations in style and behavior will be nonlinearly linked with the ups and downs of a person's effectiveness and level of functioning, creative and otherwise. Such nonlinear couplings indicate that the moment-to-moment changes in lives' patterns can be very interesting, changing suddenly, difficult to steer, and defying prediction and tight control.

A nonlinear dynamical system is capable of chaotic behavior, now speculated to be relevant to the creative process (Richards, 1996; Schuldberg, 1999) and to psychopathology as well (e.g., Gottschalk, Bauer, & Whybrow, 1995; Hoffman, 1987). The behavior of nonlinear dynamical systems is richer and more complicated than the patterning that can be described in simple narrative trajectories of progress and triumph or tragedy and defeat. Nonlinear dynamical systems can accommodate story lines of multiple forms, straight line (as special cases or as emergent properties) and otherwise. Such models can even, I suspect, generate trajectories that encompass and reflect the fractured vision and fragmented productions of modernism.[1]

We can refer to the changes or motion of a system as changes in the system's state, and we can model and describe these paths in a state or phase space. *Attractors* refer to regions where a system tends to linger, and I have argued elsewhere that the notion of attractors is useful for conceptualizing artistic genres as well as where a story is at a particular moment (Schuldberg, 1999).

Systems that are technically in chaos exhibit "strange" attractors in phase space: They are never both in the same place and going in the same direction more than once. A la Heraclitus, in chaotic systems one can never be at the same point in phase space twice. In other situations, the motion of a system can define other types of attractors (e.g., manifesting the repetition of a periodic attractor). Trajectories can have forms that may be "classical" or ballad-like, sometimes modern and fragmented, sometimes starkly transgressive. Local structures in the paths of such systems, the attractors, are sometimes single points, sometimes cyclical, sometimes strange and ever new.

Nonlinear systems models can be constructed by linking together familiar and fairly simple off-the-shelf psychological models that are already well known. When we look at the interactions of several dynamic psychological processes at once, familiar models combine to become capable of seemingly discontinuous change and unexpected surprises. Such a somewhat complicated view of creativity—as emerging from several relatively simple but nonlinearly coupled psychological subsystems—emphasizes the potentially novel, inventive properties and texture in the everyday, mundane aspects of our lives.

Importantly, creative processes can generate stories or works with nonnarrative forms, without heroic progression, perhaps better exemplified by the blues song than by many other forms (Willeford, 1985). In Muddy Waters's miniature masterpiece, the short 1949 song "Little Geneva," the singer begins by "standing at my window" and ends up—as he misses "Little Geneva"—"on my bended knee" (Waters, 1949/1987). This song is more than a concrete narrative account of the progression from standing to kneeling. Rather, it is a brief—deep rather than wide—instantiation, in music and language, of intense yearning ("I miss my Geneva so bad, so bad this morning") and, one suspects, an explication of much more about the resonance and condition of everyday life. The song possesses great stillness and echoes that we can barely grasp; its nonprogressive trajectory tells much about what comprises a piece of art.

Forms of thinking, forms of affect, and forms of relationship ebb, flow, and interact. Social factors pull and shove us, but human personalities tintinabulate after these influences withdraw, and the roles we assume shift and resonate for a long time, even after we move into solitude. The behavioral music we produce embodies, but is not strictly predictable from, our past interactions, surprising even us at times.

[1]In his commentary, Sass (2000–2001) wonders whether nonlinear dynamical systems models can also account for revolutionary science or reproduce the distanced and metaperspectives of modernism and postmodernism. I suspect that they can. One intriguing possibility concerns reframing this second-order capacity as a form of mathematical recursion, which can contribute to specifying models with interesting dynamics in behavior.

References

Barron, F. (1972). *Artists in the making.* New York: Seminar.

Battersby, C. (1990). *Gender and genius: Towards a feminist aesthetics.* Bloomington: Indiana University Press.

Becker, G. (1978). *The mad genius controversy: A study in the sociology of deviance.* Beverly Hills, CA: Sage.

Becker, G. (2000–2001). The association of creativity and psychopathology: Its cultural–historical origins. *Creativity Research Journal, 13,* 45–53.

Butcher, J. N., Dahlstrom, W. G., Graham, J. R., Tellegen, A., & Kaemmer, B. (1989). *MMPI–2 (Minnesota Multiphasic Personality Inventory–2): Manual for administration and scoring.* Minneapolis: University of Minnesota Press.

Canguilhem, G. (1991). *The normal and the pathological.* New York: Zone.

Davis, G. A., & Subkoviak, M. J. (1975). Multidimensional analysis of a personality-based test of creative potential. *Journal of Educational Measurement, 12,* 37–43.

Edwards, A. L. (1970). *The measurement of personality traits by scales and inventories.* New York: Holt, Rinehart & Winston.

Gottschalk, A., Bauer, M. S., & Whybrow, P. C. (1995). Evidence of chaotic mood variation in bipolar disorder. *Archives of General Psychiatry, 52,* 947–959.

Hoffman, R. E. (1987). Computer simulations of neural information processing and the schizophrenia–mania dichotomy. *Archives of General Psychiatry, 44,* 178–188.

Kinney, D. K., Richards, R., Lowing, P. A., LeBlanc, D., Zimbalist, M. E., & Harlan, P. (2000–2001). Creativity in offspring of schizophrenic and control parents: An adoption study. *Creativity Research Journal, 13,* 17–25.

Lovejoy, A. O. (1948). On the discrimination of romanticisms. In A. O. Lovejoy (Ed.), *Essays in the history of ideas* (pp. 228–253). Baltimore: Johns Hopkins University Press.

Ludwig, A. M. (1995). *The price of greatness: Resolving the creativity and madness controversy.* New York: Guilford.

Ogilvie, J. (2000–2001). On self-conceiving: Philosophical yearnings in a schizophrenic context. *Creativity Research Journal, 13,* 87–94.

Prentky, R. A. (1979). Creativity and psychopathology: A neurocognitive perspective. In B. A. Maher (Ed.), *Progress in experimental personality research* (Vol. 9, pp. 1–39). New York: Academic.

Prentky, R. A. (1980). *Creativity and psychopathology: A neurocognitive perspective.* New York: Praeger.

Prentky, R. A. (1989). Creativity and psychopathology: Gambolling at the seat of madness. In J. A. Glover, R. R. Ronning, & C. R. Reynolds (Eds.), *Handbook of creativity* (pp. 243–270). New York: Plenum.

Prentky, R. A. (2000–2001). Mental illness and roots of genius. *Creativity Research Journal, 13,* 95–104.

Richards, R. L. (1981). Relationships between creativity and psychopathology: An evaluation and interpretation of the evidence. *Genetic Psychology Monographs, 103,* 261–324.

Richards, R. (1996). Beyond Piaget: Accepting divergent, chaotic, and creative thought. In M. A. Runco (Ed.), *New directions for child development: 72. Creativity from childhood through adulthood: The developmental issues* (pp. 67–86). San Francisco: Jossey-Bass.

Richards, R. (2000–2001). Creativity and the schizophrenia spectrum: More and more interesting. *Creativity Research Journal, 13,* 111–132.

Richards, R., Kinney, D. K., Lunde, I., Benet, M., & Merzel, A. P. C. (1988). Creativity in manic depressives, cyclothymes, their normal relatives, and control subjects. *Journal of Abnormal Psychology, 97,* 281–288.

Rogers, C. R. (1961). *On becoming a person.* Boston: Houghton-Mifflin.

Runco, M. A., & Richards, R. (Eds.). (1997). *Eminent creativity, everyday creativity, and health.* Greenwich, CT: Ablex.

Sass, L. A. (1992). *Madness and modernism: Insanity in the light of modern art, literature, and thought.* New York: Basic Books.

Sass, L. A. (1994). *The paradoxes of delusion: Wittgenstein, Schreber, and the schizophrenic mind.* Ithaca, NY: Cornell University Press.

Sass, L. A. (2000–2001). Schizophrenia, modernism, and the creative imagination: On creativity and psychopathology. *Creativity Research Journal, 13,* 55–74.

Schuldberg, D. (1994). Giddiness and horror in the creative process. In M. P. Shaw & M. A. Runco (Eds.), *Creativity and affect* (pp. 87–101). Norwood, NJ: Ablex.

Schuldberg, D. (1999). Chaos theory and creativity. In M. Runco & S. Pritzker (Eds.), *Encyclopedia of creativity* (Vol. 1, pp. 259–272). New York: Wiley.

Sontag, S. (1977). *Illness as metaphor.* New York: Vintage.

Strauss, J. S., Rakfeldt, J., Harding, C. M., & Lieberman, P. (1989). Psychological and social aspects of negative symptoms. *British Journal of Psychiatry, 155*(Suppl. 7), 128–132.

Suleiman, S. R. (1998). *Creativity and exile: European–American perspectives.* Durham, NC: Duke University Press.

Szasz, T. S. (1974). *The myth of mental illness: Foundations of a theory of personal conduct.* New York: Harper & Row.

Walsh, J. A. (1990). Comment on social desirability. *American Psychologist, 45,* 289–290.

Walsh, J. A., Tomlinson-Keasey, C., & Klieger, D. M. (1974). Acquisition of the social desirability response. *Genetic Psychology Monographs, 89,* 241–272.

Waters, M. (1987). Little Geneva. On *The real folk blues* (Chess CD CHD 9274). Universal City, CA: MCA Records. (Recorded July 1949)

Welsh, G. S., & Barron, F. (1963). *Barron–Welsh Art Scale.* Palo Alto, CA: Mind Garden.

Willeford, W. (1985). Abandonment, wish, and hope in the blues. *Chiron, 1985,* 173–206.

Wittgenstein, L. (1958). *Philosophical investigations* (G. E. M. Anscombe, Trans.). New York: Macmillan. (Original work published 1953)

Wright, W. (1994). *The social logic of health.* Hanover, NH: Wesleyan University Press.

Wynne, L. C., & Singer, M. T. (1963). Thought disorder and family relations of schizophrenics: II. A classification of forms of thinking. *Archives of General Psychiatry, 9,* 199–206.

Creativity Research Journal
2000–2001, Vol. 13, No. 1, 111–132

Creativity and the Schizophrenia Spectrum: More and More Interesting

Ruth Richards
Saybrook Graduate School
University of California, San Francisco
McLean Hospital and Harvard Medical School

ABSTRACT: There is great promise in the articles from this special issue and their focus on schizophrenia-spectrum disorders and creativity. It becomes all the more important, then, to proceed with caution and to do good service to patients, their families, and, indeed, to our greater human potential. After a note on the study of bipolar disorders and creativity, I introduce 8 general considerations regarding creativity–pathology relations, followed by 8 specific points about the theoretical articles on schizophrenia spectrum. I bring in findings from the only empirical article in this set that actually involves participants at risk for schizophrenia, for which I was co-investigator. It is possible that familial schizophrenic risk carries "creative advantages" distinct from (and potentially combinable with) those related to bipolar disorders, advantages that are again broad and valuable in everyday life and from which we may all learn. However, one must take care to define issues fully, replicate important data, and to not "throw out the baby with the bath water" by creating artificial either–or situations between schizophrenia-spectrum and bipolar-spectrum disorders. There may be new worlds that await us in situations we are only beginning to understand.

In 1996, at the American Psychological Association (APA) annual meeting in Toronto, I was sitting with Louis Sass and David Schuldberg in a restaurant, and they asked if I would be a discussant for a symposium on schizophrenia-spectrum disorders and creativity. I said, "Yes I will—but I think it's all bipolar."

Well, at least that's how it had seemed at the time.

Actually, almost 20 years ago, in a monograph on creativity and psychopathology (Richards, 1981), I had concluded that schizophrenia "was typically associated with individual or family creativity ... but its levels were generally lower than those of affective psychosis" (p. 306). These were the days, however, when a heterogeneity of conditions were being lumped together under the designation of schizophrenia, so that one could not draw firm conclusions. I also had to add, "In the only study using more restrictive diagnostic criteria, sampling bias was such that nonappearance of schizophrenia cannot be interpreted" (p. 307).

At that time, Kinney and Matthysse (1978) had already proposed the possibility of a compensatory advantage to genes that increase vulnerability to various behavioral disorders. In a happy conjunction of interests, I began work with Kinney and others (at McLean Hospital and Harvard Medical School) on the assessment of everyday lifetime creativity (Kinney, Richards, & Southam, in press; Richards, Kinney, Benet, & Merzel, 1988), to explore whether creative phenomena may reflect such a compensatory advantage, with a focus on the spectrum of bipolar disorders (Richards & Kinney, 1990; Richards, Kinney, Daniels, & Linkins, 1992; Richards, Kinney, Lunde, Benet, & Merzel, 1988). We prepared to study schizophrenia as well, all in conjunction with Kety and associates' (e.g., Kety, 1983; Wender et al., 1986) remarkable Danish adoption studies. At the same time, in the *Diagnostic and Statistical Manual of Mental Disorders* (3rd ed. [*DSM–III*]; American Psychiatric Association, 1980),

---

I wish to thank Dennis Kinney, Stanley Krippner, Sandra Russ, Louis Sass, and David Schuldberg for their helpful suggestions.

Correspondence and requests for reprints should be sent to Ruth Richards, Saybrook Graduate School and Research Center, 450 Pacific Avenue, San Francisco, CA 94133. E-mail: rrichards@saybrook.edu.

two of the criteria for the hypomanic phase of cyclothymic personality disorder involved productivity and sharpened and unusually creative thinking. At first unknown to us, Andreasen and colleagues (Andreasen, 1978; Andreasen & Canter, 1974; Andreasen & Powers, 1974) and Jamison, Gerner, Hammen, and Padesky (1980) had also published critical studies. It was one of these fertile times of semi-independent and mutually reinforcing efforts.

The next decade or so brought varied positive findings and many interesting perspectives on affective disorders and creativity from different researchers (see Richards, 1981, 1990, 1997, 1999a; see also Akiskal & Akiskal, 1988; Eysenck, 1993; Jamison, 1989, 1990, 1993; Kinney et al., 2000–2001; Ludwig, 1992, 1995; Richards & Kinney, 1990; Richards et al., 1992; Richards, Kinney, Lunde, et al., 1988; Runco & Richards, 1997; Schuldberg, 1990, 1999). Some principles from this work now seem potentially relevant to schizophrenia as well. Jamison's (1993) influential book, *Touched With Fire: Manic–Depressive Illness and the Artistic Temperament,* was welcomed as a great gift by bipolar clients I worked with, as was Jamison's (1995) later, and autobiographical, *An Unquiet Mind.* Indeed, in just over a couple of decades, the work on bipolar disorders and creativity went from relative obscurity—or mindless rejection—to mainstream acceptance, even reaching the editorial page of *The New York Times* ("Making Art of Madness," 1993).

Now here we are, at the dawn of a new millennium, with a highly promising perspective on creativity and the schizophrenia spectrum. There are even new data (Kinney et al., 2000–2001) that are consistent with older but less methodologically rigorous data showing higher creativity among healthier relatives of schizophrenics (e.g., Heston, 1966; Karlsson, 1970; Kauffman, Grunebaum, Cohler, & Gamer, 1979; Richards, 1981). Our data were still forthcoming when Sass and Schuldberg first proposed this collection, and it has been rewarding indeed to see this fresh new perspective emerge from theory on creativity in the arts and humanities and data from more general samples on primary process and thought disorder even as our creativity results on relatives of schizophrenics became available.

Our data, from Kinney et al. (2000–2001), have linked an advantage for everyday creativity to a subtle clinical picture, two-plus schizotypal signs in a (relatively healthy) sample at risk for schizophrenia. We looked at such subtle possibilities in the first place because of our success in finding creative advantages linked to subtle clinical or subclinical manifestations for bipolar disorders in the affected individuals or their relatives.

As with bipolar disorders, this evidence on schizophrenia-related features is consistent with a compensatory advantage, one perhaps operating among the better functioning relatives of the more severely afflicted; one may compare the situation for carriers of sickle cell anemia (e.g., Richards, Kinney, Benet, & Merzel, 1988), where the full-blown syndrome can be devastating, yet the carrier state can be rather mild, with the additional compensatory advantage: resistance to malaria. Such an advantage involving creativity, this time, could show a curvilinear and optimal relation with pathology, as Schuldberg (2000–2001) also pointed out, and a relation consistent with our proposed inverted-U association between creativity and psychiatric symptomatology (Richards, 1999a; Richards & Kinney, 1990; Richards, Kinney, Lunde, et al., 1988; see also Eysenck, 1993; Schuldberg, 1990). Where symptoms are concerned, there is a key intermediate range, and more is not necessarily better. We will continue to touch base on findings with bipolar disorders to see where the latter may inform the new work on the schizophrenia spectrum.

Moderation seems to be key. Turning to state and trait effects, creativity has been linked with milder clinical states in bipolar disorders and with mild mood elevation in particular. It has also been tied to milder overall disorders or ongoing trait characteristics (Richards & Kinney, 1990; Richards et al., 1992; Richards, Kinney, Lunde, et al., 1988; see also Andreasen, 1987; Eckblad & Chapman, 1986; Eysenck, 1993; Jamison, 1990; Schuldberg, 1990). These should be important areas as well in the study of schizophrenia-related creativity.

Beyond this, it was found, initially to my surprise, that not all "normalcy" is created equal. Psychological normalcy itself can predict for creativity, when linked with a positive family history of bipolar disorders (Richards, Kinney, Lunde, et al., 1988). Coryell et al. (1989) extended this by finding a general advantage for achievement (and not specifically creativity) in the first-degree relatives of bipolar individuals. This breadth of effect is important, and critical, too, is the presence of a creative advantage in everyday life. The discussion, whether about schizophrenia or bipolar disorders, is after all not (only) about eminent artists and their exceptional expressions, be their work romantic or postmodernist in nature. It is potentially about anything and everything that we do.

Findings on normals tell us something else and something critical: Creativity will not necessarily (or not always) be linked with great pain and suffering. One may argue in fact that creativity often opens the door to psychological wholeness, transformation, and healing and to ongoing personal growth and evolving concern toward a greater whole. Such effects may help explain the intertwining of creativity with illness and even aspects of its evolutionary significance (Goodwin & Jamison, 1990; Kinney, 1992; Rhodes, 1990; Richards, 1981, 1993b, 1997, 1999a, 1999c, in press-a; Runco & Richards, 1997; see Eysenck, 1993, for a contrary viewpoint). So one should not necessarily assume that we are concerned primarily with illness. We may be—or we may not.

Road Sign: Proceed With Caution

Now enter this proposed and vitally important connection between creativity and individual or familial schizophrenia. At its most interesting, this relation may involve direct links between schizophrenia-related thought processes and key aspects of creative ability. This is what Sass (2000–2001) and Ogilvie (2000–2001) compellingly propose for certain intellectual and artistic activities that could benefit from features including a schizotypal hyperreflexivity and alienation. Beyond such issues of thought process and cultural creativity, there are important underlying possibilities of familial factors, genetic and even evolutionary effects, involving a more broadly applicable creative process that may occur in the population at large.

This connection with creativity—and perhaps not just for certain artists with schizotypal features, but in general—is such an important possibility that we must proceed with caution and put the picture in the proper frame. We do not want to make a mistake and saddle patients with yet another expectation or create unrealistic hopes for patients' families. Yet, it would be tragic indeed to miss an opening into an important and healthy realm of human possibility that we have previously overlooked.

We must also take care, as Sass (2000–2001; Sass & Schuldberg, 2000–2001) and Becker (2000–2001), in particular, do, to address the bigger picture of creativity as conceived and defined within a complex and evolving society. We also need to resist those who would bring simplistic or premature closure to the discussion. After a recent meeting of the APA, I was concerned to hear an attendee talk about creativity and schizophrenia versus creativity and bipolar disorders. He thought these were mutually exclusive. This was not the content he had encountered, and it is certainly not the position of the articles in this issue (see Sass & Schuldberg, 2000–2001), yet this was the message that was received. One may seize too readily on false dichotomies in a culture bred on distinctions and competition.

A quick look at results on everyday creativity and at arguments that suggest genetic factors, thus looking beyond creative arts and the eminent, opens us to new sorts of questions, as discussed later. The very existence of the mosaic of ways in which creativity can arise, from health, illness, or this pathology or that, may carry powerful implications for human consciousness and for better adaptation in a troubled world (Richards, 1993c, 1996a, 1996b, 1997, 1999b).

Many Roads to Creativity

I first note with caution that many other factors, motivational factors as well as ability-related ones, indirect as well as direct, nonspecific as well as specific, can mediate a creativity–psychopathology relation (Richards, 1981, 1990, 1997, 1999b). These can appear in multiple and overlapping forms as well, as is detailed later. There is promise in these potential relations but also a caveat. It can make a huge difference whether a relation involves everyday or eminent creativity (e.g., artistic or nonartistic endeavor) or is focused more on work or leisure. In addition, a relation with schizophrenia-spectrum pathology may assume a role in a broader picture of multicausal creative patterns and roles within an evolving society. The larger cultural picture is also relevant.

Eight Questions for the Researcher or Scholar

Here I list eight considerations, drawn from our group's research experience with bipolar disorders, primarily, and framed as questions. These are followed by eight directed points in the next section, linked to the provocative theoretical articles in this issue. The concerns involve: (a) everyday versus eminent creativity; (b) evolutionary versus culture-bound origins of pathology; (c) artistic versus nonartistic creativity and vocational versus avocational focus; (d) ability versus motivation as source of a creative advantage; (e) five-part typology showing the many roads to creativity, including direct and indirect effects of psychopathology on creativity and vice versa; (f) nonspecific pathology-linked factors in creativity; (g) specific pathology-linked factors (including biopsychosocial components) plus evolutionary implications; and (h) the issue of psychological normalcy in persons at risk and subclinical effects within families.

1. Do Results or Arguments Pertain to Eminent Creativity, Everyday Creativity, or Both? Are There Different Implications, Depending on Which It Is?

First, I discuss some definitions for reference. *Everyday creativity,* or the creativity of everyday life, can be defined in terms of its outcome, using two general criteria (after Barron, 1969): *originality* (unusualness within a social context) and *meaningfulness* (requirement that the contribution communicate to others and not be random or idiosyncratic). This definition underlies the Lifetime Creativity Scales (Kinney et al., in press; Richards, Kinney, Benet, et al., 1988; Richards, Kinney, Lunde, et al., 1988). It lends itself to people's wide-ranging everyday activities at work and leisure, including, to be sure, those activities in the "traditionally creative" fields of the arts and sciences but also a little of everything else, be this in homemaking, entrepreneurship, teaching, manufacturing, landscaping, mechanical repair work, child rearing, or any other activity that allows for original thought and performance.

Eminent creativity, by contrast, involves creative accomplishments that are recognized by society at large, or a professional field; the creative person responsible is often recognized as well. Indeed, eminent creative work is that which many people stand in awe of, and it is frequently in the arts or sciences. These are the socially recognized contributions that have, for instance, won the Pulitzer Prize, been produced on Broadway, sold for high price at auction, become a bestseller, or which, within a professional field, have won honors or awards, been funded, published, received multiple citations, or garnered other forms of widespread recognition. Sometimes the criteria for such widely recognized creativity are made explicit, but sometimes they are not explicit at all. We may find cultural forces silently yet powerfully at play.

Can there can be different relations to pathology for everyday compared to eminent creativity? The answer seems to be *yes* (e.g., Richards, 1990, 1997, 1999a), at least for bipolar-spectrum disorders and for persons in the arts. (This bipolar spectrum extends from milder cyclothymic mood swings to severe depressions combined with mild "highs" [Bipolar II disorder] and full-blown, manic–depressive illness [Bipolar I disorder], each of these alternating with periods of normalcy. Infrequently hyperthymic highs and full mania are also found in isolation. Depressions too, from mild dysthymias to severe major depressions, are included in the spectrum if there is a history of bipolar disorders in the family.) We can ask if the distinction between everyday and eminent creativity is as critical for schizophrenia as it is for affective disorders.

With creativity and bipolar disorders (Richards et al., 1992; Richards, Kinney, Lunde, et al., 1988), for instance, the strongest creative advantage in everyday life has appeared among persons at risk who are relatively better functioning (e.g., cyclothymes, including Bipolar II persons by today's criteria, and normal relatives), by contrast with Bipolar I or manic–depressive individuals. For these studies of everyday creativity, the participants were selected using only diagnostic criteria and, hence, were more reflective of the general population and of the subpopulation with mood disorders than were a handful of eminent people selected for creative distinction. Indeed, their activities also varied across a wide gamut, including not only arts and handicrafts but also homemaking, entrepreneurship, teaching, or inventing. One highly creative auto mechanic even designed his own tools. (One must, therefore, seek to understand a creative advantage related to risk of bipolar disorders in a general way; it is not confined only to the arts and humanities, never mind to expressions that fit a romantic literary context.)

The elite group in the arts has shown particularly severe affective disorders in conjunction with creative eminence (Ludwig, 1992, 1995; Runco & Richards, 1997). For instance, a full 80% of Andreasen's (1987) creative writers had a major mood disorder, and half those with bipolar disorders had Bipolar Type I (manic–depressive). Other findings are supportive (see Ludwig, 1995; Richards, 1997). Keeping in mind that eminent participants were selected for creative success, they may represent a better functioning subset within their particular categories (Bipolar I or II disorders or unipolar depression) and level of severity than the typical clinical client. Yet, they show serious morbidity and mortality, with as high as 20% successful suicides for untreated bipolar disorders (see Andreasen, 1987; Jamison, 1990, 1993). This is startling. (Happily, a treated bipolar disorder can have a dramatically more positive prognosis with the treatments now available.)

Turning to schizophrenia, the three empirical articles in this issue all involve everyday creativity. Included is our own research on creativity in people carrying schizophrenic risk (Kinney et al., 2000–2001); this is the only article that deals directly with schizophrenic families and persons at risk. Schuldberg's (2000–2001) and Russ's (2000–2001) valuable research on abnormal thinking or primary process was conducted with more general populations. Let us not then automatically generalize results to eminent creators selected for accomplishment.

2. Is There an Evolutionary Creative Advantage That Can Cross Cultures and Manifest Differently Across These?

With bipolar disorders (or schizophrenia), one is also talking about a heritable spectrum of disorders with widespread prevalence across cultures. Because of this, an evolutionary and genetic advantage has been proposed (e.g., Andreasen, 1987; Goodwin & Jamison, 1990; Richards, 1981, 1990, 1997). Wilson (1992), in citing twin concordance, adoptee and family risk studies, noted that the strong genetic component in manic–depressive illness is not only "highly selected" but also "may prevail at five hundred times the adjusted mutation equilibrium rate" (p. 88). A high prevalence beyond the expected mutation rates supports the preservation of certain characteristics with adaptive benefits through the process of natural selection.

One speaks of an adaptive advantage that would operate down through the generations and across a variety of people and cultures. One is not talking about (only) a brief flourishing of artistic modes in a certain Western cultural context but about a phenomenon that can cross and, indeed can shape cultures. Of relevance is the wide range of activities of creators carrying the reproductive advantage that may help maintain the genes in the population (see also Richards, 1997). We cannot place the evolutionary (i.e., reproductive) burden on the shoulders of the eminent person, however remarkable he or she may be. An evolutionary advantage will operate largely, and by definition, at the grass-roots level, that is, at the level of everyday creativity.

With schizophrenia, the question of an evolutionary advantage is once again raised. There are multiple indicators of a genetic component to schizophrenic risk, based on twin and adoption studies. Plus, there is evidence of less severe manifestations of this risk, with the milder schizotypal disorder a primary example (see Kety, 1983; Kety et al., 1994; Kinney et al., 2000–2001; Richards, 1981). Is there a compensatory advantage, and how does it manifest both at the eminent and everyday levels of creativity?

3. Do Results and Arguments Apply to All Areas of Endeavor, or Should Artistic and Nonartistic Work Be Distinguished and, Similarly, Vocational and Avocational Creativity?

In this issue, we find compelling arguments linking schizotypal thought, in particular, to certain forms of creativity in the arts and the humanities, including philosophy. If this finding has validity, how does one generalize this discussion to hard sciences, leadership, politics, business, home hobbies, or any other type of endeavor beyond the humanities?

Psychopathology, including high rates of affective disorders, is frequently reported among artists but is not so common among nonartists (Juda, 1949–1950; Ludwig, 1995; Richards, 1981, 1990). Of particular note is Ludwig's historiographic study of more than 1,000 creators across 18 different occupational areas. Social scientists, physicists, and businesspersons, among other nonartists, appeared relatively healthy on the average. How may schizophrenic risk manifest differently, one may ask, within such artist and nonartist groups? This could be an interesting question. Again, among Ludwig's eminent creators there was one definitive predictor of psychopathology: a career in the creative arts.

One also needs to consider work-related versus leisure-related creativity. There are preliminary data for understanding how both bipolar-related and schizophrenia-related creative advantages may manifest. In studies (Richards et al., 1992; Richards, Kinney, Lunde, et al., 1988), greater work-related than leisure-related everyday creativity among persons with bipolar-spectrum disorders was found, which is supported by the writings of Akiskal and others (Akiskal & Akiskal, 1992; Akiskal & Mallya, 1987).

Just the opposite was found for the schizophrenia-spectrum individuals (Kinney et al., 2000–2001). It was in the privacy of their spare time that creativity could bloom. There was notably greater leisure-related than work-related creativity (Kinney et al., 2000–2001). It is a matter of choice, the venue in which one expresses one's creativity, and this may be related to motivation for creativity, for instance (see Richards, 1990; Richards & Kinney, 1989), or to occupational drift into work or social environments in which particular styles of creative talent can bloom (Richards, 1981). What are the critical factors? Researchers and theorists may want to think about vocational and avocational contexts for creativity. Among other things, leisure activity can be more relaxed, free-form, self-scheduled, and less vulnerable to critical judgment and real-life public consequences for one's performance and could attract people with high levels of social anxiety or awkwardness, as may be found in the schizophrenia spectrum.

4. Does the Creative Advantage in Question Involve Ability or Motivation? How Do You Know?

Just because one is discussing affective disorders does not mean all effects are affective, as Russ (2000–2001) and Schuldberg (2000–2001) also point out. Schizophrenia-related factors need not all be cognitive, as is seen in Sass's (2000–2001) seven postmodernist features and their schizotypal parallels. Indeed, with bipolar disorders, factors that raise the odds of creativity can be cognitive, affective, or motivational (Goodwin & Jamison, 1990; Jamison et al., 1980; Richards, 1981, 1990; Richards & Kinney, 1990). These can involve richer associative process, greater depth and subtlety of feeling, and in the realm of motivation, greater confidence, conviction, or energizing potential.

The general literature on creativity abounds with motivational and shaping factors that can affect later creativity (R. B. Albert & Runco, 1986; R. S. Albert, in press; Richards, 1981; Runco & Pritzker, 1999). Health, illness, early difficulty, early advantages, and creative role models—what does it take to bump us out of the comfort of the status quo and convince us that a better life purpose may be found in thinking anew?

One motivational factor important to eminent creativity may involve a "standing apart" from the mainstream (Richards, 1990, 1997; Richards & Kinney, 1989). After all, challenging the status quo may hold great social costs. It can be easy to go along, to sit passively on the beach, sipping one's lemonade, or to sit quietly in a group, giving the response the leader wants to hear. It may also be relevant to creative ability. What does it take to grease our neurons a bit so that our new ideas, once welcomed, may come forth more readily? This availability may be spurred by cognitive factors but could also be fueled by energy, motivation, and creative courage, which could help bring one closer to a creative "edge of chaos" (e.g., Marks-Tarlow, 1999; Richards, 1996a, 1996b, in press-b; Zausner, 1996). With schizotypal conditions, we should not assume we are dealing solely with, for example, one exclusive mechanism that enhances creative ability (as with an overinclusive cognitive style). However valid any one factor may be, we should stay open to other motivational, ability, or situational factors that may also contribute.

5. Are You Addressing Possible Indirect as Well as Direct Effects of Psychopathology on Creativity and of Creativity on Pathology? Which of Five General Categories of Effect Might Be Relevant?

It is worth repeating: There is no one road to creativity (e.g., see Richards, 1981, 1990, 1997, 1998). Among other things, one need not be ill (or healthy) to create. Yet, one often hears sweeping generalizations of relation, for example, "creativity and madness." As a simplification in the complex realm of situations in which creativity and psychopathology are inevitably intertwined, one can talk, in the abstract, about five different types of direct and indirect relation. Again, this is by means of simplification. Included are (a) direct effects of psychopathology on creativity, (b) indirect effects of psychopathology on creativity, (c) direct effects of creativity on psychopathology, (d) indirect effects of creativity on psychopathology, and (e) the situation of a third factor that affects both areas independently. Of course, effects can be (and often are) multiple and overlapping. Table 1 gives examples of how such phenomena can play out in the case of bipolar disorders. Many such explanations could apply to people with schizophrenia-spectrum disorders as well.

Note how complex the reactions can be to a creatively different person who moves about in a reactive culture. Unicausal events are vanishingly rare. Any single phenomenon may have biopsychosocial roots, and these will create their own ricochet of reactions, which should be viewed as part of a larger systems picture. Creativity is our most complex human contribution to an evolving cosmos. The evolution of information, or of culture, may well be part of our task (R. S. Albert, in press; Csikszentmihalyi, 1988; Dawkins, 1976; Richards, 1996b, 1997).

Indeed, our psychological and creative diversity may be to the evolution of information and culture what our biological diversity is to genetic evolution and physical survival (Richards, 1997). In an information age, one may increasingly posit the importance of our human creativity to our greater purpose and very survival (e.g., Barron, 1969; Richards, 1999c; Wilber, 1997). As the contributions in this issue amply illustrate, the diversity represented by a schizotypal origin of creativity, taken along with other forms, may further

Table 1. *Typology of Creativity and Psychopathology: Application to Mood Disorders*

Typology	Application
Direct Relation of Pathology to Creativity (P > C)	Psychopathology can contribute to content and process of creativity. Consider John Ruskin's loosely associated writings about his manic episodes or William Styron's moving accounts of his depressions (see Richards, 1997).
Indirect Relation of Pathology to Creativity (P > T > C)	Pathology may lead to creative expression, as in cathartic writing, which in turn may come to enhance perspective, empowerment, psychological and physical health, and a greater giving to others. Early writings of John Cheever once helped this Pulitzer Prize-winning author deal with a difficult family situation; it later came to help a great many others. Regarding the environment, pathology may also drive occupational drift, bringing persons into career situations (e.g., flexible, unsupervised, nonconformist work) where their creativity can blossom.
Direct Relation of Creativity to Pathology (C > P)	Artistic creativity, in particular, may elicit unsuspected material, anxiety, and decompensation, one reason that humanistic psychologist May (1976) wrote *The Courage to Create.* However, note, too that under the right conditions, such short-term distress can ultimately lead to health, as in an indirect relation of pathology to creativity, shown in row 2.
Indirect Relation of Creativity to Pathology (C > T > P)	Consider conflicts that are not worked through, as in row 2, but lead to internal or external difficulties and to subsequent escape. Substance abuse is one common attempt to flee inner demons. Then there is external disapproval of the creative child or adult who is perhaps ostracized or ridiculed, lacks support, decompensates, and copes badly or escapes.
Third Factor Affecting Both Creativity and Pathology (C < T > C)	One compelling example involves familial liability or risk for bipolar disorders (or schizophrenia), here listed as a third factor. This could independently raise the odds of overt pathology, creative accomplishment, or both, as in the normal first-degree relatives of bipolar persons who show a creative advantage.

Note: P and C signify pathology or creativity, respectively, or some aspect thereof. T signifies a separate third factor that may mediate between or separately contribute to pathology and creativity. Effects can also be multiple and overlapping.

open our eyes and our options in a postmodern (and post-postmodern) world.

6. To What Extent Do You Posit Nonspecific Factors, Linked to Pathology, in a Relation With Creativity?

A pathology–creativity link need not be specific, applying only to people with schizophrenia-spectrum or bipolar disorders, for example, or to those who use a particular form of associative process. It may be specific, but it may not. There are multiple reports linking a range of pathologies or adversities to creativity (e.g., Goertzel & Goertzel, 1962; Heston, 1966; Juda, 1949–1950; Ludwig, 1992; Richards, 1981). Included are bipolar and unipolar mood disorders, to be sure (all of which may relate to a bipolar risk in a family), various specific and nonspecific psychoses, and a range of anxiety and personality disorders. For persons with certain advantages and supports, coping with adversity can be a spur to creative accomplishment (e.g., Jamison, 1993; Kinney, 1992; Pennebaker, 1995; Richards, 1998; Runco & Richards, 1997; Zausner, 1996). This case falls under the question of whether there is an evolutionary creative advantage that can cross cultures and manifest differently across them: Pathology leads indirectly to creativity. Earlier, I (Richards, 1997, 1999a) applied a model of acquired immunity to this process. Some who cope with adversity may develop yet further creative abilities by virtue of their resilient coping, and at the same time the creative motivation to try to transform situations in the future, rather than flee from or blindly react to them (fight and flight reactions; see also Richards, 1994a).

One also finds the possibility of a final common pathway in which diverse disorders lead to similar information processing phenomena. An example may be overinclusion, which I discuss further later (see Andreasen & Powers, 1974; Eysenck, 1993; Goodwin & Jamison, 1990; Prentky, 2000–2001; Richards, 1993a, 1994a). These examples relate to the direct case of pathology leading to creativity in the typology. Similarly, the motivational impetus some may get from being different, from standing apart from the mainstream, may facilitate creativity across diagnostic categories. We should not automatically assume that a creativity–psychopathology relation is specific to a certain diagnostic condition, never mind a particular mechanism. This should be investigated.

7. By Contrast, to What Extent Do You Posit Pathology-Specific Factors in a Relation With Creativity? Might Certain Ones Carry Evolutionary Significance for Affected Individuals or Relatives?

When a creativity–pathology mechanism is specific, familial, and even in part genetic with the chance of evolutionary effects, one may be onto something important. This is one great promise of this issue. As noted, we have investigated a possible compensatory advantage to bipolar-spectrum disorders (Richards, 1997; Richards & Kinney, 1990; Richards, Kinney, Lunde, et al., 1988), and now the schizophrenia spectrum has been investigated (Kinney et al., 2000–2001), and these could involve genetic mediation.

I elaborate a bit on an example touched on earlier. In sickle cell anemia (note this may be a simpler genetic model), the homozygotes, who inherit from both parents, typically develop a severe anemia with multiple medical complications and early death. The larger number of heterozygotes, or carriers, may have a mild anemia at worst. In addition, they have a notable compensatory advantage: resistance to malaria. Hence, a compensatory advantage may be carried genetically in families, despite the fact that some members become severely ill, because of survival value of the condition for a larger number of relatives, who do not carry the full burden of illness.

It was along these lines that we hypothesized that persons carrying familial bipolar risk with only intermediate pathology might emerge most creative and looked for a similar phenomenon for schizophrenia. It is a real strength that Kinney et al. (2000–2001) took as participants the adoptees of schizophrenic parents, people who may well carry the risk for schizophrenia but would not have shared the critical environment. Hence, the mild symptom pictures (two or more schizotypal signs) investigated may well be linked to a familial vulnerability and genetic risk. Indeed, within a relatively healthy range, the number of schizotypal signs was itself correlated with the creativity criterion. This seems very much an effect related to the specific disorder.

This study (Kinney et al., 2000–2001) was not designed to compare genetic and environmental effects. Notably, key supporting data were also found among control participants, persons drawn from the rest of the population, perhaps from our friends and neighbors who do not carry this schizophrenic risk. Something important seems to be happening here, something different from the creativity effects with bipolar disorders and related this time to the presence of schizotypal signs. The fact that these effects may be relevant to the general population is consistent with the work of Russ (2000–2001) and Schuldberg (2000–2001). There is very much evidence of an inverted-U effect, again consistent with Schuldberg's spectrum of effects. However, let us still not jump too automatically to concluding what the critical factors may be.

8. Are You Thinking About Psychological Normalcy and Subclinical Effects on Creativity Within Families at Risk for Schizophrenia?

At times, illness may not even be the point. How important indeed that creativity may not, even in the context of psychiatric disorder, require pain and suffering for its actualization (Cropley, 1990; Richards, 1998). One of our more significant findings, looking at everyday creativity in individuals at risk for bipolar disorders (Richards, Kinney, Lunde, et al., 1988), was alluded to earlier: The psychiatrically normal relatives seemed also to show an everyday creative advantage, along with others who lacked the most severe symptom picture. How interesting, really, that Kinney et al. (2000–2001) found a creativity effect linked with milder symptom pictures but much milder. The presence of two or more schizotypal signs rests on the normalcy side of an inverted-U. We should not jump immediately to the conclusion that this is pathology or that it has to be. We should not assume that any characteristics that are abnormal are, therefore, pathological (see Richards, 1996a). In the model of compensatory advantage, the passing of the strength or advantage down through the generations may even be the critical point. The suffering of certain strongly affected individuals (such as the sickle cell homozygote) or even of the so-called carrier is the tragedy.

To summarize, in this section, I have considered some key perspectives on a creativity–psychopathology relation that may help us sharpen our vision. We may get more out of our analyses if we consider the relation of results to (a) everyday and eminent creativity; (b) the potential for and mechanism of possible evolutionary effects; (c) an artistic or nonartistic focus and a work- or leisure-related focus; (d) factors of ability and motivation; (e) direct and indirect effects; (f) nonspecific factors related to pathology; (g) specific factors related to pathology, including the possibility of genetic effects; and at an extreme, (h) the possibility that pathology may even be an epiphenomenon of different type of process. Against this background, one may proceed to issues raised by these articles.

Eight Specific Questions Related to the Theoretical Articles

The theoretical articles in this issue are original, often ingenious. They push our understanding of creativity and its conditions in our culture, including those evident reasons one creates in the first place and the subjective experience that is involved. They reframe aspects of schizotypy that may commonly be seen as all negative. These articles represent an important contribution. Where they satisfy, they do so exceptionally well. Where they do not, they appear not to go far enough, for instance by focusing on a subpopulation (e.g., eminent persons or artists only) or subphenomenon (creativity in the humanities only, a single hypothesized mechanism, a single level of severity of illness, or a cultural phenomenon), without necessarily acknowledging where the position fits within a larger societal picture or biopsychosocial range of effects. If we are to uncover possible evolutionary effects of schizotypal phenomena over time and culture, this bigger picture seems essential to understand.

Because I cannot cover all the interesting questions that arise, I focus on eight areas related to this bigger picture and compare the schizophrenia-spectrum and bipolar disorders where useful. The issues involve (a) limitations of cultural explanations for a creativity–psychopathology relation involving genetically mediated illness; (b) taking seriously the severity and pain involved; (c) problems in generalizing from pathology-related phenomena in eminent artistic creativity to everyday and to nonartistic creativity; (d) explanatory value of viewing results in terms of creative diversity and multiple cultural roles, with the current schizotypal phenomena serving as part of a larger picture; (e) overinclusion as one, but only one, potential explanatory factor of the link with creativity; (f) postmodernism, schizotypy, and creativity as a fertile conjunction, specifically in the arts; (g) further varieties of creative and schizotypal relation, with a possible post-postmodernist effect; and (h) potential for creativity when bipolar-spectrum effects are joined with schizophrenia-spectrum effects beyond either–or reasoning to potentially fertile conjunctions.

1. When Culture Is Invoked to Address a Link Between Creativity and Major Psychopathology, How Specifically Can This Be Argued, and How Great Are the Factors Left Unexplained?

Becker (1978, 2000–2001) showed compellingly how time and culture may help determine who we see as talented and how the association of pathology with creativity may in part reflect cultural values. These are key points supported by fascinating historical data. For example, as early as ancient Greece, according to Becker (2000–2001), Aristotle linked extraordinary talent with a "melancholic temperament." In the Renaissance, artists assumed trappings of moodiness so as to bolster the impression of unusual capacity. Subsequent to an Enlightenment emphasis on rationality, there was, in the romantic era, a linking of madness with poetic and artistic creativity. These few examples do not do justice to the full picture and depth of discussion. We are, in any case, asked to consider how prevailing norms and values can influence both society's expectations of artists' behavior and artists' own (conscious or unconscious) styles and self-expectations. Pathology may, therefore, at times seem more relevant to creativity than it really is. We may thank Becker for alerting us to these possibilities. We can then ask: How much do they explain, how well, and how much is left over?

First note that over many centuries, eminent artistic creativity has been linked with psychopathology of one kind or another, at least in popular thinking, be this affective or not, psychotic or not, schizophrenic or not. Surely, there is something going on here that one may take seriously. Let us note, secondarily, that there may be historical alterations or drift in the unusual behaviors considered to have merit. The stated bias (or expectation) in the modern world, according to Becker (2000–2001), is toward psychosis, carried over from the romantic era to our own. This is extremely important, particularly if it is taken to support any current change or expansion in views of creativity from earlier times. Because many of us do not have backgrounds in historical research and methodologies, it would behoove us to become more familiar with the methodologies employed and the sorts of evidence used to support the validity of such statements, as well as understand the support for a possible change from, for instance, a more affectively linked symptom picture to thought disorder or psychosis (if this is, in fact, an implication). What are the alternative interpretations, and how are they eliminated? We need to be able to exercise critical thinking about such findings, never mind to have the important opportunity to forecast trends for the future. Becker could help us in the future by telling us more about the method, as well as the conclusions of his work.

In fact, is it possible to ask even more detailed questions? How would one bring one's methodology to address whether prevailing views reflect or amplify and further the progress of a move to postmodernist culture (as characterized in this issue)? What more can we learn about specific abnormalities that may be more expected, or tolerable now, and particularly compared to the romantic era? What is their relevance to aspects of schizophrenia-related (or other) pathology? Furthermore, what about heterogeneity or mixed pictures? Is there only one answer? As Becker (2000–2001) noted, one can find interest in "madness" (as then defined) in Plato's time. Is there not still interest in depressive moodiness or exultant highs today? I particularly like Becker's use of "sane melancholic" in reference to the Renaissance. In addressing artistic stereotypes, should we not also include a mixed cognitive–affective picture (and related clinical syndromes)? Might we also find the coexistence of more than one so-called pathological style (as discussed later) as a fertile societal mixture? (What about normalcy?) How does all of this relate to creativity and the bipolar, or the schizophrenia, spectrum of disorders? Becker's article raises important questions, which we should address with care.

As it occurs, Kinney et al. (2000–2001), in a study in which I was involved, present data from outside the arts and on everyday people, suggesting that schizophrenic risk may indeed be relevant to creativity and in ways that cultural explanations cannot fully subsume. The connections between creativity and pathology in this issue and elsewhere (e.g., Runco & Richards, 1997) tend to involve a much milder and nonpsychotic type of pathology, be it schizotypal or affective. In other words, it is not psychosis at all that appears relevant but some much more subtle phenomena. The adopted-away offspring of schizophrenics who showed two or more schizotypal signs were those who tended toward higher everyday creativity, and these were people who did not even merit a full schizotypal diagnosis. The fact, too, that these were adoptees raised apart from their schizophrenic parent speaks to biological, more than cultural, factors.

Let me further underline how multidetermined both creativity and major psychopathology may be, involving biological, psychological, and social factors (Eysenck, 1993; Runco & Pritzker, 1999; Runco & Richards, 1997; Simonton, 1984). If some people, either historically or at present, have flaunted their pathologies, we should not assume that this is all that is happening or that everyone is doing it. If some people seem to make too much of their moodiness and despair, for instance, when things do not seem that bad to us, let us not automatically assume we are right. Let us not further ignore those suffering people who may feel even worse than we think, have told us nothing, and are on the brink of suicide. There are numerous such people, very much at risk, as any mental health professional can attest.

One may call on the five-part typology mentioned previously (and see Richards, 1981, 1990, 1999b) as a further reminder of multicausality as well as heterogeneity of causation of these associations with creativity. First, the case of creativity leading indirectly to pathology or to maladaptation is only one of five general types of patterns. Beyond this, certain artists may assume a moody demeanor to enhance their sensitive or creative image precisely because there really is something to this association. It need not all be part of a self-conscious romantic attempt to provide an artistic culture with a unique image. The pattern may also be related to an occupational drift into special vocational niches more tolerant of eccentric personal or working styles (see Richards, 1981).

Also, one should recall that these are the artists; what do these arguments tell us about scientists, teachers, or business executives? How valued is a demeanor of eccentricity or mild abnormality in these cases? For the everyday (not eminent) creative person, across fields, the pressures toward nonconformity should be even less. One should recall that everyday creators are the typical subjects studied in this journal issue. They are also the typical clients who come to health professionals for assistance; we very much need to be concerned with their creativity and its origins if this may represent a strength for them and a hope. They are also the ones who will pass on any genetic advantage, and this has very likely occurred with some success across diverse cultural periods.

Thus, Becker (2000–2001) made some very important and original points that should make us think carefully about culture, but we should also look beyond these (as Becker himself said) to a more complex and multicausal field that affects the big picture.

2. Considering the Pain of Affective Disorders, Can the Severe Pathology Be Explained by Cultural Forces or Conscious or Unconscious Wishes to Display Symptomatology?

A few more comments on affective pathology and its origins and effects seem in order in view of the high prevalence and morbidity and mortality of these disorders. Comments can apply as well to the schizophrenia spectrum. We need to take people's pain seriously, whether as healers, scholars, or humane persons. If occasional individuals demonstrate their moodiness, idiosyncrasy, eccentricity, or tendencies toward thought disorder as a demonstration of artistic potential (for whatever reason), how dreadful if we should romanticize their condition and suffering. With affective disorders as examples, consider the intense pain involved (e.g., Brent, Kupfer, Bromet, & Dew, 1988; Goodwin & Jamison, 1990), the self-loathing, guilt, helplessness, paralysis, or agitation. Clients are not doing this for fun. These are lives we are dealing with. Very few people are being self-serving or image-conscious when they kill themselves. One out of five untreated people with bipolar disorder actually takes his or her own life (Goodwin & Jamison, 1990; Jamison, 1993), making it all the more tragic that many do not seek treatment when it is available and quite helpful. Clearly, a great many more people think about suicide than actually try it, and quite a few do try but do not succeed.

Note an important point, of the offspring of bipolar parents more will have a "pure" unipolar depression than a bipolar type of disorder (Akiskal & Akiskal, 1992; Akiskal & Mallya, 1987). Therefore, it is very important to ask clients if they have bipolar disorder in their family. One should be thinking about depressions as well as bipolar mood swings here. The corresponding figure for successful suicide of untreated unipolar depression is 15%. This must be taken seriously.

Depression against the background of a family history of bipolar disorders may also show particular relevance to creativity. In a small preliminary study (Richards et al., 1992), the everyday creativity of depressed people without a bipolar family history (i.e., without a relative having a bipolar disorder) was compared to the creativity of those with such a family history (Richards et al., 1992). Depressed individuals in the first group showed higher everyday creativity than those in the second. Thus, it was not a depressive picture per se that predicted higher creativity but having bipolar disorder in the family. To diagnostic assessors, the surface presentation was comparable in the two groups. Now, cultural views of illness, its appearance, and relation to creativity seem relatively less important, both because of a focus on everyday creativity (not the arts) and because of evident surface similarities between groups. What allowed for prediction of creativity in fact is what ran in the family. There is something more general going on here with bipolar disorders and perhaps, as it now appears, within the schizophrenia spectrum.

Considering the suffering involved, the high prevalence of bipolar-spectrum disorders makes an evolutionary effect even more likely, perhaps involving a compensatory advantage. How else does one explain such great human costs, undiminished down through the generations?

Note too, with familial and genetic contributions, one may well expect biologically based factors leading to creativity–psychopathology links beyond cultural factors, with benefits including the potential for originality as it might manifest in future times and places, including different cultural settings. Furthermore, pathology per se may not be necessary to the relation in the first place, as per results with the normal relatives of bipolars. When psychopathology is present, let us take care to see it in its entirety, in its real human manifestations, and to treat it with care.

3. Has One Factored in the Adaptive Advantages of Having Many Different Roads to Creativity or Advantages in the Diversity of Forms this Creativity May Take? Might There Be Social Niches Even to Formalize Such Varied Routes to Innovation?

Again comparing bipolar- and schizophrenia-spectrum disorders, let me reemphasize the large and healthier subset of people carrying the risk. Consider how prevalent bipolar-spectrum disorders (including depression with a bipolar family history) may be. Looking beyond the major psychopathologies, Akiskal and Mallya (1987) estimated that 4% to 5% of the population may be at risk for developing a bipolar-spectrum disorder. These disorders include (unipolar) subaffective dysthymias and hyperthymias as well as (bipolar) cyclothymic presentations. Depression, as mentioned, is more common than mood swings among the relatives of bipolar individuals, and subaffective dysthymias are in turn more common than milder bipolar mood swings. To some people, again, such high numbers suggest a phenomenon of evolutionary importance, one persisting over the generations, and not a mere phenomenon of a cultural moment.

Consider now that persons in the bipolar spectrum may be filling a general social role or, as Tooby and DeVore (1987) put it, a "cognitive niche." Here is the role of creative instigator, with different forms of provocation arising, perhaps, in different cultural eras. Like a fire under a kettle, these people may warm things up. They are among our natural resources, representing one or more nonconformist subgroups of the population who present a broader, if sometimes bizarre, vision, which others may more judiciously modify or select from, toward what we hope is a social good. Such a process has been termed *cultural brainstorming* (Richards, 1997). Idea generation is separated from the function of the critic, as in a brainstorming group, and wild ideas are generated first, followed by critical selection. However, in this societal case, there is a strategic division of labor, with these two functions being lodged in different groups of people.

Here, too, lies a potential control mechanism for stability and change. If the initiators are getting too wild, they may be called abnormal and their ideas pathologized. If a little more change is needed, one may loosen up on standards and perhaps even give a deviant person a grant. There are qualitative as well as quantitative issues, changes of kind as well as degree. All contributes to a complex balance. Perhaps the articles in this issue and the ingenuity they represent are reflective of a useful opening up, a healthy broadening of possibilities in the new millennium at a time of creative need.

However, remember to keep the full range in mind. If Viewpoints A and B are in favor today and Viewpoints C and D are in favor tomorrow, there may well remain some intermittent enclaves of Viewpoints A and B. One may shift, for instance, from a romantic to postmodern framework in one's immediate community but find this is still one of several extant cultural forces in the larger society, never mind down the block. Indeed, not everyone has coffee on university campuses, nor does everyone share the same philosophical concerns. The overriding evolutionary point is that it is variability that leaves us most able to adapt to changing circumstances.

The contributors to this special issue deserve our thanks for their insight and highly effective consciousness raising about the relevance of schizotypal pathology and its relevant traits to creativity, an awareness that may increase our cultural adaptation, and we need it. None of them suggest, however, that we take the romantic poetry off the shelf. This is a mosaic of multiple possibilities. Furthermore, those who are lacking diagnoses altogether will still have a chance to innovate. As I have said, there can be many roads to creativity.

4. To What Extent Does Overinclusive Thinking Explain the Link Between Creativity and the Schizophrenia Spectrum?

One may now consider overinclusion as a factor in creativity, as effectively argued by Prentky (2000–2001). Here is a factor related in part to biological and perhaps genetic factors. Prentky most particularly addresses issues of genius (eminent creativity) and suggests that the abnormal cognitive style in general and overinclusion specifically may apply to more than one diagnostic group. He suggests this is consistent with his neurocognitive model. How useful is this explanation, and how complete is it?

Overinclusion has been much studied as a factor linking psychopathology with creativity, beginning with Andreasen and colleagues (Andreasen & Canter, 1974; Andreasen & Powers, 1974) and including a diversity of research as well as other views of its genetic and psychopathologic relevance (see Eysenck, 1993; Richards, 1993b, and multiple other commentaries in the same issue). *Cognitive style* may be defined as a mode of information processing affected by certain personality trends (Richards, 1994a; Runco & Pritzker, 1999). It can be viewed in terms of a range of classification rules employed in categorization; rules may also be vague, changeable, or primitive (Richards, 1981, 1996a, 1997). Overinclusion has been associated with originality and creative response in normal individuals as well as individuals within various psychodiagnostic groups, although the qualitative nature of the response may differ (see Richards, 1981, 1997).

How well might overinclusion explain creativity in the context of schizotypal risk? Andreasen and associates (e.g., Andreasen & Canter, 1974; Andreasen & Powers, 1974), Goodwin and Jamison (1990), and others have reported pathology-specific patterns. Findings on creativity were discouraging for schizophrenia compared to bipolar disorder. Yet, only severe schizophrenic pathology was considered. Of great interest, pathology-specific thought patterns could be seen in patients' normal relatives, as per the work of Holzman and associates (e.g., Holzman, Shenton, & Solovay, 1986; Shenton, Solovay, Holzman, Coleman, & Gale, 1989); using their Thought Disorder Index, they have also done fine tuning on differential thought characteristics by diagnosis, which could be useful in Prentky's (2000–2001) further discussions. Indeed, there is a muted manic-type thinking, schizophrenic type and schizoaffective type, that one sees in the unaffected family members. Might this help explain elevated everyday creativity in normal relatives? Comparing such patterns to the A-type and C-type thinking discussed by Prentky would be of interest. Russ (2000–2001), consistent with Schuldberg (2000–2001), also shows profiles or types of distinct and sometimes aberrant cognition, now in the population at large. Indeed, McConaghy and Clancy (1968) found familial patterns of allusive thinking, as Prentky notes, consistent with a certain degree of overinclusive (if not overly loose, and unfiltered) thinking and in as much as 10% of the population. Are these persons more at risk for schizophrenia as he suggests? Why not for another pathology?

It would be useful to know even more about how Prentky's (2000–2001) characterization of A-type and C-type thinking fits with all this literature, with underlying personality types such as he initially addresses, and with other risk factors for schizophrenic pathology. Presumably, overinclusion is not the full explanation. We also need to know what moderating factors may help a person turn such unusual thinking to creative purposes, as Prentky also points out. To the extent that Prentky's view is reminiscent of Eysenck (1993), who posited a more general pathological phenomenon across diagnoses, linked to creativity and to his proposed psychoticism dimension, we need to know how these two viewpoints may relate and what general aspects of overinclusion might support this generality of effect.

Prentky (2000–2001) wisely recommends further research. One would do well to allow for the following:

1. *Heterogeneity of cause:* Keep in mind affective and motivational and direct and indirect causes and the full range of biopsychosocial variables that may contribute.
2. *The issue of distinct types of overinclusion:* How general are the effects or how specific?
3. *A mechanism allowing normal relatives to carry some of the deficits:* How exactly does his model of dysfunction allow for subclinical and perhaps positive productive effects, and what of persons not at risk for schizophrenia who seem to show the creativity effect, too, related to their abnormal and schizotypal thinking? (This of course needs replication.) How might the general population fit in this model? Can such a cognitive style be modeled and environmentally transmitted; can it be genetically transmitted?
4. *Issues of everyday versus eminent creativity:* Issues of evolutionary advantage speak at minimum to an effect at the everyday level needed to allow genetic transmission. Prentky believes such genetic factors lie in "the realm of speculation." However, twin and adoption studies have given very strong support to presence of genetic factors, both in affective disorders and schizophrenia (Goodwin & Jamison, 1990; Kety, 1983; Kety et al., 1994; Kinney et al., 2000–2001; Wender et al. 1986); their relevance to overinclusion and creativity could be more fully studied.

Finally, one should recall that creative advantages that influence the evolution of information, or *memes* (see Dawkins, 1976), can interact with and also help influence biological evolution; consider the people who discovered fire and the people who did not when the freezing winter came. Whereas the eminent creators addressed by Prentky (2000–2001) may influence a culture through their memes, one must also address the everyday person who will ultimately pass on the reproductive advantage through their genes. How does this occur? What is the interaction? We need to understand the whole system. Prentky raises important points about overinclusion and its importance, which, above all, direct us to further work that is needed.

5. What Are the Implications for Eminent Creativity if Postmodernism and Schizotypy Share Some Features? Does This Apply to Everyday Creativity in the General Population as Well?

In the work of Sass (2000–2001) and Ogilvie (2000–2001), original and provocative thinking was found regarding a connection of schizotypal phenomena to creativity, most particularly in relation to the arts and humanities. The arguments are compelling and believable, especially for this subpopulation. Sass presents features of postmodernism and related views of creativity that may indeed be relevant to schizotypal experience. One may wonder, in the receptive cultural environment described by Sass, whether the prevalence of schizophrenia-spectrum phenomena may actually increase (or, perhaps, as a diagnosed entity, actually decrease) by virtue of being less culturally pathologized.

Sass (2000–2001) links schizotypal phenomena as well to biologic hypotheses about the cognitive functioning of schizophrenics, suggesting that one consider their effects as potential advantages instead of deficits. This could be consistent with the model of compensatory advantage (Kinney et al., 2000–2001) and yield some interesting and testable hypotheses.

Ogilvie (2000–2001), drawing on Wittgenstein, looks from the inside out and notes features including hyperreflexivity and profound schizophrenic conflicts about agency, self, and the reality of the world within which one acts. The distance, perspective, and sometimes third-person vantage point of the schizophrenic may allow some analysis (rather than absorption) and the hope of creative agency. However, this process further threatens the self and degrades the reality or consensual reality of what is observed. In exercising this kind of creativity, then, the very presence of the creating self and the experience of creation become concerns to address. One may profitably do phenomenological studies to address these possibilities.

Data (Kinney et al., 2000–2001) have linked subtle schizotypal signs (but not frank schizophrenia) with creativity. Granting provisional prominence to Sass's (2000–2001) and Ogilvie's (2000–2001) viewpoints over other types of creativity–pathology links that may exist (see five-part typology), we may ask how and to what extent they manifest explicitly for the person with mild or subclinical schizotypal phenomena and for the normal person with or without a schizophrenic family history. Furthermore, regarding Sass's work, what is the creative advantage for everyday as well as eminent creativity? Each author could bring much to such questions and may, thereby, extend the theory.

One does well to think in terms of continuum models, as per Schuldberg (1990, 1999, 2000–2001), who noted the existence of a vertical continuum of severity with psychopathology. Pathology may therefore come in different gradations, as may phenomena of thought disorder and with a particular function relating these. Schuldberg (1999) also looked beyond quantitative presence of a quality (present, absent) to qualitative profiles or patterns involving combined pictures of affect and cognition in a complex dynamic systems framework. A rich tapestry of presentations were proposed. Russ (2000–2001), too, shows shades of what may in some people be called *abnormal* but can also represent varied and normal operations of our primary process, drawing on key affective as well as cognitive phenomena. Primary process is not a single thing like an apple or orange. It is a construct including a wide range of possibilities for mental operations of a person within context. Patterns for creativity could certainly be distinctively different for the schizophrenia versus bipolar spectrum.

Again, the studies by Schuldberg (2000–2001) and Russ (2000–2001) drew participants from the general population. These were not schizophrenics, relatives of schizophrenics, or even persons known to have psychopathology. When, indeed, does deviant thinking become pathology, when is it useful abnormality, and what may certain forms of psychopathology have to do with it? How may it increase adaptation in the originality of everyday life if it plays a broader evolutionary role? When and for whom may schizotypal-like characteristics be combined with other modes, say, with a touch of bipolar cognitive style? As I wrote these comments, I kept visualizing a patient I once knew, a very gentle and thoughtful, highly articulate man, bright and well educated, who had been diagnosed as schizoaffective. He was said to have once written some penetrating things about Wittgenstein. My wish is that he will do so once again.

Let us look further at how schizotypal features may contribute to creativity. Sass (2000–2001) reminds us of our changing worldviews as they intersect our views of pathology and our normative experience in a culture and a world that we are increasingly realizing is made (constructed), not born. We each have our own personal slice of infinity, our finite condensation. How readily we can focus on this, neglect everything else, and not even know that we do it. As whole cultures, too, we agree on regularities, rules, indeed what will exist, and what we will not even notice consciously, at least here between us in this consensual life space (e.g., Richards, 1993b, 1999b). In all of this, each of us, or our ego, may be taken as a fixed quantity and reference point at coordinate (0, 0, 0), the central spot from which space and time are measured in this consensually validated universe. If in fact each of us, at every moment, cocreates the world, never mind ourselves (see Marks-Tarlow, 1999); well, we are just not going to notice. There it is, we may say, and there it is going to remain.

Does schizotypal thought provide more movement and possibility amidst this limited life space? So it may seem. Sass's (2000–2001) seven postmodernist features (and also modernist features, as he uses the term) have evident parallels in schizophrenia-spectrum experience, an evident resonance, as he puts it. The features involve (a) an adversarial stance, relativism, fragmentation, and passivization; (b) loss of "worldhood of the world" (becoming subjectivized or devoid of value); (c) loss of temporal flow or narrative unity; (d) intense self-reference; and (e) detachment and emotional distancing. Building on this, Ogilvie (2000–2001) characterizes the schizophrenic person as a philosopher of a sort, showing hyperreflexivity and autistic alienation, struggling to find agency, meaning, and self in his or her life space.

Now assume that the pathology can be down-regulated and utilized adaptively, say, in a postmodern challenge to the consensual present. One can electively distance, shift, question (self and world), and reframe. Imagine a pinch of this schizotypal skew in a sensitive artist with flexible access to this as one cognitive style (Richards, 1981) among others. This can involve Kris's "regression in the service of the ego" (as cited in Richards, 1981) or, as Sass (2000–2001) pointed out, nonregressive control mechanisms that can exist along with nonregressive forms of original vision. We are seeing, increasingly, many new recipes for and forms of creativity (see also Richards, 1996a, 1996b, 1999b, in press-a; Russ, 1993, 1999, 2000–2001; Sass, 1992; Schuldberg, 1999, 2000–2001). Sass (2000–2001) and Ogilvie (2000–2001) remind us that schizophrenic illness is not necessary to manifest these tendencies so that any of us may also display them. Indeed, we are products of our culture. Here are vivid colors any of us may elect for our own artistic creative palettes.

6. Are There Not Other Ways in Which Schizotypy May Contribute to Creativity? Might These Include a Post-Postmodernist Viewpoint?

It may be useful to broaden the cultural framework of possibilities. Consider contexts in which what some Westerners call seriously abnormal might not only be seen as positive but might also be sought, favored, and celebrated. Examples include shamanic experience across diverse indigenous cultures and certain features of meditative experience in the contemplative disciplines. These two examples can highlight (a) the cultural relativism of normalcy, (b) possible manifestations of schizophrenic risk apart from aspects of postmodern thought described by Sass (2000–2001), and most particularly, (c) the wide range or variation of possible creative presentations for even one particular risk. Such adaptive diversity is needed if evolutionary factors are at play. Despite different times and cultures, the risk must be kept alive (e.g., for schizophrenia) in the gene pool. Creative advantages may play out in very different ways in different cultural contexts (see also Becker, 2000–2001); not only may they diverge from a postmodern relativism as they cross cultures, but they also may even at times carry the potential to approach a more changeless and fundamental core of reality. As James (1902/1958) wrote,

> In mystic states, we both become one with the Absolute and we become aware of our oneness. This is the everlasting and triumphant mystical tradition, hardly altered by clime or creed. ... (Across cultures) an eternal unanimity which ought to make a critic stop and think. (p. 321)

First, note that shamans are humanity's most ancient spiritual, psychological, and medical practitioners and exist across diverse cultures (Harner, 1980; Walsh, 1990). The term *shaman* comes from *saman* in Siberia and means "one who is excited, moved, raised" (Walsh, 1990, p. 8). One should note that shamans within and across cultures are not a homogeneous group, nor need their experience be similar (Walsh, 1990). One may consider, however, two types of event: (a) the initiation crisis (including painful symptoms and unusual experiences) that mark the beginning of a shamanic calling for some persons (the minority) and (b) the shamanic journey, in which the shaman alters her or his state of consciousness and journeys to other realms, experiencing rich imagery and visions and the presence of spirits, to help an individual or community.

According to psychiatrist and anthropologist Walsh (1990), the shamanic journey "should in no way be confused with psychosis" (p. 85), although the "initial crisis is less clear" (p. 86). Only a small number of shamans do have an initiatory crisis, however, and only some of these may involve psychotic features. Walsh suggested the condition would most likely be an atypical or brief reactive psychosis or schizophreniform psychosis and not classical schizophrenia. (Note that the first two terms have also been used in the past for affective disorders; e.g., Goodwin & Jamison, 1990; Richards, 1981.) In fact, the "vast majority of shamans cannot be diagnosed as mentally ill" (Walsh, 1990, p. 86).

Yet, we might profitably wonder how many shamans show milder clinical or subclinical characteristics and have a family history of a major psychiatric disorder. Perhaps some ongoing schizotypal characteristics, as one example, could aid in the elective process of intermittently entering trance or reaching an altered state and destabilizing and repatterning their consciousness. It appears a question worth asking.

It is particularly significant that "shamans often end up as the most highly functional members of the community and, according to Eliade, 'show proof of a more than normal nervous constitution' ... Shamans ... function exceptionally well as leaders and healers of their people" (Walsh, 1990, p. 90; see also Harner, 1980). Indeed, the brave facing of unknown factors can lead to health and resilience; implosive therapy has been compared to aspects of shamanic journeying (Walsh, 1990). Shamans show control and great skill in subsequently altering their consciousness. They may regulate attention through breath, imagery, music, movement, vocalizations, rites, and rituals; this is characterized by a controlled flow of awareness (Krippner, 1997). The shaman's work is highly creative. They undergo initial trials to heal and grow; they dare to depart from the ruts of ordinary reality to bring back broader perspectives for all of us.

Instructive as well is Krippner's (1997) multidimensional set of criteria for cross-cultural classification of dissociative states. Certain of these can be positive indeed, including states that facilitate creative inspiration (see Grosso, 1997). In general, creative dissociation can be said to include "the mind's evolved ability to escape, transform, and possibly transcend the limitations of ordinary reality" (Krippner, 1997, p. 195). The outcome here is positive contribution, not pathology.

The exact criteria for dissociative states are less important here than the complexity they represent. However, for reference, they combine Heinze's (1997, 2000) cross-classification of levels of volitional control by an awareness and dissociation dimension with a classification of ego-based experience or transcendence and an evaluative dimension based on personal or cultural norms. What emerges is a rich mosaic of presentations and culture-related phenomena. The main point is that it depends. Across cultures, there is no absolute normal or abnormal standard for human behavior or experience, not even for what modern Westerners think are exceptionally bizarre phenomena. Our human possibilities are rich beyond measure.

Now consider a mild schizotypal profile in a functional Westerner in a state involving unusual perceptions, magical thinking, odd speech, and fluid boundaries. Might this facilitate creative thinking? Might it catalyze postmodern types of thought as characterized in this issue? Are there other choices as well? Most likely, it depends.

Following up, let us speculate about certain meditative experiences within the world's great wisdom traditions (e.g., Austin, 1998; Goleman, 1977; James, 1902/1958; Smith, 1991) and the possible utility of schizotypal traits as framed by Sass (2000–2001) or Ogilvie (2000–2001) to transcend the limitations of dualistic thinking. It is worth noting Heidegger's interest in meditation, as well as Wittgenstein's view of the self as nonself. Now, imagine the meditator who views personal ego, with its self-serving focus and dependence on conceptual thinking, as impeding a deeper and nonconceptual knowing (and the emergence of a more expansive identity that speaks to loving kindness and universal compassion). Might the many perceived relativities and their conceptual packaging not then be seen as masking a greater truth? Might aspects of postmodernist thought—as Sass (2000–2001) helped address this post-postmodernist dilemma—be it through self-reflection, relativism, vivid awareness, or features including more concrete and immediate experience or a temporary detour from the relentless press of time?

Paradoxically, in this contemplation, the act of distancing may be useful but ultimately not to distance. A focus on the limited self may be useful but to transcend this self. Ironically, one's goal may first be to seize but then to jettison postmodernism, that is, to embrace fully the relativity and limits so as to vaporize them toward an absolute. Assuming this possibility, one may then wonder if a touch of schizotypal symptomatology could be helpful in getting this particular ball rolling? Could it further the creative possibilities that may arise?

7. What Might Be Involved in a Creative Advantage Related to the Bipolar or the Schizotypal Spectrum?

The aforementioned are possible outcomes in the best instances. However, as the articles in this issue suggest, the pathological process can also remain stuck in a self that is, in turn, shaky, whereas the fragmented domain it witnesses, shattered in time and space and limited to certain concrete particulars or to hyperabstraction, becomes ever so painfully present. Furthermore, it can be tied in absolute dominion to the observing self through the logic of solipsism. One may emphasize, once again, that creative outcomes are not inevitable or the norm in the presence of psychopathology but only one possibility, given a constellation of facilitating conditions (R. B. Albert & Runco, 1986; R. S. Albert, in press; Runco & Pritzker, 1999; Runco & Richards, 1997; Zausner, 1996). What indeed makes the difference?

With this caveat, let me return again to the schizophreniform and bipolar possibilities for thought and potential advantages for creativity. Again, this is not a zero-sum game, and in the next section, I hypothetically combine schizotypal and bipolar characteristics in a muted and perhaps accessible form for creativity.

Now, let us consider a hypothetical bipolar individual (or perhaps a normal relative with a touch of hyperthymia) in a state of mood elevation. This and the subsequent profile represent fanciful abstractions based on the literature (e.g., Goodwin & Jamison, 1990; Jamison, 1993; Laing, 1965; Runco & Richards, 1997; Sass, 1992, 2000–2001) and clinical and research experience; they provide a basis for discussion but do not represent realities that will necessarily occur.

This hypothetical bipolar person's energized consciousness during mood elevation casts a broad and brilliant beam on the outside world. A focus is chosen for creative processing; this develops and is transformed and elaborated, buzzing with ideas, affects, and associations, and then broadens out even to encompass (in a moment of grandiosity) the whole world. There is awareness of self but not an overt questioning of self. There is at first a tiny touch of overconfidence as the process cascades on and this builds on itself. The subjective gaze is directed outside and not typically to the inside except at times when some self-congratulation occurs for the rich tapestry that is being woven.

Now contrast the hypothetical person with features of schizotypy; here perhaps is the search of a jumping light, a narrow pencil beam, a snapshot here, a snapshot there, not tying it together but turning inward instead to question the self and the consciousness that creates this perhaps worrisome apparition. It lacks culturally shared meaning and perhaps much meaning at all. How concrete and how fearsome things may seem at times—the specks on a doorknob, the stripe on a road, the strange face of a coworker—when framed with this momentary awareness. Here is a more naked knowing, as the cultural constructions are shed. Who is this person or is there a person who is creating this frightening scene? Common language may fail to express the totality of this experience.

A contrast arises with a recent study on awareness, beauty, and survival (Richards, 1999c), an aesthetic theory in which the proposed advantages of direct knowing are adaptive and appealing. They may also be unifying and even universal in significance, following streams of signification—including fractal patterns based on chaos theory—that may have benefitted *Homo sapiens* for thousands of years. With schizophrenia-related thought, by contrast, we may find awareness with a vengeance in a personal context too undefined to hold it and that is, in itself, threatened.

Is such a schizotypal experience related to Wittgenstein's "truth of solipsism" and the "disappearance of the thinking self" (see Ogilvie, 2000–2001)? At worst, can a person flounder in idiosyncratic distress while producing a signature idiosyncrasy on an index of thought disorder? Ogilvie (2000–2001) asks how much may such a patient wish for a reality, and a self, that can be created and shared?

Sharing through creativity is one possibility for connection and grounding. Here is yet another possibility and one that is a bit more "way out." Perhaps in this world beyond words, this person senses influences from others and even from beyond the grave and feels different from other human beings. He or she uses ritual at times to ward off negative influences. To him or to her, some people and situations seem familiar, as if from prior acquaintance, and some connections seem to occur through thought alone.

Before one thinks this is entirely too bizarre (after all, these do include Schneiderian first-rank symptoms and a heavy dose of *The X-Files*), these experiences were drawn from the top eight magical thinking items that emerged when Schuldberg did a correlation at my request of Eckblad and Chapman's Magical Thinking scale with Schuldberg's (1990) creativity factor for a sample of normal college students. Creativity was operationalized and the factor was defined using measures including the Alternate Uses Test, the Barron–Welsh Art Scale, and the How Do You Think? Scale. Let me reemphasize that the sample was a group of normal college students.

The eight magical thinking items were significant at levels (ranging from $p < .02$ to $p < .0005$; *N*s = 192–

194) and accounted for between 3% and 8% of the variance. (There were many significant items for this large sample.) From the strongest correlation on down, these creativity predictors concerned (a) experiences suggestive of reincarnation ($r = .28$), (b) use of rituals to ward off negative influences ($r = .26$), (c) wondering if the dead can influence the living ($r = .22$), (d) people making others aware of them through thinking ($r = .21$), (e) the momentary feeling of not being human ($r = .19$), (f) the passing thought that others are in love with him or her ($r = .19$), (g) sensing one had known strangers before ($r = .18$), and (h) the ability to learn to read others' minds ($r = .17$). These are quite interesting leanings for a general sample compared to our more conventional thoughts.

Hence, these magical thinking items were not found to be bad predictors of creativity at all, especially for single questionnaire items. Of course, replication of effects would be useful. Do the data speak merely to a general openness of mind and an ability to toy with possibilities? Is there something more specific here, seen also in the schizotypal sample, that has particular importance for creativity (Cardena, Lynn, & Krippner, 2000; Richards, 1994b; Schimmel, 1993)? Let us keep in mind that there are alternative interpretations of this data and also keep our eyes, and also our minds, open and remind ourselves once again that normality and abnormality can be very much contextual (Richards, 1997).

8. Is There Particular Merit to a Combined Creative Advantage Related to Features From Both the Bipolar and the Schizotypal Spectrum? What May Be Involved Here?

Now let us put schizotypal and bipolar pictures together, or at least these hypothetical fragments, as a stimulus to our thinking. One may keep in mind the question of whether all of us, at times, do not show just a little pinch of this characteristic or of that, whether we are diagnosis-carrying members of a *DSM-IV* (4th ed.; American Psychiatric Association, 1994) category or not. We are all much more similar than we are different.

For this creative mix, as a binder, we may start with a little ego strength, so as to help creators modulate primary process (e.g., Russ, 2000–2001) and access the colors on their mental palette at will. Add energy and bipolar confidence to overcome inertia, get things going, and open up possibility in the public as well as private spheres (vocational as well as avocational). Now add in a potential wealth of information, perspectives, and states of consciousness, drawn from each diagnostic area. On the one hand, there is the energetic absorption and enthusiasm of the bipolar person (suitably down regulated), looking out on the world with the rich conceptual overlay of combinatory process (e.g., Holzman et al., 1986; Shenton, et al., 1989). Add to this the inward looking, immediacy, and awareness of the deconstructor of conceptual experience, who also feels the vulnerability of self in its midst. Yet, now this person has a few extra places to turn. The colors on the palette of mind can be modified, remixed, or painted over. He or she now has the equipment to do the creative job, to re-create self and world, as Ogilvie (2000–2001) said, and in some cases to do so not only for himself or herself but also as a creator who can give to us all.

Conclusion

Sass (2000–2001), Schuldberg (2000–2001; Sass & Shuldberg, 2000–2001), the other contributors, and this journal do well to present this provocative series of theoretical and empirical articles on creativity and the schizophrenia spectrum and such a rich context for discussion. Subtle effects related to the schizophrenia spectrum appear relevant to creativity, with some similarities in the abstract to effects found within the bipolar spectrum.

Further work on the schizophrenia spectrum could add greatly to our knowledge of creativity, both for clinical populations and for the population at large. Beyond this, it can alert us generally, as earlier work on bipolar disorders has done (e.g., Andreasen 1987; Jamison, 1990; Richards & Kinney, 1990; Richards, Kinney, Lunde, et al., 1988), to the strengths that may lie in the differences and to ways in which creativity and psychological problems can be usefully intertwined (and for all of us). It may also remind us to not immediately pathologize something just because it is (or we are) different and depart from a statistical norm, while raising the possibility that one may thereby see farther than one did before.

Of particular importance, it seems, is specific evidence supporting a connection between creativity and schizophrenia-spectrum disorders that operates, perhaps, via a mechanism of compensatory advantage (Kinney & Matthysse, 1978; Richards, Kinney, Lunde, et al., 1988). This possibility offers new hope to people who have suffered and young people who are at risk. One should proceed with an open mind tempered by critical judgment. On the one hand, we have limited data, and there is need for replication and extension of research findings. On the other, we have already seen examples of illness or familial risk of illness linked with creativity in related contexts (Runco & Richards, 1997). We do not want to miss out on such an important relation. Plus, it is often from our problems that we make creative gains and learn to reach from "deficiency creativity" (as per Maslow's, 1968, hierarchy of needs) to higher levels of personal growth and meaning (Rhodes, 1990; Richards, 1997, 1998).

Finally, in surveying creativity in both the schizophrenia spectrum and bipolar spectrum and the cognitive–affective–motivational styles they may each represent, we are reminded that certain complementary tendencies might perhaps increase dramatically in power when applied in concert with each other (either within the same person or same culture). Each may play a different role in the generation of originality, separately and together, and they need not be placed in opposition. They may even yield benefits together and for you and me in the general population and not just for those at risk for a major psychiatric disorder.

Let us, therefore, actively discourage misunderstandings and either–or games in discussions of creativity and schizophrenia-spectrum or bipolar-spectrum disorders. Along with the authors in this special issue, let us applaud the adaptive diversity of our creative options and the evolutionary phenomenon they potentially represent, even as we continue our investigations. Here are diverse urges toward originality, growth, and our greater possibility that may fit brilliantly into a whole that goes beyond our current understanding.

References

Akiskal, H., & Akiskal, K. (1988). Reassessing the prevalence of bipolar disorders: Clinical significance and artistic creativity. *Psychiatry and Psychobiology, 3,* 29–36.

Akiskal, H., & Akiskal, K. (1992). Cyclothymic, hyperthymic, and depressive temperaments as subaffective variants of mood disorders. In A. Tasman & M. B. Riba (Eds.), *Review of psychiatry* (Vol. 11, pp. 43–62). Washington, DC: American Psychiatric Press.

Akiskal, H., & Mallya, G. (1987). Criteria for the "soft" bipolar spectrum: Treatment implications. *Psychopharmacology Bulletin, 23,* 67–73.

Albert, R. B., & Runco, M. A. (1986). The achievement of eminence. In R. J. Sternberg & J. E. Davidson (Eds.), *Conceptions of giftedness* (pp. 232–257). New York: Cambridge University Press.

Albert, R. S. (in press). The achievement of eminence as an evolutionary strategy. In M. A. Runco (Ed.), *Creativity research handbook: Vol. 2.* Cresskill, NJ: Hampton.

American Psychiatric Association. (1980). *Diagnostic and statistical manual of mental disorders* (3rd ed.). Washington, DC: Author.

American Psychiatric Association. (1994). *Diagnostic and statistical manual of mental disorders* (4th ed.). Washington, DC: Author.

Andreasen, N. C. (1978). Creativity and psychiatric illness. *Psychiatric Annals, 8,* 113–119.

Andreasen, N. C. (1987). Creativity and mental illness: Prevalence rates in writers and their first-degree relatives. *American Journal of Psychiatry, 144,* 1288–1292.

Andreasen, N. C., & Canter, A. (1974). The creative writer: Psychiatric symptoms and family history. *Comprehensive Psychiatry, 15,* 123–131.

Andreasen, N. C., & Powers, P. (1974). Overinclusive thinking in mania and schizophrenia. *British Journal of Psychiatry, 125,* 452–456.

Austin, J. H. (1998). *Zen and the brain.* Cambridge, MA: MIT Press.

Barron, F. (1969). *Creative person and creative process.* New York: Holt, Rinehart & Winston.

Becker, G. (1978). *The mad genius controversy: A study in the sociology of deviance.* Beverly Hills, CA: Sage.

Becker, G. (2000–2001). The association of creativity and psychopathology: Its cultural–historical origins. *Creativity Research Journal, 13,* 45–53.

Brent, G. H., Kupfer, D. J., Bromet, E. J., & Dew, M. A. (1988). The assessment and treatment of patients at risk for suicide. In A. J. Francis & R. E. Hales (Eds.), *Review of psychiatry* (Vol. 7, pp. 353–385). Washington, DC: American Psychiatric Press.

Cardena, E., Lynn, S., & Krippner, S. (2000). *Varieties of anomalous experience: Examining the scientific evidence.* Washington, DC: American Psychological Association.

Coryell, W., Endicott, J., Keller, M., Andreasen, N., Grove, W., Hirschfeld, R. M. A., & Scheftner, W. (1989). Bipolar affective disorder and high achievement: A familial association. *American Journal of Psychiatry, 146,* 983–995.

Cropley, A. J. (1990). Creativity and mental health in everyday life. *Creativity Research Journal, 3,* 167–178.

Csikszentmihalyi, M. (1988). Society, culture, and person: A systems view of creativity. In R. J. Sternberg (Ed.), *The nature of creativity* (pp. 325–339). New York: Cambridge University Press.

Dawkins, R. (1976). *The selfish gene.* New York: Oxford University Press.

Eckblad, M., & Chapman, L. J. (1986). Development and validation of a scale for hypomanic personality. *Journal of Abnormal Psychology, 3,* 214–222.

Eysenck, H. (1993). Creativity and personality: Suggestions for a theory. *Psychological Inquiry, 4,* 147–178.

Goertzel, V., & Goertzel, M. G. (1962). *Cradles of eminence.* Boston: Little, Brown.

Goleman, D. (1977). *Varieties of meditative experience.* New York: Dutton.

Goodwin, F., & Jamison, K. R. (1990). *Manic–depressive illness.* New York: Oxford University Press.

Grosso, M. (1997). Inspiration, mediumship, surrealism: The concept of creative dissociation. In S. Krippner & S. M. Powers (Eds.), *Broken images, broken selves: Dissociative narratives in clinical practice* (pp. 181–198). Washington, DC: Brunner/Mazel.

Harner, M. (1980). *The way of the shaman.* New York: Harper San Francisco/HarperCollins.

Heinze, R.–I. (1997). *Trance and healing in Southeast Asia today.* Bangkok, Thailand: White Lotus.

Heinze, R.–I. (2000). *The nature and function of rituals: Fire from heaven.* Westport, CT: Bergin & Garvey.

Heston, L. L. (1966). Psychiatric disorders in foster home reared children of schizophrenic mothers. *British Journal of Psychiatry, 112,* 819–825.

Holzman, P. S., Shenton, M. E., & Solovay, M. R. (1986). Quality of thought disorder in differential diagnosis. *Schizophrenia Bulletin, 12,* 360–372.

James, W. (1958). *The varieties of religious experience.* New York: Mentor. (Original work published 1902)

Jamison, K. R. (1990). Manic–depressive illness, creativity, and leadership. In F. K. Goodwin & K. R. Jamison (Ed.), *Manic–depressive illness* (pp. 332–367). New York: Oxford University Press.

Jamison, K. R. (1993). *Touched with fire: Manic–depressive illness and the artistic temperament.* New York: Free Press.

Jamison, K. R. (1995). *An unquiet mind.* New York: Knopf.

Jamison, K. R., Gerner, R., Hammen, C., & Padesky, C. (1980). Clouds and silver linings: Positive experiences associated with primary affective disorders. *American Journal of Psychiatry, 137,* 198–202.

Juda, A. (1949–1950). The relationship between highest mental capacity and psychic abnormalities. *American Journal of Psychiatry, 106,* 296–307.

Karlsson, J. L. (1970). Genetic association of giftedness and creativity with schizophrenia. *Hereditas, 66,* 177–182.

Kauffman, C., Grunebaum, H., Cohler, B., & Gamer, E. (1979). Superkids: Competent children of psychotic mothers. *American Journal of Psychiatry, 136,* 1396–1402.

Kety, S. S. (1983). Mental illness in the biological and adoptive relatives of schizophrenic adoptees: Findings relevant to genetic and environmental factors in etiology. *American Journal of Psychiatry, 140,* 720–727.

Kety, S. S., Wender, P. H., Jacobsen, B., Ingraham, L. J., Jansson, L., Faber, B., & Kinney, D. K. (1994). Mental illness in the biological and adoptive relatives of schizophrenic adoptees. Replication of the Copenhagen Study in the rest of Denmark. *Archives of General Psychiatry, 51,* 442–455.

Kinney, D. K. (1992). The therapist as muse: Greater roles for clinicians in fostering innovation. *American Journal of Psychotherapy, 46,* 434–453.

Kinney, D. K., & Matthysse, S. M. (1978). Genetic factors in the transmission of schizophrenia. *Annual Review of Medicine, 29,* 459–473.

Kinney, D. K., Richards, R., Lowing, P. A., LeBlanc, D., Zimbalist, M. E., & Harlan, P. (2000–2001). Creativity in offspring of schizophrenic and control parents: An adoption study. *Creativity Research Journal, 13,* 17–25.

Kinney, D. K., Richards, R., & Southam, M. (in press). *Everyday creativity, its assessment, and the Lifetime Creativity Scales: The handbook of creativity.* Cresskill, NJ: Hampton.

Krippner, S. (1997). Disassociation in many times and places. In S. Krippner & S. M. Powers (Eds.), *Broken images, broken selves: Dissociative narratives in clinical practice* (pp. 3–40). New York: Brunner/Mazel.

Laing, R. D. (1965). *The divided self.* Harmondsworth, England: Penguin.

Ludwig, A. M. (1992). Creative achievement and psychopathology: Comparison among professions. *American Journal of Psychotherapy, 46,* 330–354.

Ludwig, A. M. (1995). *The price of greatness.* New York: Guilford.

Making art of madness. (1993, October 15). *The New York Times,* p. A14.

Marks-Tarlow, T. (1999). The self as a dynamical system. *Nonlinear Dynamics, Psychology, and the Life Sciences, 3,* 311–345.

Maslow, A. (1968). *Toward a psychology of being.* New York: Van Nostrand Reinhold.

May, R. (1976). *The courage to create.* New York: Bantam.

McConaghy, N., & Clancy, M. (1968). Familial relationships of allusive thinking in university students and their parents. *British Journal of Psychiatry, 114,* 1079–1087.

Ogilvie, J. (2000–2001). On self-conceiving: Philosophical yearnings in a schizophrenic context. *Creativity Research Journal, 13,* 87–94.

Pennebaker, J. W. (Ed.). (1995). *Emotion, disclosure, and health.* Washington, DC: American Psychological Association.

Prentky, R. A. (2000–2001). Mental illness and roots of genius. *Creativity Research Journal, 13,* 95–104.

Rhodes, C. (1990). Growth from deficiency creativity to being creativity. *Creativity Research Journal, 3,* 287–289.

Richards, R. (1981). Relationships between creativity and psychopathology. *Genetic Psychology Monographs, 103,* 261–324.

Richards, R. (1990). Everyday creativity, eminent creativity, and health: "Afterview" for *CRJ* special issues on "Creativity and Health." *Creativity Research Journal, 3,* 300–326.

Richards, R. (1993a). Everyday creativity, eminent creativity, and psychopathology: Invited commentary on Hans Eysenck's creativity and personality: Suggestions for a theory. *Psychological Inquiry, 4,* 212–217.

Richards, R. (1993b). Seeing beyond: Issues of creative awareness and social responsibility. *Creativity Research Journal, 6,* 165–183.

Richards, R. (1994a). Creativity and bipolar mood swings: Why the association? In M. Shaw & M. A. Runco (Eds.), *Creativity and affect* (pp. 44–72). Norwood, NJ: Ablex.

Richards, R. (1994b). Psi Fi?—"Acceptable" and "unacceptable" research. *Creativity Research Journal, 7,* 87–95.

Richards, R. (1996a). Beyond Piaget: Accepting divergent, chaotic, and creative thought. In M. Runco (Ed.), *New directions in child development* (Vol. 72, pp. 67–86). San Francisco: Jossey-Bass.

Richards, R. (1996b). Does the lone genius ride again? Chaos, creativity, and community. *Journal of Humanistic Psychology, 36*(2), 44–60.

Richards, R. (1997). When illness yields creativity. In M. Runco & R. Richards (Eds.), *Eminent creativity, everyday creativity, and health* (pp. 485–540). Greenwich, CT: Ablex.

Richards, R. (1998). Everyday creativity. In H. S. Friedman (Ed.), *Encyclopedia of mental health* (pp. 619–633). San Diego, CA: Academic.

Richards, R. (1999a). Affective disorders. In M. Runco & S. Pritzker (Eds.), *The encyclopedia of creativity* (Vol. 1, pp. 31–43). San Diego, CA: Academic.

Richards, R. (1999b). Five-part typology (of relations between creativity and psychopathology). In M. Runco & S. Pritzker (Eds.), *The encyclopedia of creativity* (Vol. 1, pp. 717–723). San Diego, CA: Academic.

Richards, R. (1999c). The subtle attraction: Beauty as a force in awareness, creativity, and survival. In S. Russ (Ed.), *Affect, creative experience, and psychological adjustment* (pp. 195–219). Philadelphia: Brunner/Mazel.

Richards, R. (in press-a). Everyday creativity and the arts. In A. Montuori & R. Purser (Eds.), *Social creativity: Prospects and possibilities* (Vol. 3). Cresskill, NJ: Hampton.

Richards, R. (in press-b). Millennium as opportunity: Chaos, creativity, and Guilford's structure-of-intellect model. *Creativity Research Journal.*

Richards, R., & Kinney, D. K. (1989). Creativity and manic–depressive illness [Letter]. *Comprehensive Psychiatry, 30,* 272–273.

Richards, R., & Kinney, D. K. (1990). Mood swings and creativity. *Creativity Research Journal, 3,* 203–218.

Richards, R., Kinney, D. K., Benet, M., & Merzel, A. P. C. (1988). Assessing everyday creativity: Characteristics of the Lifetime Creativity Scales and validation with three large samples. *Journal of Personality and Social Psychology, 54,* 476–485.

Richards, R., Kinney, D., Daniels, H., & Linkins, K. (1992). Everyday creativity and bipolar and unipolar affective disorder: Preliminary study of personal and family history. *European Psychiatry, 7,* 49–52.

Richards, R., Kinney, D. K., Lunde, I., Benet, M., & Merzel, A. P. C. (1988). Creativity in manic–depressives, cyclothymes, their normal relatives, and control subjects. *Journal of Abnormal Psychology, 97,* 281–288.

Runco, M., & Pritzker, S. (1999). *The encyclopedia of creativity* (Vols. 1 & 2). San Diego, CA: Academic.

Runco, M., & Richards, R. (1997). *Eminent creativity, everyday creativity, and health.* Greenwich, CT: Ablex.

Russ, S. W. (1993). *Affect and creativity.* Hillsdale, NJ: Lawrence Erlbaum Associates, Inc.

Russ, S. W. (1999). *Affect, creative experience, and psychological adjustment.* Philadelphia: Brunner/Mazel.

Russ, S. W. (2000–2001). Primary-process thinking and creativity: Affect and cognition. *Creativity Research Journal, 13,* 27–35.

Sass, L. A. (1992). *Madness and modernism: Insanity in the light of modern art, literature, and thought.* Cambridge, MA: Harvard University Press.

Sass, L. A. (2000–2001). Schizophrenia, modernism, and the creative imagination: On creativity and psychopathology. *Creativity Research Journal, 13,* 55–74.

Sass, L. A., & Schuldberg, D. (2000–2001). Introduction to special issue: Creativity and the schizophrenia spectrum. *Creativity Research Journal, 13,* 1–4.

Schimmel, A. M. (1993). *The mystery of numbers.* New York: Oxford University Press.

Schuldberg, D. (1990). Schizotypal and hypomanic traits, creativity, and psychological health. *Creativity Research Journal, 3,* 218–230.

Schuldberg, D. (1999). Creativity, bipolarity, and the dynamics of style. In S. Russ (Ed.), *Affect, creative experience, and psychological adjustment* (pp. 221–237). Philadelphia: Brunner/Mazel.

Schuldberg, D. (2000–2001). Six subclinical spectrum traits in normal creativity. *Creativity Research Journal, 13,* 5–16.

Shenton, M. E., Solovay, R. R., Holzman, P. S., Coleman, M. A., & Gale, H. J. (1989). Thought disorder in the relatives of psychotic patients. *Archives of General Psychiatry, 46,* 897–901.

Simonton, D. K. (1984). *Genius, creativity and leadership: Historiometric inquiries.* Cambridge, MA: Harvard University Press.

Smith, H. (1991). *The world's religions: Our great wisdom traditions.* New York: Harper San Francisco/HarperCollins.

Tooby, J., & DeVore, I. (1987). The reconstruction of hominid behavioral evolution. In W. G. Kinsey (Ed.), *The evolution of human behavior: Primate models* (pp. 183–237). Albany: State University of New York Press.

Walsh, R. N. (1990) *The spirit of shamanism.* New York: Putnam.

Wender, P. H., Kety, S. S., Rosenthal, D., Schulsinger, F., Ortmann, J., & Lunde, I. (1986). Psychiatric disorders in the biological and adoptive families of adopted individuals with affective disorders. *Archives of General Psychiatry, 43,* 923–929.

Wilber, K. (1997). *The eye of spirit.* Boston: Shambhala.

Wilson, D. (1992). Evolutionary epidemiology. *Acta Biotheoretica, 40,* 87–90.

Zausner, T. (1996). The creative chaos: Speculations on the connection between nonlinear dynamics and the creative process. In W. Sulis & A. Combs (Eds.), *Nonlinear dynamics in human behaviour* (Vol. 5, pp. 343–363). London: World Scientific.

For Product Safety Concerns and Information please contact our EU
representative GPSR@taylorandfrancis.com
Taylor & Francis Verlag GmbH, Kaufingerstraße 24, 80331 München, Germany

www.ingramcontent.com/pod-product-compliance
Ingram Content Group UK Ltd.
Pitfield, Milton Keynes, MK11 3LW, UK
UKHW050757180926
475701UK00007B/1101

* 9 7 8 0 8 0 5 8 9 7 3 9 5 *